Parenting, Inc.

Parenting, Inc.

HOW WE ARE SOLD ON $800 STROLLERS,
FETAL EDUCATION, BABY SIGN LANGUAGE,
SLEEPING COACHES, TODDLER COUTURE,
AND DIAPER WIPE WARMERS—
AND WHAT IT MEANS FOR OUR CHILDREN

PAMELA PAUL

TIMES BOOKS
Henry Holt and Company • New York

Times Books
Henry Holt and Company, LLC
Publishers since 1866
175 Fifth Avenue
New York, New York 10010

www.henryholt.com

Henry Holt® is a registered trademark of
Henry Holt and Company, LLC.

Copyright © 2008 by Pamela Paul
All rights reserved.
Distributed in Canada by H. B. Fenn and Company Ltd.

Library of Congress Cataloging-in-Publication Data
ISBN-13: 978-0-8050-8249-4
ISBN-10: 0-8050-8049-2

Henry Holt books are available for special promotions and
premiums. For details contact: Director, Special Markets.

First Edition 2008
Designed by Kelly S. Too

Printed in the United States of America
1   3   5   7   9   10   8   6   4   2

For Beatrice and Tobias

CONTENTS

Parenting, Inc.

The Mother Load

When she was seven months old, my husband and I seriously considered enrolling our daughter, Beatrice, who has no hearing impairment, in baby sign language class. Oh, we did have some initial doubts: If Beatrice was busy learning how to fold and pleat her fingers into signing gestures, wouldn't that take time and attention away from learning to speak? Wouldn't being able to communicate through signs remove any incentive to talk? But our misgivings were brushed aside by the baby signing professionals and their acolytes. Signing is like crawling, they explained. Just as crawling gives your baby that taste of movement that motivates her to walk, signing inspires the voiceless communicator to learn how to verbalize. Not only do signing babies speak earlier, but research indicates they have higher IQ scores, by an average of twelve points, at age eight, they pointed out.

Baby signing—for babies who can hear perfectly well—had become so popular that we also felt prodded by a competitive impetus: Everyone else seemed to be signing their children up. Our friends Paul and Ericka had a daughter who signed; she waved and poked her chubby hands about whenever she wanted to speak her mind. A genius! Shouldn't Beatrice have the same advantage? Any parent can understand why we were tempted. We all want to provide our children with every opportunity and are eager to get a sense of what's going on inside our preverbal babies.

Still, the classes were expensive. Plus, it would take time away from work in order for me to commute to wherever it was that baby signers convened, surely not in my neighborhood, where most parents struggle to afford quality day care. As an alternative, we could allocate precious weekend time to the classes, allowing both my husband and I to attend, but even the thought of adding one more thing to our pittance of "time off " made me weary. Either way, on top of everything, we would have to teach the babysitter how to sign too, and when would we ever find the time to do that? Wouldn't Beatrice get frustrated if her caretakers didn't understand what she was trying to "say"?

On the other hand, there were incentives to get Beatrice started on language skills immediately. Getting into preschool in New York City is cutthroat. Many applications include ample space in which to list the "classes" two-year-olds have attended before they've even enrolled in their first school. How could I forgo an activity that might provide the decisive advantage? I would kick myself ten times over for my neglect. If Beatrice proved to be an "accelerated learner," we could potentially enroll her at a magnet public school later on, rather than a private school, either one a necessity since our neighborhood is bereft of good public schools. This would in turn free up money for our other children's education, in case they didn't get into a good public school.

If Beatrice didn't "measure up," the tuition for private nursery school alone would run up to $30,000 a year; if we had three kids, the price of education would eventually eat up a six-figure income each year. Suddenly, it seemed that if Beatrice didn't baby-sign, we wouldn't have enough money to afford three kids, something my husband and I, both products of large families, would like.

Or so my snowballing logic went. Like all parents, I am confronted every day with complex spending decisions for my children. And I can drive myself nuts trying to weigh the pros, cons, and costs. No matter what I do, someone else seems to be doing enviably more or improbably less, and either way, their child and family seem all the better for it.

But with the sign language conundrum, I had the benefit of finding an answer through my job as a journalist. While researching a story on cognitive development for *Time* magazine, I came upon a comprehensive review of studies on baby signing. Contrary to what I had been led to believe by the baby signers' websites and brochures, the evidence is all over the place. Some studies even showed signing babies to be *worse* off than their non-gesturing counterparts. After an interview with one of the review's authors, my husband and I decided to bypass the whole thing. (Our daughter speaks just fine and, at age three, gesticulates in her own, invented ways.)

Making these kinds of decisions—choosing what *not* to do or buy for our baby—isn't easy. Saying no runs counter to all our instincts as parents and to everything the parenting culture tells us. Aren't we supposed to do everything we possibly can for our children? Doesn't this frequently mean sparing no expense? Many parents already feel tremendous guilt for working long hours and spending less time than they would like with their children. Now add to that a layer of guilt for not spending as much money on them as we could. With every *no*, you can hear the judgments and recriminations, be they imagined or actual: *What are you going to do with that money instead? Go out to dinner more often? Buy yourself more clothes? Sock money away in your retirement fund*—before *taking care of your own children?* We are pressured to spend by the cautions of experts, the advice of parenting pros, and the endless and frightfully persuasive marketers proclaiming that certain goods, services, activities, and environments ensure a happier, smarter, healthier, and safer child. A more emotionally secure and socially successful child. A better baby.

. . .

AT THE TIME WHEN WE FEEL MOST DISABLED AS DECISION makers—by experts, advertisements, product overload, our own niggling doubts—the need to make reasoned decisions is greater than ever. Raising kids today costs a fortune. Rather than plot family size based on any number of factors—one's ideal conception of family, the kind of life one wants to lead, the disruption that pregnancy and child rearing might bring to one's careers, the terrifying thought of traveling to visit grandparents with a full brood in tow—often the decision about whether to have one child, or more, pivots on the question: Can we afford it?

This just seems wrong. How can money be what makes or breaks such a personal decision? "Why can't we just have a kid the way our parents did in the seventies?" asked a friend I've known since my early twenties—I'll call her Ava. She wasn't referring to giving birth on a leftover hippie commune, nor did she especially hanker for a child outfitted in an orange velour ensemble and bowl haircut. She simply wanted to be able to afford having a baby, perhaps two, as so many of our parents did, almost unthinkingly, just a few decades ago. Whether or not to have kids and how many were choices that once could be made without poring over Quicken and breaking into a premature sweat about college costs. Sure, everyone has always complained that "kids are expensive," but when people said it in the 1970s, they often meant that in a period of rapid inflation sugar cereals cost twice as much as cornflakes and that store-bought Halloween costumes were overpriced. Many parents didn't even worry about college tuition until their kids were in junior high, and the money needed to cover it today would barely pay for preschool, even adjusted for inflation.

Despite oil lines and inflation, raising a child in the 1970s was cheap. Even during the supposed heyday of family life, in 1958, parents spent about half what they spend now, the equivalent of $5,470 on goods and services ($800 in 1958 dollars) during a baby's first year.[1] The major cost creep can be dated to the 1980s, when the baby boomers entered parenthood, and started to become parents, and prices continued to spiral upward during the 1990s as the boomers' spending on their kids hit its peak. According to the U.S. Department of Agriculture (which of all government bureaucracies, is the one that tracks these things), the cost of raising a child born in 2006 from birth to the age of seventeen is $143,790 for parents in the lowest income group (households earning less than $44,500 a year) and $289,390 for parents with the highest incomes (those earning more than $74,900 and an average income of $112,200).

Still, it's hard to get a realistic sense of just how much children cost. Experts agree that though the government estimates try to account for housing, food, transportation, clothing, health care, childcare, education, and miscellaneous goods and services, the Department of Agriculture lowballs these costs by a long shot. For example, the government expects parents in the wealthiest group to spend $2,850 on childcare and education during the first two years of a baby's life,* while the National Association of Child Care Resource and Referral Agencies, a network of more than 805 child-care resources and referral centers, reports that the average cost of childcare for an infant—no matter how much the parents earn—ranges from $3,803 to $13,480 a year.[2]

Costs spiral much, much higher in major urban areas. According to a 2006 report in *USA Today*, the cost of childcare is leading parents nationwide to make major lifestyle adjustments: relocating, changing jobs, and selling homes. One Boston couple, the husband a software support engineer, the wife in communications, had to move and buy a new house in an area where they could find day

*This number is particularly misleading because only half the families interviewed for the survey spent any money at all on childcare or education. These families probably cared for their children themselves or had a family member take care of them. The result is that the "average" figures reported in the study are inaccurate for those families who *do* spend money on child care and education.

care for under $850 because the $1,500 to $2,000 monthly price
tag where they had been living in Boston was unaffordable. "We
went into shock," the mother complained. "That's like a second
mortgage."[3] In major cities, nannies charge between $400 and
$750 a week, depending on experience and skills (licensed drivers,
for example, earn more). Nannies typically charge $50 a week for
each additional offspring. In New York or San Francisco, it's tough
to find a caregiver who will accept less than $500 for a forty-hour
week (which doesn't allow much time for a parent's commute or
overtime). That means $26,000 a year—not $2,850. And that's if
you're paying your help illegally. To hire someone on the books
costs an additional $6,000 or more annually, once you count taxes,
benefits, and insurance. When many of today's parents were growing up, live-in help was within the reach of upper-middle-class
families. Now such arrangements are exclusive to the truly wealthy,
though substantially more families today require two working parents and often need near-around-the-clock childcare and household maintenance to make such work arrangements possible.

In addition to what parents have to pay out of pocket, there are
the amounts we are supposed to set aside in those savings ac-
counts for college. Adding government figures for middle-income
families (those earning between $43,200 and $72,600 per year), to
estimates from the College Board, it takes about $500,000 to raise
a child from birth through college, assuming the child goes to a
public university. If she gets into the Ivy League, parents can bank
on a tab of $635,000—not factoring in inflation.

Most of us are already behind. A 2006 poll of 2,239 parents
found that although 79 percent of parents who expected their
child to attend college also expected to have to pay for some or all
of it, more than half had barely gotten started: 26 percent had
saved less than $5,000 and 32 percent had not saved anything, de-
spite the fact that personal financial advisers suggest putting aside
a minimum of $1,000 a month for each child, starting at birth, as
much as many parents pay for their monthly rent or mortgage. If

you've got two kids and need to put aside $2,000 every month, you may as well own two homes.

This sounds bad enough, yet the numbers don't tell the full story.

For one thing, the cost of raising children is rising far faster than our earnings. Estimated household income rose 24 percent during the past ten years, while the cost of raising a child rose 66 percent. That leaves even couples who make decent salaries belaboring the decision to have children based on the bottom line. Again and again, couples in their midtwenties to their midthirties say they don't feel they can afford to have kids until at least one of them is making a six-figure salary.

Prospective parents are wrestling with this conundrum from the tony streets of Cambridge, Massachusetts, to the suburbs of Cleveland, Ohio. Recently married and well into her thirties, my friend Ava and her husband, Colin, wanted a baby, but their circumstances looked grim. Colin, a freelance writer, had no health benefits, and Ava had quit her job to pursue a more flexible, child-friendly self-employment. The little savings they had were earmarked for a down payment on a home, once the housing market cooled off. Having a baby seemed to require winning the Lotto or uncovering a lost millionaire aunt. This wasn't a case of bemoaning the cost of a designer stroller. Ava and Colin—two college-educated professionals—actually thought that unless things changed, they would not be able to afford a family. Not a *single* child.

In the *Wall Street Journal*, columnist Terri Cullen publicly debated whether to have another child largely in terms of its financial impact: Since much of the baby gear used by her firstborn had been given away, Cullen was faced with the sticker shock of having to buy everything all over again. "With no shower for a second baby, we'd have to foot a bill that would amount to more than $5,000 ourselves." Adding up the costs in child care, education, baby food, and diapers, she realized:

All those new costs and years out of the workforce would cut into our ability to save—for retirement, college, an emergency, or otherwise. It's a tradeoff [my husband] Gerry and I are reluctant to make. Ultimately, the arguments against another baby carried the day: I'd love to have one more child, but it doesn't make sense for our family.

If a financial columnist at the *Wall Street Journal* can't make it work, is it any wonder that two typical professionals in their thirties would be dismayed at the thought of supporting a child? Unnerved by the numbers but overcome with parental yearning, Ava and Colin went ahead with their procreation plan, and Ava got pregnant. Like so many other parents, they would just have to figure out how to afford it.

Then there were the weighty, long-term problems to tackle. Would Ava's salary cover the cost of child care, let alone help provide for her family? Would they have to move farther away from their work opportunities in order to afford a house big enough for their family? Would they be able to take a vacation sometime in the next decade? Just how much would they have to give up in order to have a child? These questions of work arrangements, child-care, and housing are enough to send any parent into a state of despair. In a 2005 survey of 1,568 mothers by iVillage, 37 percent said they would need more than an additional $50,000 each year in order to significantly improve their quality of life with their children.[4] When asked what they would change to become better mothers if time, money, and stress were not obstacles, 38 percent said they would quit work, work less, or become stay-at-home mothers. Eighteen percent wanted to spend less time doing housework and more time with their children.

But soon Ava and Colin were grappling with the other concerns and fears that consume modern parents, and the price tags spun well beyond their stomach-churning Quicken-induced nightmares. Why did everyone seem to have at least two strollers?

Would it be feasible to purchase one model without compromising their baby's comfort, mobility, and safety? How many toys—and what type—does a toddler need to develop well? Are more expensive car seats significantly safer? They dwelled on mundane questions like what brand of bottle to choose and whether pricey formula with supplemental docosa hexaenoic acid (DHA) actually improves cognitive development. They debated the benefits of organic layettes.

Because those scary government numbers do not take into account all the extras that many parents deem necessities after the appearance of that second strip on the self-pregnancy test. They don't include, for example, the cost of maternity clothes; of new home purchases and moving expenses (extra space is often in order); of childbirth education and newborn care classes; of prenatal vitamins and extra fresh fruits and vegetables (organic, please!); of Glider breastfeeding armchairs; of "babymoon" vacations and baby showers. When the *Wall Street Journal* looked at the suspect government figures in an effort to make them somewhat more realistic, it added costs such as sporting equipment and tutoring (which is no longer just for the wealthy—the average income of a family seeking tutoring for a child is between $50,000 and $70,000) and came up with a total cost of raising a child to age seventeen that ranged from $800,000 to $1.6 million (in 2007 dollars).[5]

A million dollars to raise a baby. "Having kids is a privilege," financial planner Rich Chambers declared.[6] A privilege?! When I was growing up, children were not considered a luxury item. But in major American cities, having three or four children is practically an ostentatious display, akin to owning a pied-à-terre in Paris and a country retreat to boot. "Three is the new two when it comes to having kids," Amanda Uhry, founder of Manhattan Private School Advisors, told me. Her job: helping frazzled New York City parents get their kids into hypercompetitive preschools for a fee of $10,000.

· · ·

THIS PARENTAL MONEY WARP HAS DISTORTED OUR ENTIRE AP-
proach to raising children. That million-dollar estimate doesn't account for the uneasy combination of guilt and desire that has
become the artisan-bread-and-butter of the parenting industry. It
doesn't factor in the thousands of potential saviors that loom before worried parents in baby gear catalogs or the enticing amusements heralded in parenting magazines, piled on shelves at baby
emporiums, and charmingly displayed in specialty gift shops. It
doesn't calculate the pressure to buy something because everyone
else's child seems to have one. Today, the "mom market" is said to
be $1.7 trillion, with the toy industry for babies between birth and
age two alone generating more than $700 million a year. "Parents
will do anything to provide for their children. Marketers now
know that this category has tremendous opportunity for growth,"
said Jan Studin, publisher of *Parents* magazine.

The marketing pitch to parents is usually predicated on fear—
and it starts right away and relentlessly. Advertisements scare
women senseless about all that can go wrong in pregnancy in order
to sell supplements, classes, massage therapy, shopping therapy,
and pillows, when a bath and a tub of chocolate would probably
suffice. Parents are bludgeoned over the head with statistically
warped safety warnings in order to sell childproofing gear,
strollers, changing tables, helmets, restraining devices, and high
chairs. We are inundated with articles about early childhood development that trumpet the need for children's cognitive stimulation in order to sell toys, DVDs, video games, computer programs,
extracurricular activities, programmed family outings and vacations, and a host of products bleating "sensory overload!" in moving, shaking, music-making primary colors. Books, tutors,
teachers, test prep companies, and admissions officers startle parents into action with scare stories about the merciless competition
of school entry requirements and academic performance and the
need for every child to find his ideal "learning environment," in

which he can meet and exceed his abilities—all to sell parents on sky-high tuition, tutoring fees, test-taking courses, test prep books, and consultant fees.

We are terrified of what might happen if we don't do "something" (that is, everything) for our kids, and too often this translates into buying something or hiring someone. Not only am I all too aware of this as a parent, I know this from the inside, having worked in the parenting business myself. From 1994 to 1997, I edited and managed a book club for parents of children ages three to seven at Scholastic. I had the advantage of witnessing how companies market to parents, capitalizing on their hopes, worries, and fears. (It was an ironic position for a woman in her mid-twenties who had never even held a baby.) We sold parenting books, activity books, children's nonfiction, educational toys, games, and "manipulatives"—all with the goal of helping parents "foster their child's emotional, social and cognitive development."

There are more places to buy these products and services than ever. The 1990s saw the birth of the baby superstore retail category with chains like buybuy BABY (the store name, sadly, says it all), which has stores measuring up to sixty thousand square feet, selling over twenty thousand products. Babies "R" Us, founded in 1996 and merged with the Baby Superstore chain in 1997, now has 218 stores nationwide, adding approximately eighteen stores per year. According to Alan Fields, coauthor of *Baby Bargains*, "The juvenile-products industry has tripled its size in terms of dollars . . . You can see that when you walk into a baby store. It overwhelms and frustrates new parents." Business owners have a rather rosier take: "Having a kid is very overwhelming," says Jeffrey Feinstein, the owner of buybuy BABY. "When you can walk into one store and there's so many items that can help you with a problem or help make the job of parenthood easier—one, you don't feel alone, and two, you're happy to have a selection of items to try and see which one works for you, because all babies are different and all parents have different preferences."[7]

Still . . . twenty thousand baby products in one store alone?

· · ·

IN THIS BOOK, I WILL EXPLAIN HOW THE ACT OF REARING CHIL-
dren has been turned into big business, requiring thousands of
dollars where hundreds once sufficed and filling our playrooms,
storage bins, and hallway closets with products our own parents
never dreamed would exist. I will seek answers to questions such
as: When did child rearing become "parenting" anyway, which
sounds exactly like what it is—an industry? How has the profes-
sionalization of parenting led to an avalanche of products and services targeted to parents? Which goods and expert opinions are
worthwhile? How can a parent figure that out when we are understandably susceptible to messages telling us that we should, ought
to, really must consider, absolutely cannot forget to, better not
avoid, truly must remember to buy, sign up for, enroll in, take advantage of this or that?

This book is not about how anxious parents are—though that's
partly why we succumb to excess expenditures for our kids. It's not
about how difficult raising kids is—though the difficulties parents
experience can motivate our purchases. It's not about whether
moms should or should not work—though our lifestyle choices *do*
affect consumer decisions. And it's not about how little social and
institutional support parents get nowadays—though our lack of
support may lead us to buy products and services to compensate
for that absence.

Most important, this book is not about making parents feel
even more guilt-ridden and anxious than they already do. I do not
claim to be the perfect parent. I have no doubt that years from
now, I will berate myself over my own parental misbehavior, and
one day, I am sure my children will do it for me. But as a journalist
reporting extensively on childhood and family issues, I've uncovered facts that I would not have otherwise known about raising
children. I've been lucky to have had the opportunity to talk to
hundreds of experts—psychologists, neuroscientists, pediatricians, educators—and to learn from their research.

To get an understanding of what's worth spending money on and what's exploitative, unnecessary, or harmful, I interviewed the entrepreneurs, managers, product developers, and marketers behind the parenting products. I talked to parent coaches, private tutors, prenatal yoga instructors, learning center instructors and owners, product managers for toy companies, founders of luxury baby goods lines, and advertising executives.

Many people who get into the parenting biz are parents themselves, moms-turned-entrepreneurs (*mompreneurs*) or smart, dedicated professionals who see a need and set out to fulfill it. I have spoken to start-up founders, consultants, and CEOs who are earnestly trying to make the lives of fellow parents easier and to enrich the lives of their children. I have no intention of demonizing all the businesses that serve parents' needs. Some of the products and services they provide are extraordinarily helpful. Unfortunately, however, many others aren't. We've been told that a whole range of products and services are necessary components of our child's life and our family's well-being. We assume that various services will give our children a leg up or support them in ways we couldn't do ourselves. Often, we're quite wrong.

Still, I continued to shop for my children even when I was diaper-pail-deep in my research for this book. Besides the ridiculous and misleading products I uncovered, products to condemn and services to scoff at, I kept finding magnificent things for babies—practical, time-saving, intriguing—or just too adorable to resist. I marveled at some of the innovations that we take for granted, but that previous generations somehow managed without. Where would we be—*dare we even think about it*—without the sippy cup? So I also talked to hundreds of parents. They overwhelmingly complained that not only are they strapped for time, which means they can't sort through the various marketing claims and read all the child development research; they're strapped for money.

There are serious reasons behind the price of parenthood that have nothing to do with this marketing—the rising cost of living, the lack of affordable childcare and health care, the punishing increases in college tuition—circumstances parents can do little to alleviate. There's also been a massive increase in marketing directed to children, a phenomenon that can distract parents from the ability to see the ways in which businesses target us directly.[8] Rather than be controlled and consumed by the marketing pitch, we *can* cut down on spending without shortchanging our kids. Sometimes, spending a lot on children isn't just unnecessary; it's counterproductive.

Every parent I know is struggling to figure out how to afford a family without succumbing to the spiral of consumption that characterizes modern parenthood. While we can't just have kids the way our parents did in the 1970s, at least not in financial terms, as my friend Ava hoped, we don't have to go broke for our children either. As I learned in the research for this book, it simply requires taking an informed approach to the mammoth power of the parenting industry, and, as Dr. Spock once advised, many expert exhortations ago, learning to trust ourselves.

1

Gearing Up

Keen to start off on the right bootie, you make sure to register at Babies "R" Us or your local baby emporium. Your list will likely include a full set of baby bedding: sheets, mattress liners, quilts, blankets, bumpers, dust ruffle, and a high-quality crib mattress. You will choose between a bassinet or a cosleeper, then select your crib, changing table, baby armoire, and glider. You'll want to purchase cushiony piles of receiving blankets, all-cotton onesies, hats, mittens, socks, pants, sweaters, and Robeez shoes. Then the hooded towels, extrasoft baby washcloths, patterned burp clothes, silky blankets, and bibs. Of course, you need the best in transportation: the safest car seat, a lightweight, easy-to-transport stroller, and a sturdier model with more features for neighborhood use. Plus a bouncy seat, a swing, a Gymini playmat, a Jumperoo, a scatter of rattles and teethers, and a pride of stuffed animals. You'll require a nursery school's worth of developmental toys: creatures with hands to tug and buttons to press, toys that "build cognitive skills" and "foster brain development," and a special black-and-white, high-contrast, patterned "Stim" mobile to hang over the crib in order to stimulate vision. You purchase white noise

machines, video baby monitors, and digital camcorders, ready to
track and trouble over every minute.

Then you have a bouncy little baby. During the first few groggy
weeks, you might agonize over breastfeeding, hiring three different lactation consultants, buying all manner of salves and implements to mend feeding woes: nipple cream, nursing pads, breast
shields, a breast pump, and a series of bottles and latex nipples.
You might purchase formula (two different brands) and then soy
formula for the baby who refuses regular. Frustrated and weary,
you might join a new mother's support group, hosted by a postpartum doula, for $15 a week. Bleary-eyed and somewhat depressed,
you might then hoist your exhausted limbs to postnatal yoga twice
a week, $12 per visit. "Soon," you think, "I can start Mommy and
Me yoga."

Six months will pass by in a haze of firsts and "Ugh, agains."
Certain expenditures, the kind you laugh at before you have a
child, suddenly seem reasonable. You might decide, for example,
that your wobbly baby needs assistance learning to sit upright and
purchase a plastic bébéPOD ("ergonomically designed to promote
proper posture while helping your Baby learn to sit"), pediatrician-
approved and -recommended, for $44.99. Or one of several com-
peting models that purport to do the very same thing. At some
point, despite your efforts, you might get that nervous itchy feeling
that parents so often do, that a child isn't quite . . . hitting all his
milestones at quite the right time. A friend's son is only five months
old and can already sit up by himself, whereas your six-month-old
can barely tripod and tips over within seconds. Someone else's
daughter kicks her legs every time she's Bjorn-bound; your baby's
hang limply. Could he be understimulated? Perhaps it's time to buy
an exersaucer. Or one of those jumpy-swing things that hang in the
doorway. Perhaps the baby needs new toys to stir his interest instead of lying placidly on his back, staring at the ceiling fan. Surely
there is something out there that can somehow make a baby's life
better, the best that it can be.

Call it the anxiety of underspending.

One dazed morning only a couple of months after my first child was born, between her daily round of naps, meals, and twenty-minute-long waking periods, I e-mailed my friend Holly, a seasoned mother of two. Both of us were following the same scheduling program, which encouraged us to play with our infants during their brief wakeful moments. I had dangled the requisite mobile over her bassinet, but my two-month-old looked away; she likewise seemed indifferent to her activity mat, with its cheery amusements swinging overhead. Was I playing the right way and with the right toys? "I feel like I'm not stimulating her enough," I typed out to Holly with my left hand, my right hand cradling Beatrice against my breast. "She seems sleepy and disinterested. Should I be doing more? Should I be taking her out more? Playing with her differently?"

"STOP THE GUILT," Holly responded immediately. "CALL ME RIGHT NOW."

Still clutching Beatrice, I phoned Holly at her office. "Listen," she said. "There is nothing you need to do with your baby except talk to her and hold her and give her some time lying around staring at whatever she wants to stare at." Our own mothers had not worried about having the right toys and playing the right way, Holly reminded me; they didn't feel compelled to do half the "enriching" activities, like perching colorful toys around the crib and piping Mozart MP3s into the nursery, that today's parents have been told they must do. Instead, they sequestered us in playpens and ran errands and cleaned the house and chased after our siblings while we drooled on the nearest surface. We were able to weather such "indifference"; both Holly and I managed to grow up emotionally unscathed and establish fully developed adult lives.

I knew Holly was right. I had said the same thing myself before I gave birth. What happened? When had I, like so many others, slipped off the edge of reasonableness into foolish dithering? I was now one of *those* moms—the ones who scrolled through Target.com perpetually searching for learning toys and just the right baby carrier. And *those* moms had probably been just like me—previously rational consumers who were driven to buy Mr. Whoozits and black-and-white striped soft blocks that squeak in a quest to ensure our children's proper visual development and auditory discrimination skills.

The anxiety of underspending has turned us into parenting gearheads, ever ready to purchase the perfect equipment to outfit our babies. As the gear becomes more specialized, we need more of it, and once nonexistent products and services are now considered essential. In the 1970s, for example, few people owned car seats. Today children are strapped by law into an armada of foamy seats and boosters well into elementary school. More than two kids, and you need a minivan to harness the equipment. Every parent totes a squirt bottle of antibacterial purifier in her pocketbook where soap and water once served. According to one survey, one in three parents sends their children to school with a bottle of it.[1] (The old ten-second rule—if it's on the ground for ten seconds or less, no problem—would send them into apoplexy.) Moms used to carry bottles and diapers around in old canvas totes; now any woman worth the cover price of *InStyle* fantasizes about an array of diaper bags to suit various outfits and occasions. Whereas disposable diapers (for those who didn't stick with cloth) were once tied up in a leftover produce bag and tossed in the garbage, they are now masterfully sucked into a Vipp diaper pail, where galvanized liners "lock in" odors to the tune of $168. And they can be pre-packaged inside Diaper Baggies, onetime-use small plastic bags with zipper closure, promise to add even more plastic and debris to the nation's mass of diaper detritus. New items materialize each year: the Splash Shield to keep bathwater in the tub; the Shopper Topper to stick on top of grimy grocery cart handles; the Original Crumb Chum, to cover a toddler in bib from chin to waist, across the lap, over the legs, and down to the toes. You would think our children never take baths.

Somehow, the parents of today's parents managed to raise their children without such accoutrements. When my brothers and I complained of boredom growing up, our mother told us to go outside or to play in a converted porch filled with old furniture, broken household items, crayons, and battered toys passed down by a neighbor. Our favorite game, Jump the Roof, involved piling old chairs and junk, covering them with a blanket, convincing the cat to come inside, then climbing atop until the entire thing collapsed. My mother supervised us when she could (she might have spent more time had she known exactly what we were up to), but she didn't make a daily ritual out of floor time and song-and-dance instruction. There was no Music Together; instead, my brothers and I spun around the living room, arms outstretched to make ourselves dizzy, to the tune of the tornado on the *Wizard of Oz* soundtrack, one of the few "children's records" we owned. Of course, it's easy to wax nostalgic over the glory days of youth, and certainly all was not rosy, yet we bargain-basement kids turned out just fine. Miraculously, none of us broke a bone or even sprained an ankle, and we all managed to get into good schools.

Like other mothers, my mom tried to eat well during pregnancy but allowed herself to billow out under a poufy maternity smock. Her approach to pregnancy and its aftermath was decidedly low-key; it had not yet been determined that pregnant moms require frequent massages and acupuncture. Once delivered from the womb, children were issued wooden blocks and figurines, toy fruit that could be pushed around in a mini shopping cart, a Barbie, or maybe a Baby Alive. We ran around in unisex overalls and plain turtlenecks, and at the kitchen table we were stuffed into cheap plastic boosters or piled onto a stack of books and cushions. Growing up, some kids got piano lessons or ballet if their parents were particularly ambitious; the rest joined Little League, ran around the block playing kickball, and rode bikes. Many mothers today would panic over a child left to dawdle unattended, squandering hours away alone or in the unsupervised company of other neighborhood kids, the children of "just anyone."

But then, even those glowing childhood memories have now been commodified, as marketers draw on the nostalgia for a carefree youth to sell a dizzying array of products. Notes one trade magazine, "The challenge for marketers and advertisers is defining what happiness means to mothers . . . Advertisers look for help in defining a mother's sense of happiness by recreating her own happy childhood in ads." This "nostalgia marketing" allows companies to "take mothers down memory lane in an attempt to help them relive childhood experiences that can be re-created for their own children." All in the name of enticing us to buy increasing numbers of increasingly complex gadgets when what many of us actually long for is the simplicity of our own comparatively unencumbered youths.

THE PARENTING BUSINESS IS ALL ABOUT EXTRAVAGANZAS, AND for expectant parents and the parenting business, the baby shower is the auspicious start to a juggernaut of spending. What originated as an informal affair for close friends and family has become a massive celebration for friends, extended relatives, and coworkers. Party planners have turned the shower, a formerly demure occasion for bequeathing dainty outfits and pastel-colored keepsakes, into themed events. "People love to celebrate the different stages of life," says etiquette expert Peggy Post. "Traditionally, baby showers were small and intimate, just the way wedding showers used to be. But we live in a consumer society and people love to shop."

This modern baby shower arrives with fanfare, complete with theme (bunnies, things that go, ladybugs), color scheme (modernist, baby blue, gender-neutral orange), and several carefully engineered baby registries. The shower embodies everything we want our baby to be and everything we dream about as a parent, to embrace everything we loved about our childhoods and inveigh against all that we disliked. Where we choose to register and for what comes to symbolize the type of parent we want to be and the way in which we want to raise our children. By the time giddy expectant moms get down to actually setting up a registry, a baby's arrival—in terms of worldly goods—can seem fraught with implications that few feel prepared to consider.

"You walk into Babies 'R' Us, and you're just so overwhelmed because you have no idea exactly what you need," recalled Brooke Houghton, a thirty-five-year-old from Chicago who gave birth to a baby girl in 2007. The first time she made a go of it, she ran out in a panic after fifteen minutes. "There was just so much equipment I hadn't even considered!" The next time, she brought along moral—and practical—support. "A friend who already had kids took me to help out, but I was still overwhelmed." Houghton's friend gave her the store "gun" to zap bar codes on items, automatically entering them into her registry, and pointed to various items she thought Houghton would need. "But it kept going on and on, and I was embarrassed because I didn't want my list to be too long. I was afraid I would look greedy." Her friend insisted she include things like a high chair and a travel seat, even though Houghton wouldn't need them for months. "She was like, 'Trust me. You don't want to have to buy these things yourself. So if people want to get them, let them get them for you.'" Houghton drew the line at the breast pump. "Surely, that's something I can get for myself!"

Claire Varrelmann, a twenty-eight-year-old expectant mother from Madison, Wisconsin, figured she knew what she was getting into when she embarked on her baby registry. "I had come along with several girlfriends to register for their first babies, so I didn't think it would be a big issue for me," she said. "But when I went into Babies 'R' Us by myself, I just couldn't do it." Varrelmann, too, had to return to the store with a friend in tow, even though Babies "R" Us assigns expecting moms a dedicated salesperson who provides a handy, preprinted shopping list and the easy-to-wield gun scanner. In the end, she consulted the store's checklist and asked friends for advice. "I'm usually a great decision maker, but in this situation there are just so many choices," she explained. "There are ten different swings to choose from, and trying to differentiate between the features on each and decide which you really need can be overwhelming to a first-time mom." She tried to enlist her mother's guidance. "But my mom couldn't believe all the stuff out there—everything from the monitor to the Diaper Champ. She could figure out what they were, but she didn't have any of this when she was a new mother." Indeed, Varrelmann's mother felt the need to consult with another new grandmother to get a primer on what equipment *she* needed to have on hand for family visits, meeting with her adviser at one of her daughter's four baby showers.

Yes, *four* baby showers. And it's hardly unusual anymore. Stores report that women are having at least two and often three showers: one for friends, one for family, and one in the workplace. In Varrelmann's case, the first baby shower was hosted by her best friend from college, in her husband's hometown, Clear Lake, Iowa, so that Varrelmann's mother-in-law and her extended family could attend along with their friends. The second was in Madison, hosted by a few girlfriends in the area, and intended mostly for Varrelmann's friends and her side of the family. A third, with a "Sweet and Sassy" theme, was hosted by three girlfriends from work, with colleagues invited to attend on a weekday afternoon. Finally, neighbors on her block planned a shower barbecue for Varrelmann and her cow-breeder husband, Caleb, so that they could join in the festivities as well.

To handle the downpour, Varrelmann, by then adept with the scanner gun, created three different registries, turning to Target and Pottery Barn Kids in addition to Babies "R" Us, and following a precision plan. She divided her needs into three categories. First, there were the big-ticket items: the car seat, stroller, bouncy seat, Pack n' Play, and baby swing. Next were necessities: diapers, onesies, a first-aid kit, a grooming kit, a Diaper Genie, and a diaper-wipe warmer. Finally, there were the "fun items": decor for the nursery, car-seat toys, a nightlight, a baby book, a Gymini play-mat. "It's a little overwhelming," Varrelmann repeated. "I live in a house that's over a hundred and twenty years old, and we don't have a lot of storage. I keep worrying about how we'll put things away like the bathtub. It all adds up."

For baby gear manufacturers, it also adds up—in a good way. Registries have mushroomed in the past ten years into a $240-million business, up 9.6 percent between 2004 and 2006 according to research firm Mintel International. Baby specialty stores and retailers like Wal-Mart and Target view baby showers, espe-cially the trend toward hosting more than one per pregnancy, as a major opportunity. "Smart retailers see baby registries as an initial touchpoint and a way to grow with a woman and her family," said David Morris, a senior research analyst at Mintel. According to Joel Hernandez, a Babies "R" Us promotional coordinator, new parents get about 60 percent of the items they register for.[2] Many then buy the remainder of their list themselves. Encouraging a massive registry pays off either way.

Registries are ballooning to include ever more expensive items. They're the fastest growing part of the business for minichain Gig-gle, which consists of four stores and a website, with sales up more than 30 percent a year. "People still spend more on a wedding present," said Ali Wing, founder of Giggle, "but the amount peo-ple spend on a shower gift has increased in the last five years, from an average of forty dollars to sixty dollars per gift to a new stan-dard of sixty dollars to seventy-five dollars." (Nationwide, accord-ing to Mintel International, the average price of shower gifts rose from $22 in 2002 to $26 in 2006—less than upscale Giggle but an 18 percent uptick.) When Wing started her company in 2002, par-ents were sensitive to the fact that they should have an appropri-ate range of items and prices. "People felt that if they put their crib on their registry it was offensive. Now they're putting on thousand-dollar cribs."

Joe Mediate, CEO of KooKoo Bear Kids, an online, catalog, and retail marketer of children's rooms and gifts located in suburban Roswell, Georgia, has also observed the shift. "People are buying fewer necessities nowadays and instead looking for the 'Wow' gift," he said. "Years ago, it was diapers and onesies from Target. Today, people want to make a statement." At his stores, expectant parents create registries averaging fifty to sixty items long, including $1,500 cribs and $2,000 bedding sets. "It's amazing the gifts people are giving, but people *want* to give them," he told me, a bit befuddled. While the most registered-for item in Amazon's baby store is diapers, people have begun shopping outside the "baby store" to register for items in outdoor gear, for baby backpacks, and consumer electronics. "Electronics are a very big category with baby registries," said Mark Randall, vice president of toys and baby products at Amazon. "People are requesting video cameras, digital cameras, and iPod docking stations for their nurseries."

Even the more affordable retailers have noticed parents registering for bigger-ticket gifts. According to a spokesperson for Target, people will pool together to purchase the items. "As women have entered the workplace, the office often goes in together on one big gift," said Emilia Fabricant, president and chief merchandising officer of Babystyle, a web retailer and national chain. (To think that only a decade ago, having a child and taking maternity leave was something female employees did as surreptitiously as possible.)

The drive to buy is intense, said Jessie Jury, thirty-three, who works for a technology firm from home in Homewood, Illinois. "At first I thought it was because I was pregnant and so I was more aware of all the products being sold out there," Jury said. "But I realized that society is just baby crazy these days. There are so many new things coming out constantly, and there's this pressure to give your child the best start. It's hard to weed out what's really good and what's hype." And someone is always telling you about all the things you absolutely must buy. When I mentioned in an e-mail to a passing professional acquaintance that I was pregnant with my first child, she e-mailed back an inventory of "required" items that sent me into a hyperventilating tailspin. In its gearhead relish and brand-name-dropping, it rivaled the "new parents' checklist" at Babies "R" Us, which prepares parents for the daunting task of having a baby with its list of more than a hundred registry "essentials."

WHAT TO TAKE TO THE HOSPITAL

FOR THE BABY: Undershirt (for the umbilical cord), 2 diapers, 2 outfits (in case of spit-up on one), bootie/socks, sweater, mittens (so they don't scratch themselves and their hands stay warm), hat, blanket, bunting, car seat, bottle, pacifier, infant car seat (I like the Graco Snug Ride, which fits into the Snap and Go, an infant stroller).

FOR THE MOTHER: Toiletries, 2 nightgowns, 1 bathrobe, slippers, 1 outfit to go home in (you will probably not fit into prepregnancy clothing, so bring a loose-fitting outfit or maternity wear), underwear (bring 2 bras, and if you are planning to breastfeed, don't forget nursing bras and pads), your own pillow and pillowcase, your own towel, address/telephone book, a calling card, a couple of large shopping bags to bring home gifts or supplies provided by the hospital. Also, don't forget the video camera and camera with film.

NURSERY BASICS
Bassinet (optional—I used this for three months)
Crib with bumper pads
Glider/ottoman
Lamp
Changing station
CD/cassette player
Lullaby CD/tapes
Mobile (good to make sure it plays three songs and has primary
    colors; babies see red and black first)

Clock

2 waterproof crib pads

3–4 fitted crib sheets

Dust ruffle

Comforter (for decoration; you won't use this for the baby for probably the first year)

4 changing pad covers

4 crib and stroller blankets

5 receiving blankets

Nursery monitor

Lots of antibacterial soap (for each bathroom)

BABY GEAR

High chair (not until the baby is sitting up—around five to six months old)

Diaper bag

Infant car seat

Bouncy chair

Swing (I like the Fisher-Price one with the lights and fish)

Activity center

Pack n' Play (portable play yard and sleeping place)

BABY CLOTHES

6–10 T-shirts (until the umbilical cord falls off, usually within five to ten days)

6–10 body suits (for after the umbilical cord falls off)

6–10 onesies (for sleeping)

4 gowns (I didn't like these as the baby moved more; it rides up the legs)

1–3 sweaters (of varying weight)

6 pairs of socks

1 snowsuit

1 warm hat

mittens

24 hangers

BATH

Infant tub

4 hooded towels

6 baby washcloths (Carter's are small and soft)

Baby wash

Baby lotion

Baby shampoo

DAILY-CARE ITEMS

2 newborn pacifiers

2 packages of disposal diapers (get both the type for before and
after the umbilical cord falls off)

Baby wipes

Diaper Genie and refills

Changing pad

Infant Tylenol

Thermometer

Nasal aspirator

Saline drops

Nail scissors or clipper

Comb and brush

Protect mittens

Diaper-rash cream (I like Triple Paste the best)

BREASTFEEDING

Nursing bras

Nursing pads

Nursing shirts

Medela breast pump

4 8-oz. plastic bottles (Dr. Browns or ones with a curve to prevent
gas)

4 4-oz. plastic bottles

Breast milk storage bags

1 dozen burp cloths

Boppy pillow for nursing

Nursing cream for soreness

Bottle drying rack

Mylicon gas drops

BOTTLE-FEEDING

10–12 8-oz. bottles (stage 1 nipples; get the starter set)

4 4-oz. bottles

1 case of formula (I like Similac with iron, DHA, and ARA)

4–8 small cloth bibs

Dishwasher basket

Joy dishwashing liquid (to wash bottles)

Bottle and nipple brush

Insulated bottle holder for travel

Powder formal dispenser

Boppy pillow for feeding

Mylicon gas drops

Bottle warmer

TOYS

Gymini (primary colors: red, white, black)

Rattles

Stuffed animals

CD/cassette player

Soft books

DVD/videos

Developmental toys

THINGS TO KEEP IN DIAPER BAG

Portable changing pad with a place for ointment, wipes, and
    diapers

1 change of clothes

Small plastic bags for wet diapers

Bottle

Formula in dispenser (a can is good too)

Bottled water for powdered formula

Extra blanket

Pacifier

Toys and books

Sunscreen

Hat

Emergency medical information

I frankly had no idea what half these item were and felt sick-ened by my own ignorance. Faced with such a catalog of the oncoming consumer binge, some expectant mothers feel queasy. When Roxanna Hakimi, thirty-four, was pregnant in 2005, she made the pilgrimage to her local buybuy BABY superstore in Rockville, Maryland. "I had a breakdown," she recalled. "There were so many things there that I had no idea what to choose." She left after about fifteen minutes and returned two weeks later with her husband, but his support didn't make things easier. "We felt like it was our wedding registry all over again. How could we ask people to buy us these things? We ended up registering for a lot of silly trinkets that everyone suggests you buy and getting the big things ourselves or as gifts from our parents." After Hakimi's son was born, she packed up the bottle sterilizer, bottle warmer, diaper wipe warmer, and a slew of other products and returned them. "There's so much baby gear out there that one does not need. It's this huge moneymaking machine." Thirty-one-year-old Stephanie Morris, who gave birth to a girl in 2007, tried to keep her two reg-istries to the basics. "I was astounded by how much is out there for newborns," she said. "I heard it was similar to the wedding indus-try, but I still wasn't prepared. After walking around the store in a stupor, Morris retreated and did some research on- and off-line to figure out what she actually needed. "It's really easy to get sucked into thinking you need everything."

But for Big Baby, registries are the gift that keeps on giving. Once reserved for the firstborn, showers are becoming a ritual for second-time moms. According to research conducted by Babies "R" Us, 37 percent of so-called experienced moms create registries, a number that has increased significantly in recent years. According to Amazon, grandparents are adding their own items onto their child's registry; Babies "R" Us has even seen the creation of "grandparent registries." "There are so many more products available for moms that when they have a second child, the market has changed and they want to register again," said Deborah Derby, president of Babies "R" Us. "Everyone wants to get the latest and greatest for baby."

The ante keeps getting raised, and if you abstain, it's hard not to feel that your baby is (relatively) deprived. "A kid is now a status symbol in a way that it wasn't before," explained Marian Salzman, chief strategy officer for the advertising behemoth RSCG Worldwide. "People define themselves as architects of family life." The mentality fostered by our consumption-driven culture is: The more we spend on our children, *the more we care*.

WHEN IT COMES TO CARING FOR A BABY, THERE COULDN'T BE A more loaded phrase than "the brand you trust." Most women start buying baby gear during the third trimester, so more companies are trying to appeal to women early in their pregnancies, hoping to establish a loyal relationship between mother and brand that will last well into her child's life. In 2006, for example, eighty-year-old Playskool, a company long associated with preschoolers, expanded into baby care in order to better cultivate maternal devotion. "For a brand all about infants and toddlers, establishing a connection with moms is critical," said Lorrie Browning, general manager of preschool toys at Hasbro, which owns Playskool.[3] Babies in Playskool Plushies diapers can have their tushes wiped by Playskool wipes and chug milk from Playskool sippy cups long before they're ready for Mr. Potato Head.

"It's all about customer acquisition," explained Andrew

Moreno, a retail manager for Hollister, which manufactures breast pumps. Products and companies help expectant or new mothers retain their business as their children grow up. Breastfeeding equipment, for example, has become a source of growth for companies aiming for the mom market. Between 2004 and 2006, Evenflo Company's breast pump sales rose 29 percent as the company, which manufactures everything from children's toys to exersaucers, pushed efforts to brand itself onto new mothers through its breastfeeding accessories.[4] A 2007 report in the *Wall Street Journal* noted that while breastfeeding has "traditionally been associated with maternal bonding, immunities and nutrition," for some companies, "it is all about business plans, market share and product placement." Ten years ago, only one double electric portable breast pump was available in the United States; today there are more than twenty.

Babies "R" Us hosts a series of special in-store events to pull expectant and new moms through its doors. Super Baby Showers feature "local experts" who help expectant parents, relatives, and friends host a proper baby shower, including, of course, advice on what to buy. There's a breastfeeding and maternity workshop to facilitate the purchase of all manner of feeding paraphernalia. Johnson & Johnson, a company most closely associated with bathroom products like shampoo and baby powder, capitalizes on the opportunity to extend its reach into the nursery by sponsoring Crib Notes, an in-store seminar on getting a child to sleep. The store's Baby Safety Expo features safety seminars and product demonstrations. All of this is carefully orchestrated with an eye toward building "relationships" with women on the brink of motherhood and capturing loyalty.

Grandest of all baby shopping experiences, and dwarfing the retail superstores, is the hulking American Baby Faire, a roving exhibition sponsored by Babies "R" Us that alights at large convention centers in major cities across the country nearly every month. Billed as the largest baby exposition in the country, Baby Faire offers live entertainment, free giveaways, and, above all, an enormous consumer product show. "We showcase tons of products, and they're all presented by experts," said Aija Erglis, the show's director. "You can really talk to the people who designed the product before you go home and make educated assessments about what you need for your baby."[5] Baby Faire includes a pavilion where expectant parents can attend additional "buying opportunity" seminars on topics such as car-seat safety and nursery design.

More than a hundred exhibitors offer activities and product samples to lure parents to their wares, and children and grandparents are granted free admission. At the 2007 Baby Faire in Dallas, Palmer's Cocoa Butter Formula hosted what it called the World's Largest Baby Butter Massage, in which three hundred babes were manipulated under the guidance of the author of *Baby Massage for Dummies*. Needless to say, many of the featured products and services are for sale. Every effort is made to ensure parents are comfortably accommodated and ready to spend. Food stations abound. There are special nursing lounges and "diaper depots." Amply sized aisles beckon stroller pushers. Kids can be ferried from "super spiral bouncer" to a twenty-four-foot-high "Old Woman in the Shoe" slide to the "action center filled with toys." There's a baby derby relay, cosponsored by Huggies, in which parents can determine whose baby crawls the fastest. An estimated fifteen thousand people attend each event. As one mommy blogger recounted in her online diary,

> I thought this sounded like a really great idea until I researched it on-line. I had a panic attack looking at the pictures. It's basically a Babies "R" Us but TEN times as big because it's at Dallas Market Hall . . . Everyone knows that registering at Babies "R" Us nearly sent me on a drinking binge, so I can only imagine what would happen if I went to the American Baby Faire.[6]

The enormity of Baby Faire amply demonstrates that there's a lot more gear out there for parents. Take just one product category—soap—a seemingly straightforward purchase, and the explosion in goods and brands is clear. There used to be just one or two kinds of soap for our youngest bathers, either Johnson's Baby Wash or a bar of Dove. Today there are dozens to choose from. Parents can turn to one of the "basic" brands—Gerber, Playtex Baby Magic, Aveeno, Aquaphor—or choose from a throng of specialty products, each with its cutesy name and charmingly adorned package: Doctor Bobby Body Wash ("created by a pediatric dermatologist," $14), Butt Naked Baby Essentials Oatmeal Bath ($15), Cocoon Gentle Body and Hair Wash (with chamomile, lavender, and lemongrass, $9), Propoline Baby Mild Wash for Hair and Body (with olive and chamomile, $12). Parents can venture into upscale luxury baby lines from Kiehls, Mustela, and Davies. They can go earthy with wholesome products like Avalon Organics, Baby Botanicals, California Baby, and Burt's Bees. The profusion has propelled baby soap sales, up 17 percent in 2005, to almost $100 million in sales a year.[7]

That's just stuff to clean your kid; when you include baby lotion, baby cream, baby moisturizer (yes, it's true), baby oil, cradle cap shampoo, regular baby shampoo, baby powder, petroleum jelly, and diaper cream, there are hundreds of infant toiletries available, adding up to a $548-million market. From a chemical point of view, most of these products are the same, containing simple ingredients to either wash or lubricate, with dyes and scents and botanicals mixed in to make the product pretty and sweet. But the boutique label on a delicate bottle of lavender-scented crème pour le bébé is so much more appealing than the jumbo jug of bubble-gum pink Baby Magic from CVS. Shouldn't your baby have Kiehls too? As a parent, it's hard to resist.

The truth is, most babies don't even need baby cream, powder, or lotion; unless they have a dermatological condition, their skin is naturally soft and supple. While the products are concocted to appeal to parents, many contain dyes, scents, and other chemicals that have never been tested on infants; there is no FDA for toiletries, either adult or infant. A number of the chemicals in baby products may be allergenic; some are suspected to cause or exacerbate eczema. Many baby shampoos, for example, often contain 1,4-dioxane, a chemical deemed by the Environmental Protection Agency to be a "probable human carcinogen."[8]

No matter what a container includes or leaves out, baby-care products offer high margins to the companies that create them. As with adult cosmetics, the cost is largely in the marketing and packaging, and customers clearly fall for the frippery. Between 2005 and 2006, drugstore spending on baby ointments increased 14 percent; spending on bath products increased 10 percent and on lotion sales 9 percent.[9] In order to further nurture this profitable market, companies have begun to market "toddler care" products in their brand lines. "The expansion of baby wipes into toddler potty training, hand and face clean-up products, and bath-time products is a great way to grow the category," said Cathie Petak, category manager for Rockline Industries, a private-label baby-care manufacturer. "The [toddler] segment has historically been unaddressed, and the current offerings help fill a void," confirmed Tammy Stewman, a marketing category manager for Cumberland Swan, another manufacturer. As a result, sales of such diaper wipes grew 7 percent in 2005 to $64.6 million a year. New products like "youth pants," geared toward older bed wetters, have generated 25 to 33 percent increases in revenues.

Parents naturally grab at anything that appears tailored to their child's needs at a particular developmental stage, no matter how idiosyncratic or brief. As Matt Rinaldi, president of the private-label manufacturer Arquest, explained, "An important part of marketing these new products is to include developmental nomenclature on the packaging that signals that the products are designed to address specific performance and fit needs in their child's stage of life."[10] A special toy for clumsy nine-month-olds or a funny-shaped spoon for fourteen-month-olds who insist only on using forks can seem like rational, even essential, purchases at a given parenting moment. When my second child had trouble sleeping during his first few months, I purchased a round of attempted fix-its: two sleep sacks (the latter to bypass the faults of the first purchase; it zipped up easily, matched the room temperature in the nursery, and skipped the carcinogenic flame retardants), a sleep positioner, a white-noise machine, and anything that promised to make him sleep, now, *please*. Parents are particularly keen on finding the right gear for a given challenge if they are working long hours and don't have the time to spend tending to the problem themselves. We are all looking to purchase *solutions*.

IN THE SWIRL OF GEARING UP, THE MOST MUNDANE PRODUCTS are sold with an intimidating barrage of high-tech promise. Cleaning, once accomplished with towels and trashcans, boasts state-of-the-art implements and measures to eradicate the slightest indication of bodily waste that are nothing short of astounding. The Diaper Genie II Advanced Disposal System proffers a "revolutionary patented Air-Tite Odor Barrier System" with a seven-layer barrier film that makes diaper odor "virtually disappear." Implementing a zero-tolerance toward germs is a mini-industry in itself. The makers of the Germ Guardian Nursery Sanitizer ($69.99) warn, "Germs can be passed on toys, especially moist soft toys, where a wet environment is the perfect breeding ground for germs." The device pledges to kill 99.9 percent of the treacherous microbes skulking around on bath toys, bottles, and teethers in thirty minutes.

Much of the seemingly indispensable baby gear seems barely useful to begin with, and it's almost too easy to find downright useless products to disparage. A set of finger-puppet children's cutlery transforms mealtime into showtime, with children sticking their fingers into the stems of smiley-faced spoons and knives— well and good until some zealous toddler forks another child's eye out. There's the $31.99 Twilight Turtle, a stuffed animal with an orange shell that glows in the dark ("individually hand painted"), which projects images of stars onto a child's bedroom ceiling, helping her identify eight constellations while easing fear of the dark. It's one of the top-selling items in Amazon's Baby Store. Farewell, $2.99 night-lights. The company also offers a Sleep Sheep that makes soothing sounds and a Lavender Lab that releases a soothing scent. (Given that lavender has been found to stimulate female breast development in boys, the spritzing puppy may be the last thing you want to put in your little boy's room.)[11] For children with sophisticated musical taste, there's the iCrib, a compact sound system compatible with MP3 players. A "stroller rocker" to help a baby fall asleep is also available, to the delight of 52 percent of moms (according to a Parents.com poll); a whirlpool bath spa is considered a must-have for one-third of moms. Finally, there's the TP Saver, a gadget that prevents wayward children from unraveling toilet paper off its roll. Invented by Tamara Monosoff, a mother with a doctorate in education and a former Clinton White House staffer who founded the Mom Inventors website in 2003, the TP Saver sold thirty thousand units in its first year, with receipts of about $1.5 million,[12] and relieved many parents of the onerous task of reminding children to "leave the toilet paper alone!"

Perhaps the TP Saver won't last. After all, the aisles of baby emporiums are littered with the vestiges of baby products once deemed crucial but now considered obsolete. The formerly universal walker, for example, is now widely shunned despite the efforts of walker manufacturers to adopt and advertise new safety standards. (Between 1990 and 1994, an average of 23,000 walker-related injuries occurred each year; in 2003, 3,200 were hurt.) Often there is good reason to discard. While parents and babies loved the freedom walkers afforded, according to at least one hospital study, walkers may in fact *delay* walking and other motor skill development.[13] In the 1960s and '70s, mothers swore by travel-friendly wicker changing tables, which could be easily folded. A little too easily. One mother who raised five children back then told me about her fourteen-month-old daughter inadvertently collapsing the contraption, which toppled her onto the floor, breaking her nose. You don't see those tables anymore.

But companies are constantly conceiving new gear to replace the must-haves of yore. Every year at the 2006 Juvenile Products Manufacturers Association show, awards are issued for the most innovative debuts. In 2006, recognized products included the Strollometer, "the world's first computer/speedometer designed to fit any stroller," and the go-go Kidz Travelmate, an attachment that hooks to toddler car seats, allowing them to be rolled along with one hand, a blessing to any parent who has lugged the unwieldy, twenty-pound Britax Marathon through an airport. Another industry gathering, the All Baby and Child Expo, an annual convention in Las Vegas, is the fastest-growing trade show in the nation, with more than seven hundred exhibitors in over 450,000 square feet of exhibit space, each bent on getting a piece of the $6 billion spent each year on baby equipment.

New products continue to wend their way from trade show novelty to consumer ubiquity. When today's mothers were babies, most were likely nestled on their own mothers' hips when they weren't being pushed in a stroller. In the mid-1970s, the Baby Bjorn carrier won the endorsement of doctors, who ballyhooed the importance of eye-to-eye, physical contact between a baby and his parents, and by the 1990s, the Baby Bjorn was the established carrier of choice; the use of slings, a low-tech rival, was confined to earthy mamas in San Francisco and Santa Fe. Today, any mom with a penchant for Dr. Sears–style baby-wearing can choose from dozens of sling manufacturers, with carriers available in fleece, mesh, cotton, silk, linen, or heavy wool, in every conceivable color, print, and size. There is a profusion of kangaroo pouches, designer Bjorns, and Ergos. And we can hoist our babies behind: Nearly half of the country's 75 million recreational hikers are parents, propelling sales of sports-related child carriers to $10 million in 2005.[14] The fanciest are framed carriers, retailing for as much as $250, which look like serious camping gear but are often seen on parents' backs as they trek up and down urban sidewalks. To my embarrassment and occasional shame, the entryway to our house is jam packed with a stroller/car-seat travel system, a toddler car seat, a sports stroller, a Snap 'N Go, a double stroller, an umbrella stroller, a Baby Bjorn, a Kangaroo Korner pouch, and a baby backpack. There's another stroller in the basement, which seemed rational of the time of purchase. A trip to the local zoo requires a careful negotiation of transit gear depending on our mode of travel, the babies' nap status, and an assortment of other variables.

Modes of baby transport are no trivial matter. Shuttling children around is nothing new, but the frequency and means have altered dramatically in the last twenty years. Parents are *constantly* leaving the house, what with Americans spending an average of one hundred hours a year commuting and children enrolled in a weekly average of four activities outside the home. In the early 1980s, when car seats became widely available, the days of kicking and fighting for space in the backseat of the family station wagon ended (though the struggles of parents to fit multiple children in anything short of a mini-van had only just begun). The shift in family transportation has been dramatic. Today, driving a child without a car seat is against the law; and every year, nearly 5 million car seats are sold across the country. According to the Fatality Analysis Reporting System, infant seats for babies under one reduce the chance of dying in a crash by 71 percent and seats for children ages one to four decrease the death rate by 54 percent. (By comparison, seat belts alone lower the death rate 47 percent for children under age five.) Still, it's not easy for the average parent to weigh all the safety precautions and statistics. Though car seats save children in accidents, they may create problems as well. A few small-scale studies have shown that young babies are in danger of asphyxiating in their car seats when their heads slump forward while sleeping, cutting off their oxygen supply. And a frightening 2007 study by the Ecology Center, an Ann Arbor–based research organization, discovered that chemicals including PVC, brominated flame retardants, and lead are found in car seats, possibly contributing to developmental and liver and thyroid problems in children.

Shopping for a car seat can feel like purchasing climbing equipment for a trip up Mount Everest. Products come complete with multiple safety assurances, stamps, codes, and endorsements, and each advertises itself as the safest, most proven seat on the market. "Be Over-Protective," urges an advertisement for SafeGuard, "the most advanced child seat in the world." The SafeGuard boasts "more safety features than any other seat on the market" and includes "aircraft aluminum construction" and "headrests designed for important side-impact protection." When I walked into my local baby store and told one of the clerks I was looking for a toddler car seat, I was immediately accosted by the store's car-seat "specialist," a salesman who reeled off *Consumer Reports* statistics rapid-fire while escorting me to the top-ranking Britax Roundabout, a mammoth chaise retailing for $219.

"Uh, I don't care about safety," I gently interrupted.

The salesperson looked as if he'd been shot.

"You don't care about *safety*?" he repeated, trying to regain his breath.

"No, I'm looking for something light and easy to carry," I explained. "I don't have a car, so I'll be taking it in and out of rentals and borrowed cars all the time. I mean, they're all basically safe, aren't they?"

The salesman leaned forward and whispered excitedly, "That's exactly right," he said. His whole body visibly relaxed. He set down the sheaths of photocopied papers and promotional brochures that he'd been flapping about. With a conspiratorial gleam in his eye, he unloaded what must have been long pent-up frustration over peddling car seats, careful to keep his voice lowered to a whisper. "We all survived without any seats at all, right?" It was as if he'd been momentarily freed from the endless manufacturer guarantees and recalls; the rabble-rousing press that freaks out every time a safety lapse occurs; the anxiety-ridden parents fearful that the wrong purchase could send their infants flying out the window if they took a sharp left; the threat that perhaps he could somehow be blamed if something, somewhere went terribly wrong. We proceeded to look for a chair that I could disengage and unload easily, and that wouldn't whack my spine out of alignment when I tried to haul it through an airport. (Lugging around a car seat of any size is no small endeavor, which is why the Sit n' Stroll, a car seat that converts into a stroller of sorts, has become wildly popular, its low-slung passengers visible hurtling through airports and in and out of taxicabs on busy streets.) The chair I ended up buying, which is perfectly safe, saved me over $100.

Safety isn't the only factor when it comes to selling child-car equipment. The biggest car-seat manufacturers offer dozens of fashionable covers so that parents can match their gear to the color scheme of their cars and sell additional car-seat bases separately to simplify the complicated handover from Mom's to Dad's car. Disturbingly, the obesity rate in two- to five-year-olds has more than doubled in the last thirty years, and, according to a 2006 study in *Pediatrics*, "Tipping the Scales," more than 280,000 American children are too big for a standard car seat. In response, companies have created plus-size car seats like the Britax Husky, with wider buckets and longer straps for children weighing up to eighty pounds. There are even car seats made for stuffed animals (Joovy's "Just Like Mine," $30) so that strapped-in only children aren't deprived of company while harnessed in.

Of course, it's not likely that a child would be truly alone given the flotilla of mobile accoutrements available to transform the car seat into a baby-friendly entertainment zone. There are car-seat mirrors and car-seat video cameras (so as to observe a rear-facing baby's facial expression while the parent is parallel parking), car-

seat toys and activity centers, in-car television sets, car-seat mo-
biles, attachable snack trays, and car-seat clip-on blankets. There
are devices to protect the baby from the car, like a car-seat comfort footrest ($24.95), which promises "no more painful dangling
legs," and a seat-belt adjuster pad ($8.95) that "feels good against
little tummies," unlike "rigid plastic and metal buckles." And there
are devices to protect the car from the baby, such as the car-seat
protector ($19.95), designed to eliminate stains and dents from
bulky car seats and their sloppy inhabitants, and the Toys on the
Go Backseat Organizer ($16.95), which drapes over a front seat,
with plenty of pockets for books, DVDs, and other diversions. The
National Highway Traffic Safety Administration, which meticulously regulates car seats and other backseat child restraints like
booster seats and seat belts, has no jurisdiction whatsoever over
any of these products. With all the caution and oversight devoted
to the car seat itself, parents essentially buy and use their accessories at their own risk.

THE NUMBER OF GADGETS DEVOTED TO KEEPING OUR BABIES
safe, contained, and entertained en route is dwarfed by the number of gizmos designed to keep our babies alive when out of the
car. Parents need just one visit to what's alternately called the Wall
of Fear or the Wall of Death in their local baby store—rows of
gear to secure every door and drawer, pad each pointy corner and
unpleasant surface, and blockade every staircase—to terrify them
into a buying frenzy. Even if they veer clear of their retail pur-
veyor of doom, they can become well versed in the threats online,
at specialized Web sites like Perfectly Safe. Divided into "safety
zones" like Electrical, Fire, and On the Go, the site sells such necessities as a soft-cornered toy box, to ensure your baby never
bumps his head against a harsh corner, and The Bilby, a $27.95
shopping-cart liner for mothers who worry about their children's
comfort and protection from germs while trundled through the

grocery store. It's hard to imagine many parents, on top of dealing with mounds of groceries, eager to drag a pile of fabric as big as a sleeping bag to the supermarket, but there *is* a market for the thing, and several varieties exist. As there is for Walking Wings ($25) by Upstart, a harness to strap onto your child while he's learning to walk, so as to prevent any conceivable mishap or tumble.

Katharine Hepburn used to tell a story of her carefree youth in which she climbed to the top of a tall tree in her backyard as a young girl, A neighbor spotted her and went running to her mother, frantic. "Mrs. Hepburn," the neighboring mother cried out in alarm. "Kathy is all the way up at the top of that tree!"

"I know," Hepburn's mother blithely replied. *"Don't let her know that it's dangerous."*

We are a far way off from such wanton times. According to historian Peter Stearns, author of *Anxious Parents: A History of Modern Childrearing in America,* the view of American children as inherently vulnerable is a distinctly twentieth-century phenomenon, which we have gingerly escorted into the twenty-first century. And their vulnerability has become increasingly loaded. It wasn't until the 1920s that the ideas of risk and accident were redefined as not *really* accidental but the result of parental incompetence.[15] That shift in blame exacerbated the need to do whatever it takes to keep babies safe. Simultaneously, accidents involving children became more common. Many of the inventions and appliances of twentieth-century life increased children's susceptibility to certain types of harm (cars whizzing by, surge protectors, vacuum-sealed refrigerators, you name it). By World War II, accidents were the leading cause of death among young children.[16] Businesses rushed to attend to children's vulnerability, real and perceived, with child-proof devices requiring parental implementation and often supervision, and have been pumping out new ones ever since.

As a consequence, our children are more watched over, hovered over, and breathed-down-the-neck-over than previous generations. Baby monitors have become increasingly high-tech and high-priced, to the point where using a standard audio monitor seems as primitive as waiting until a baby wails loudly enough to be heard from downstairs. For $200, the Philips DECT monitor scrambles the signal of its wireless device—heaven forbid the neighbors try to listen in to a baby's tantrums—and acts as a two-way monitor so that parents can coo "Hush-a-bye" to their infants from any room in the house. An advertisement in an airplane mall catalog hawks a baby-monitoring system that includes up to three cameras. "With this state-of-the-art baby monitoring system, you'll not only hear what's happening in the nursery—you'll see it in full color on a wireless handheld, 1.5" monitor." The voice-activated device includes infrared technology so that parents can scrutinize their baby, even in total darkness.

When you're not home, you can use the ultimate in paranoid devices, the In-Reach Child Tracking System, which enables you to monitor how far your child wanders, be it at the playground or at the mall. Parents determine a preset boundary, and an alarm sounds if your child steps beyond her limit. The "triple alert system" also goes off if the child presses the "panic button" on her unit or if the child's SensorBelt is removed. *Bing, bing, bing!* Also to be filed under Paranoid Parenthood is the NY Nanny Cam Company service, which for a fee of $1,200 will monitor your entire home and stream it live to a private website. "You're instantly in your home, eyes and ears," said the company's founder, Rhyder McClure. "With the technology we have now, it's bordering on irresponsible for parents not to take advantage of it."[17] (Poorer parents can shell out $299 for a teddy bear with a spying camera hidden within its furry tufts.)

Even in the relatively secure home environment, each room has its own cavalcade of safety paraphernalia. The bathroom is a dangerous place, a fact of which most parents are well aware. Marketers are perhaps even more aware, which is why we can buy such things as the Sudsy the Hippo Faucet Protector ($12) to prevent us from ever having to warn our toddlers against hitting their foreheads on hard metal spigots. A rubber duck with built-in thermometer warns parents when the water is "TOO HOT" for their bathing infant.

If anything, the nursery, that supposedly cozy and peaceful childhood refuge, seems most fraught with peril. A major area of focus is sleep: getting babies to fall asleep, ensuring they stay asleep, and, above all, making sure they don't die in their sleep. Dozens of products aim to prevent Sudden Infant Death Syndrome (SIDS) by wrapping and wedging a baby properly on his back. The HALO SleepSack wearable blanket 2-in-1 Swaddle was created by a parent who lost an infant to SIDS. Advertisements feature a gold seal from First Candle SIDS Alliance, designating the HALO its "#1 Safe Sleep Product." The copy assures us that the HALO is used in hospital nurseries nationwide and is the top choice of parents and leading experts.

"Why does your baby need our Movement Sensor?" asks an advertisement for the BébéSounds Movement Sensor with Sound Monitor, an ultrasensitive under-the-mattress contraption. Because BébéSounds detects a baby's slightest movements, even while she sleeps, and issues an alarm if no movement is detected for twenty seconds. The very *idea* that such a product exists is enough to distress any parent who doesn't have one; you can't help but think: *Wait—how would I have any clue if my baby didn't move for twenty seconds without this thing?* An even more overt play on fear dominates the commercial for the Babysense V infant motion monitor. We open to the camera panning over a dark bedroom where a couple lies fast asleep, oblivious to their infant's impending doom. "If your baby stops breathing, you won't know it," warns an ominous voice, reminiscent of those used in political attack ads. "Unless you're prepared for *the unthinkable.*" We see a glimpse of a mobile hanging over a crib where a baby lies on its belly, inert. An alarm sounds, and the couple dashes frantically to the nursery, drumbeats quickening. "Protect your baby with Babysense V—it's a matter of life. *Your* baby's."

Not only are we terrified of the bough breaking; we're ob-
sessed with the cradle itself. Bassinets, cosleepers, Moses baskets,
cribs, and toddler beds have become major household invest-
ments. In 2005, the children's-home-furnishings business at the
top twenty retailers was $8.7 billion, up 5.4 percent from the pre-
vious year.[18] Parents are warned never to buy a used crib or accept
a hand-me-down one, though chances are most cribs built in the
last ten years live up to current federal safety standards. Though
the majority of baby furniture—60 percent—is purchased at off-
price retailers, such as Wal-Mart and Target,[19] buying baby furniture is still a costly and time-intensive endeavor. The range of
safety rules is enough to confuse any parent. Are Jenny Lind spin-
dles a hazard or an adorable retro embellishment? Are there any
bumpers designed to fit a sleigh-style crib? On top of that, we are
seduced by the variety of styles, colors, fashion statements, and
parenting philosophies embedded in each arrangement. Are we
earth mama cosleeper types? Do we fancy ourselves nostalgic for
the old-timey comforts of a Moses basket? Or would we prefer a
proper British snow-white wooden crib, which we can fantasize
presided over by a proper British baby nurse?

The latest upgrade in the sleep arena involves deluxe baby mattresses, filled with all the embellishments of high-end adult-sized
bedding. Latex, quality inner springs, "memory foam," and organic materials have become popular features for the tiniest sleepers, who, let's face it, probably couldn't care less. Mattresses can
run up to $700. One even offers a built-in, battery-operated vibra-
tor to help soothe colicky babies. While soft mattresses have been
associated with increased SIDS risk, other deluxe features are
"more catering to the parents' preferences than to the child," according to Gary Smith, chairperson of the American Academy of
Pediatrics Committee on Injury, Violence, and Poison Preven-
tion.[20] Fact is, a baby can sleep indefinitely in a Pack n' Play, which
has no mattress at all, as I found out when my son was ready for a
crib but my daughter wasn't ready to give hers up for him. Letting

a baby sleep in there—even for as long as six months—is fine, my pediatrician assured me. It makes sense when you consider that previous generations didn't have such things as toddler beds; as inadvisable as it seems, infants were known to sleep in dresser drawers for want of a larger space.

Quite plainly, safety sells. Given parents' understandable concerns for their children's welt being, it's no surprise that manufacturers are adding safety features to all manner of products and jacking up prices accordingly. Explains one market report, "Ever more efficient, safer products will not only carry much higher price-points, increasing household investment; the constantly improving technology will motivate many parents to go out and buy such products new, as opposed to picking up outdated versions second-hand, or accepting them free from a neighbor."[21] Don't say you haven't been warned.

WAY ABOVE AND BEYOND THE BASICS OF KEEPING OUR CHILDREN alive, we spend lavishly on assuring their place in a cocoon of unimpeachable bliss. Thousands of products exist to enhance each moment of a baby's day, ensuring endless cushiony ease. We don't just offer a child a potty to pee in. We provide him with potty books, music to pee by, a special stool to rest his feet on, miniature toilet paper, toys to bring to the potty with him, and a stuffed animal with which to share the experience. Freud would have had a field day with Piddlers Toilet Targets, little floating toys ("flushable foam shapes!") for boys to aim for while they pee.

We do everything we can on the comfort front, cosseting and mollycoddling our tiny charges even when not necessarily productive or helpful. One-third of parents use teething remedies though doctors agree most are ineffective and unnecessary.[22] Prior to October 2007 when manufacturers finally removed them from store shelves, nearly half of parents used cold or cough remedies an average of five times a month, though such products were generally not recommended by physicians and have never been tested on young children.[23] "Parents tend to throw out their healthy skepticism when it comes to shopping for their children because such decisions are deeply emotional," said Lisa Spiegel, a developmental psychologist and cofounder of the Soho Parenting Center in New York. "The instinct to nurture one's child bypasses a lot of logical thinking."

It's hard to ignore that intrinsic desire to make our babies happy. It's what makes us tear out hair out in anguish and sob uncontrollably before running into the nursery to rescue a wailing baby in the midst of much-needed sleep-training. It's what causes us dash over to comfort a bawling toddler after a minor tumble, even though we know overreactions are counterproductive. It's what leads us to cycle through six different snack choices even though we know our child would be just fine with the first bag of crackers we selected. Add to this emotional backdrop a consumer parenting culture that assures us that the right equipment can minimize conflict, problems, and trouble with our children, and make them—phew, sigh, *alas*—happy. But we must still ask the question: Does it make sense to have a happy baby all the time? Of course, we all want our children to be happy. But children necessarily go through moments, even hours, and sometimes days when they are not happy—and there isn't necessarily anything wrong with that. It's when they're not happy that they learn what they need to do to content themselves. Children are remarkably resilient—if we allow them to be. "Babies don't need perfect days to grow up healthy," said Jack Shonkoff, chairman of the National Scientific Council on the Developing Child, a group of leading neuroscientists and child development researchers. "Babies need to live in a real world, a real environment, where things sometimes go well and sometimes don't go so well. They need some time to flounder by themselves and figure things out."

The profusion of safety and comfort gear prevents such inadvertent discoveries. Buy a baby wipe warmer, and you will inevitably have a baby who only tolerates gently warmed wipes, instead of raising a child to tolerate that sometimes, unpleasant as it may be, her bottom will be chilly. "This fantasy that you can provide a way to shield children from discomfort is where we've gone seriously wrong," said Lisa Spiegel. "It's almost like we've forgotten what it's like to be a human being. There's no way to avoid discomfort or unhappiness. Not only is there no way to avoid these things—it shouldn't even be a goal." Ironically, one of the results of not allowing babies to cry is that parents end up depriving them of sleep. "What's happened in the last generation is that parents have become so worried about creating any discomfort that they will gratify their needs instead of holding back and letting the child figure out how to soothe himself." Perhaps the epitome of the happy-no-matter-what product is the Time's Up/Time Out teddy bear, a $25 stuffed animal with a cheerful grin and a built-in timer on its belly to count down a child's allotted "time-out" period, thus minimizing freak-outs and frustrations. But if time-out, the popular disciplinary tactic that has largely replaced spanking, ceases to be difficult and annoying, it also ceases to be punitive and effective. We end up smiley-facing out the essential dark moments in a child's life. "Kids need to feel bad sometimes," explained David Elkind, a child psychologist at Tufts University and author of the acclaimed classic *The Hurried Child.* "We learn through experience and we learn through bad experiences. Through failure we learn how to cope."[24]

In the long-term, the baby gear deluge deprives our children of the ability to build tolerance for frustration, one of the key elements to succeeding in life. "Children need to learn to cope with stress and disappointment," Spiegel emphasized. "Never being frustrated is not what leads people to feel more in control of their lives." Parents' mistakes are far from intentional, she pointed out. The problem is that we confuse discomfort with damage, and parents are understandably worried about damaging their children. "But it's faulty thinking," she explained. "Of course, we want to avoid real traumatic events in a child's life. But now we feel like every interaction has the potential to be traumatic. People are afraid to let their babies cry, even though crying is part of the human repertoire! It's a release—and that's really important."

By catering to every wish and whim, we teach our children that their interests should always be top priority, regardless of effort or the needs of others. We teach them to be less flexible about accommodating other people and we instill a sense of entitlement. We teach them to be rigid about their preferences—making sure they get to sit on their favorite-color chair in a restaurant that serves their favorite-shape macaroni. Not surprisingly, children who are accustomed to being the center of attention, focus, and expenditure grow up constantly needing attention. As one Washington, D.C., nursery school teacher complained to Judith Warner in her book *Perfect Madness,* "I think this generation will be totally self-centered. I think they'll feel a real need to produce and have *things.* I don't think they'll have a clue about the human side of our lives."[25]

Diane Levin, a professor of education at Wheelock College in Boston who has trained early childhood professionals for over twenty-five years, coined the term *problem-solving deficit disorder* to describe a generation of young children who enter school without critical-thinking skills or even the desire to solve problems. According to Levin, "As the process for interacting with the world becomes more passive, children are robbed of the process of being an active agent in their own lives"[26] Preschool teachers report that children are easily frustrated and overly accustomed to having other people help them carry out projects. We are unwittingly inhibiting their ability to achieve a sense of autonomy, capability, and responsibility. "There's no question in my mind that we have more restless, agitated, and unhappy children because they are dependent on instant gratification, said Sharna Olfman, a psychologist and editor of the "Childhood in America" book series. "Life is boring when you haven't acquired the capacity to solve problems as basic as knowing how to fill your own time."[27]

Many experts believe we're raising a generation of narcissists. Is it any wonder, when any manner of baby gear can be customized to make sure a child is the center of her own universe? Online, you can find personalized sippy cups and binkies. Flashcards can be made to order featuring photographs of a child, his familiar objects, and the people he knows. Customized CDs with songs like "Little Emma had a farm, E-I-E-I-O" can be recorded to include a child's name in every verse. You can even order Elmo stories featuring photographs of your child as the main character. While no single item is a disaster, there has to be a limit. Children who are constantly scrutinized by their parents, their every move and mood monitored, become hyperaware of the attention. They can't help but become self-conscious. Under their parents' watchful eyes, they learn to perform rather than relax and enjoy the moment. We might do well to bear in mind the power of benign neglect, something that occurred quite easily when mothers were dividing their attentions between three or four little ones. The British child analyst D. W. Winnicott wrote about the necessity of the child *to be alone in the presence of the mother* as a condition for self-creation.

It's important to recognize the downside of padding every corner of a baby's environment. The notion that if we only have this particular corner guard and that stovetop protection unit, our babies will escape injury is a dangerous way of thinking, one that inadvertently results in other kinds of injuries. After all, if a mother thoroughly childproofs her kitchen with every cabinet lock and enclosure under guard, she is likely to be less vigilant while her child scampers around underfoot.* No matter how many safety devices one installs, nothing can prevent an enterprising toddler from doing something potentially dangerous, like climbing onto a kitchen

---

*The theory of *risk homeostasis* suggests that people crave a certain level of risk, and if we make their environments safer, they will do more foolhardy things in order to achieve it. In playgrounds that have been made safer by the replacement of seesaws with springed platforms, kids have made a new game of crashing their bicycles into the new device as hard as they can, for the fun of bouncing off.

barstool in the wrong way. Not only can abundant childproofing lead to less parental vigilance; it can also teach a child the wrong lessons about risk and safety. The toddler who is allowed to fiddle with the childproofed stove controls at home may find himself one day playing with the controls at a friend's house, where the stovetop hasn't been outfitted with a protective panel. Valuable lessons are taught with those nagging refrains of "No, don't touch that!" and "Hot!"

Worse, not every safety product is necessarily that safe, and many safety features on regular products are just corporate efforts to preempt expensive, time-consuming, and image-destroying litigation. A glance at child product recalls, posted each month in toy stores and parenting magazines, is an education in how just about anything—from a doll's nose to a high chair leg—can become an object of malice when used inappropriately. Even products meant to enhance safety can bite back. Sleep positioners, which are marketed specifically to help prevent SIDS, actually *increase* the risk of children suffocating in their sleep; the American Academy of Pediatrics recommends against using them altogether. Crib bumpers, intended to protect infants from getting their limbs stuck between the slats of their cribs, instead do more harm than good, according to a 2007 study in the *Journal of Pediatrics*. Babies have suffocated when they become wedged against the padding or are strangled by one of the bumper ties.[28] Antibacterial soap, now a staple in homes with children, can cause burns on sensitive skin if it dries on a child's hands, arms, or face. Hand sanitizer, of all things, has been found to cause alcohol poisoning in young children who inadvertently lick it off their hands (beware, thumbsuckers!). Reports of children rushed to the hospital, severely lethargic and incoherent, have emerged from poison control and emergency rooms. Now that sanitizer gels often come with enticing scents to appeal to discriminating parents, young children are more liable to slurp them off. Plain old soap and water, it turns out, has its advantages.

The reality is, kids are inconvenient, messy, difficult, and dangerous. They get frustrated, annoyed, bratty, and upset. They also get
hurt. Life with children isn't always easy or comfortable. It's full of
risks, without which we would be deprived of rewards. But in an era
in which dodgeball and even tag have been banned from school
playgrounds in places like Wichita, Kansas, and Beaverton, Oregon,
in which even sports like soccer and touch football are deemed too
rough for some schools,[29] we have lost sight of this basic truth. "If I
could do anything for parents, it would be to eradicate fear and
worry from their souls," said Joan Almon of the Alliance for Childhood. "Kids are going to get a few bruises, but chances are they are
going to do just fine. Let them breathe a little more easily. Otherwise, they become so overly programmed and safe and protected
that they never learn how to function on their own."

Another unfortunate result of inundating our homes with baby
gear, overloading our children's lives with superfluous and even
counterproductive stuff, is that it undermines parental confidence.
It suggests that raising children without a lot of equipment is out
of the realm of most ordinary human beings, or at least those with
ordinary-sized wallets. That forgoing the requisite gust is irre-
sponsible. That not buying in translates into a much more onerous
task of child rearing, one that most parents are incapable of carrying out. And when the barrage of baby tackle fails to produce the
perfect family life shown in the advertisements, parents tend to
fault themselves.

2

Target: Parents

Many thousands of baby products ago, back in 1867, parents got their first taste of manufacturers' zeal for telling them what's best for their babies. It was during that year, in his laboratory, that Justus von Liebig, a German chemist known as the "father of the fertilizer industry" for his studies on plant nutrients, cooked up Liebig's Soluble Food for Babies, the world's first commercial infant milk formula.[1] This new "soup for nurslings," Leibig claimed, was as nourishing and healthful as mother's milk and would relieve mothers of the act of nursing their infants by providing a perfectly acceptable substitute. The era of commercialized parenthood had dawned.

At first, Liebig's concoction was an unqualified flop. It was difficult to mix without creating lumps, and it didn't agree with many babies' delicate digestive systems. But Liebig brushed aside complaints, insisting that his formula contained the "very same ingredients as in mother's milk."[2]* Despite lackluster

---

*The original recipe contained wheat flour, malt flour, and potassium bicarbonate added to cow's milk. In 1915, powdered formula was introduced containing cow's milk, lactose, oleo oils, and vegetable oils. Various fortifications were added over the years: iron in 1959, taurine (an organic acid commonly fond in animal urine, as well as in plants, fungi, and some bacteria) in 1984, nucleotides in the late 1990s, and polyunsaturated fatty acids in the early 2000s.

sales, the idea proved tantalizing enough to draw competitors into the market: Meigs' Mixture, Nestlé, Mellin's Infant Food, and Ridge's Food for Infants were soon being sold to mothers as an alternative, even a preferable one, to human milk. Some doctors argued that infant formula was at least superior to wet nurse's milk, if not to the milk of birth mothers. Certainly the new formulas were an improvement on animal milk alone, which some desperate mothers turned to when their babies couldn't nurse. As the formulators tweaked their recipes and commercial milk improved, companies ramped up their sales pitch. By the 1890s, Nestlé advertisements ("Best for Babies") claimed its formula was better than milk, because "impure milk in hot weather is one of the chief causes of sickness among babies." Companies offered free samples to readers of middle-class magazines and gave out handbooks on infant care. The handbooks added the imprimatur of science by explaining the chemistry of milk and feeding in clear but relatively sophisticated language, convincing mothers and doctors alike of their healthful properties.[3]

Still, habits were hard to break, and at the turn of the twentieth century, most mothers still chose to nurse their babies themselves or to hire wet nurses when circumstances or tradition dictated otherwise.[4] It wasn't until the 1920s and '30s, when evaporated milk formula became widely available, that formula use really began to take off. Clinical studies were published showing that babies who were fed formula thrived as well as those reared on breast milk. By 1950, a majority of babies were fed home-mixed evaporated milk formula. When Similac ("similar to lactation"), introduced in the late 1920s and reformulated in 1951, and Enfamil, introduced in 1959, hit the market, they were accompanied by massive advertising and public relations campaigns. One key to their success was cementing a relationship with the medical establishment, advertising to physicians who received instructions on how to mix and dispense formula and creating the impression that formula was endorsed by medical professionals. By midcentury, formula had swept into parents' bedrooms and baby nurseries with an aura of technological know-how, medical advancement, and social progress. Mothers became convinced that formula was the modern way; breastfeeding, once considered "natural" and "maternal," was viewed as backward, unsanitary, and peculiarly "low class." By the late 1970s, more than 75 percent of babies were formula-fed.

Formula was legitimately useful, particularly as more women returned to work before their children were fully weaned. For women unable to negotiate pumping on the job or who had trouble breastfeeding, formula overcame what would otherwise have seemed like insurmountable hurdles. Formula was also invaluable to adoptive mothers, mothers with diseases that could be transmitted via breast milk, mothers on medication, and babies who were incapable of nursing. But formula makers had a problem. Research began to show that breast milk was clearly better for babies. Formula babies suffered more ear, respiratory, intestinal, and other bacterial infections; they were much more likely to suffer from diarrhea, asthma, and diabetes and had a greater incidence of obesity and a higher risk of serious food allergies. Some studies even showed lower cognitive development among babies raised on formula. From an economic standpoint, formula was also less desirable, costing mothers hundreds of dollars a year.

For this last reason, however, formula was a winner for the baby business. Over the course of the twentieth century, commercial breast milk substitutes ballooned into a multibillion-dollar industry. When birthrates dropped in the United States after the baby boom, infant formula companies turned their marketing efforts to the developing world to maintain their sales growth. Unfortunately for them, this led to another problem: mortality rates in those countries climbed as babies got sick and died from drinking formula mixed with unsanitized water or from drinking overly diluted formula fed by mothers who couldn't afford to buy the product in the recommended quantities. In 1974, OXFAM, the British relief organization, published *The Baby Killers*, an exposé of deceptive marketing practices by Nestlé, which revealed how company saleswomen in rural Africa dressed as nurses in order to promote formula feeding. In *Science,* pediatricians Derrick and E. F. Patrice Jelliffe accused formula manufacturers of "commerciogenic malnutrition."[5]

After the ensuing outcry and an international boycott of Nestlé in 1977, breast-feeding began to rebound. In response, the formula industry rejiggered its marketing efforts. DHA, ARA, and other fatty acids (derived from fungi, algae, or fish oil) were added to formula. These reformulated versions, touted as boosting children's brain power, were launched with aggressive, worldwide campaigns in magazines, newspapers, direct mail, and sampling programs. Martek, the leading supplier of such oils to the formula industry, noted in 2002 that "infant formula is currently a commodity market, with all products being almost identical and marketers competing intensely to differentiate their products. Even if Formulaid (the blend of fatty acids, DHA/ARA) has *NO* benefit, we think it should be widely incorporated into formula, *as a marketing tool* and to allow companies to promote their formula as *'closest to human milk.'*"[6]

The new campaigns depended on the results of small, inconsistent studies showing that the improved formula could surpass breast milk in its ability to promote cognitive and physical development. Martek's sales shot up 183 percent in nine months. According to the International Baby Food Action Network (IBFAN), eleven of the sixteen international formula companies jumped on the brainy-milk bandwagon. In its 2004 report on ethical violations by the industry, IBFAN notes that such companies are "selling 'intelligence in a bottle' . . . cashing in on the emotional desires of parents to have smart children"

In many parts of the world, parents are willing to pay extra for the IQ promise. It is estimated that infant formula supplemented with fatty acids cost parents an additional US$200 a year as these products are priced 15 to 30% more than standard formula. There are no independent long term studies to substantiate the benefits of added DHA/ARA to formula.[7]

The new marketing spin was a rebuff to the 1981 International Code of Marketing of Breastmilk Substitutes established by the World Health Organization. The code requires formula companies to preface their product information with statements confirming that breastfeeding is the best food for infants and that formula should only be used after consultation with health professionals. It dictates that no images of mothers or babies may appear on packets or containers. Words like *motherly* are verboten in advertisements. Commercial representatives for formula companies are not allowed to make direct contact with medical personnel, mothers, or pregnant women. Free samples and coupons are banned. Manufacturers have chosen to ignore nearly all these provisions. Luckily for them, the code has no legally enforceable power, and in the United States, the Food and Drug Adminstration regulates formula as a food product, with no jurisdiction over its health claims.[8]

The formula industry is a highly sophisticated and omnipresent machine; open a magazine for parents, and you are bombarded. When I left the hospital that was a supposed beacon of breastfeeding enlightenment after the birth of my first child, I did so toting a free diaper bag stocked with canisters of formula and coupons for future purchases. Outside the United States, marketing efforts are even more overt. In Thailand, for example, doctors, nurses, and mothers are deluged with gifts during their hospital stays and return checkups. Abbott, a major manufacturer, promotes its Formance brand for mothers or mothers-to-be in China with a leaflet proclaiming, *"Before delivery, nurture the fetus; after delivery, boost milk production,"* an assertion—in direct contradiction to all medical evidence—that using formula improves the quantity and quality of mother's milk. Though companies are forbidden from distributing materials to mothers via health facilities, many circumvent the rule by labeling brochures "for health professionals only"; they list required statements about breast milk and other warnings in small print and clearly write brochures for mothers, not trained medical providers. Nestlé blatantly labels its materials as intended to be distributed to mothers by health professionals, in direct violation of the powerless international code.

There's a reason formula manufacturers continue to be so brazen. Parents are a seductive market. Yearning for assistance and answers, full of high hopes, willing to spend money, and often vulnerable, parents are ready consumers with clearly defined needs. Formula manufacturers demonstrated that the parenting industry could transform the way millions of mothers raised their children, even persuading them to buy products that demonstrably hurt their children. They had set a powerful example.

STAN FRIDSTEIN, A FORMER ADVERTISING EXECUTIVE WHO HAD spent his career selling packaged goods, wanted to create the perfect catalog. Operationally, everything pointed in the direction of success. It was 1985, and a number of innovations taking place in the direct marketing business made launching a new catalog company a lot easier. First, there were advances in software that enabled companies to send out catalogs without hiring a whole department of IT people and raising millions of dollars to set up a computer system. A second big change occurred in shipping. When Americans want to buy something—and especially when parents want to buy something for their baby—they want it *now*, but the post office couldn't always deliver. Then FedEx, which had been primarily used for government documents and business-to-business transfers, started delivering to individuals' homes. Finally, there was the 800-phone-number revolution, which allowed customers to place orders for free at a relatively low cost to catalogers.

A thirty-one-year-old single guy with no kids, Fridstein was an unlikely candidate to run a parenting catalog, but for him it was simply a business calculation. The baby boom of the early 1980s was taking off, and Fridstein noticed what so many other entrepreneurs at the time saw: These new moms were different. They were better educated, better off, and older—and they were very pressed for time. Fridstein thought that if he could offer a catalog that sold the best, safest, easy-to-use prescreened baby gear, parents would see the value.

It seemed like a no-brainer, but Fridstein had trouble raising funds. "People were looking at me like, 'Have any direct marketing experience?' *Nope.* 'Ever run your own company?' *Nope.* 'Have any kids?' *Nope.*"

"It was truly an intellectual enterprise," he admitted. "It was more of just a great business idea than an idea that came out of passion. I wasn't this diehard skier who invents a great new ski." Fridstein went in with a partner, an accountant who handled operations, telemarketing, warehousing, and all the behind-the-scenes mechanics. Fridstein was in charge of product selection, marketing, and catalog design. "We did a lot of research. Focus groups with moms. As time went on we became pretty smart about what parents wanted. We *had* to rely on research because I had zero instincts."

Somehow, he managed to scrape enough money together. And that's how RightStart (then called The Right Start) got started. One of the first challenges was finding the people to send the catalog to. In those early days, Fridstein had to snoop around for moms. He went to Spiegel and bought the names of customers who had purchased items that might signal the presence of a new baby in the household. He went to *American Baby* magazine and bought it list of subscribers. After he got his first mailing lists together and began to bring in customers, he exchanged lists with other new baby catalogers to expand his customer base. Hanna Andersson, Children's Wear Digest, and several new toy catalogs were trying to take advantage of the same demographic trends Fridstein had picked up on. "Once there were more catalogs, it was great," Fridstein recalled. "I wasn't competitive with them, so we all traded names and grew together."

RightStart took off right away. Before the Internet, it wasn't hard to be the exclusive national outlet for a baby item from Germany or from a tiny mom-and-pop manufacturer out of Minnesota. Fridstein uncovered gems like a foam product that went into the top compartment of a shopping cart, where parents could lay down a young infant who wasn't yet able to sit up. It was the kind of gizmo that would have died in a retail store but which sold well in a catalog, where it could be appropriately displayed and explained. He traveled to juvenile shows in Asia and Europe. "It was like hunting. We'd get really excited by finding these little itty-bitty booths at [the major trade show in Germany] where some little old lady would be sitting there with an ingenious little product." Fridstein was the first retailer in the United States to sell Avent anticolic baby bottles, now a staple among American moms.

Rather than offer products that were stylish, RightStart specialized in functionality. "We appealed to people's sense of logic so they could justify why they would spend twice as much at The Right Start as they would at Toys "R" Us. It's like Mercedes. Mercedes doesn't tell you to buy their car because you will be the envy of everyone at your country club. They sell to you on safety, on the best technology. But *you* know why you're buying it." For example, when offering a new stroller, RightStart would tailor the description in a way that differentiated the stroller from what parents could then buy in their local baby stores. "You find a benefit, and you make that benefit disproportionate," Fridstein explained. "With this stroller, you can get a shock absorber that's actually used on bicycles, so that when you hit potholes, your baby won't wake up. But it's your call! If you don't want to spend the extra thirty dollars to make sure your baby won't wake up, then go get another stroller. That made it very easy for them. It's *your* decision."

The sell was rational; the decision to buy wasn't. Selling to parents wasn't difficult, in any case. "Spending on a baby is the greatest hobby on earth," said Fridstein, now a father of two. "If you're into photography, you get off in a photo store. People who have babies are dying to spend money on their kids because it's a passion of theirs."

Of course, Fridstein admitted, passion isn't the only thing that prompts parents' purchases. "The real reason people would buy things is because they wanted the best for their kids and they felt extraordinary levels of guilt because they were working. They substituted a lot of that profound guilt with what they could buy for their kids." Not that marketers could ever say so much, at least explicitly, to their customers. "You *never* sell on guilt—never ever. You *never* make a parent feel negative about being a parent. You're never going to make a sale saying, 'We know you're feeling guilty because you're out on the road all the time.' Instead, the way we did it was, 'Ms. Busy Career Woman, while you're out there running like a chicken with your head cut off, we've gone out and saved you time by picking out all the best products.' Our sell was, 'This is the best stuff available. We've done it *for* you.' And if it costs them a few more bucks, that's OK because we've provided them with convenience, time savings, and a sense of 'Well, it if it came from The Right Start, it's the best thing.'"

RightStart was picking and providing for parents so well, parents began stopping by the company's warehouse in Westlake Village, California, an upscale suburb, to shop; they didn't even want to wait for FedEx. "We were completely ill-equipped to handle it," Fridstein recalled. He and his partner decided to open a little store out of the warehouse to deal with the traffic. At the time, the average baby store was posting about $500,000 a year in sales. When RightStart opened its first store in 1990, sales hit $1.5 million in the first year. Fridstein made almost as much money from that single store out of a corner of the warehouse as he did from his entire catalog business.

The store offered access to a new category of customer. "As a catalog, if you were a mom, we could find you. If you were pregnant, we could find you. But we couldn't find your Aunt Tillie or your best friend." Given that half of all baby product purchases were gifts, expanding into storefronts allowed RightStart to reach Mom and Dad's nearest and dearest. In 1991, RightStart went public to fund a significant retail presence and beginning in 1992, opened ten stores a year. Since then, mergers, bankruptcy, and new ownership reshaped RightStart (including rebranding it from the original name, The RIGHT START).[9] The mail-order landscape and the baby business had also changed.

To keep up with baby superstores and the Internet, traditional mail-order catalogs, long a staple for frazzled moms, had been forced to modernize. The current incarnation of RightStart, for example, sends advertisements via superstore chain Destination Maternity. Parents receive e-mails geared to their child's developmental stage, each of which gets a cute label and a link to appropriate products. For babies in the "Homecoming" stage, RightStart offers a Nightlight Soother to make sleeping through the night easy. For older babies in the "Bottoms Up" stage, there's a Baby Activity Walker ("Those first steps take practice!").

Messages are tailored to appeal to parental hopes and appease parental concerns. "Positioning the company as a reliable source of information first . . . is an especially effective tactic in an area as fraught with controversy and uncertainty as parenting," advises *Marketing News*. Its advice to marketers is to "find cheerleaders for your products that can influence end-user purchases"—such as doctors and other health professionals—and to use "all available database technologies" to "hit families with mailings timed to stages of pregnancy or the child's development." In the years since the formula makers pioneered the tactic, baby-product businesses have made pediatricians' and obstetricians' offices a significant outpost for their products. Doctors are often willing participants because the companies provide information packets on health and developmental basics that can be given to expectant parents instead of having questions eat up a doctor's preciously managed time. Some OB/GYN offices allow patients to sign up to receive free information or samples from companies or hand patients "gift packs" in their second trimester. Hospitals give out coupons and sample bags to expectant parents taking childbirth or newborn education classes as well as to new mothers leaving the hospital.

Yet businesses no longer have to depend on cornering parents in the maternity wing. Gargantuan databases take note of our children's birthdays and subsequent life milestones; our mailboxes and in-boxes are packed with alerts for perfectly timed buying opportunities. In addition to using sales data for their own promotions and research, retail stores sell customer information to outside companies when parents sign up for a registry. Explains one direct marketer, "What we try to do is be in the mailbox, talking to that mom at the right time. We try to provide information before she even articulates the question." The moment a baby is unloaded from her car seat into the bassinet, formula samples land in the mailbox. When the baby is ready to start solid foods, coupons for baby food are there. As Sandy Jones, the author of *Consumer Reports Guide to Baby Products,* put it, "They spend millions to be right on top of every baby expected in the nation. Their job is to impact a mother-to-be, almost as soon as she knows she is pregnant, to build brand loyalty with coupons, free products or subscriptions to company-backed magazines."[10] That impulse purchase of a single onesie can end up clogging your mailbox with several trees' worth of catalogs a year.

Perhaps the most pervasive of the mail-order catalogs is One Step Ahead Baby, also known as the Paranoid Parent's Bible. (Fridstein sees it as a knockoff and successor to his original vision of RightStart.) When the One Step Ahead catalog promises "thoughtfully selected products to help with baby . . . every step of the way," it's nearly impossible not to find a measure of usefulness somewhere in its pages. A crib wedge for baby's neck to ease

nasal congestion and improve digestion? Perhaps that will snuffle
a child's snores. A Discovery Fun Roller to promote crawling? Just
the thing to get a baby from creep to crawl. Microfiber, terry-lined
Snuggle Bug Booties? Perfect for a chilly old house and, besides,
so cute!

Making it incredibly difficult to turn One Step Ahead into re-
cycling fodder is Karen Scott's job. Scott, a former Kraft marketing
executive, founded One Step Ahead in 1988 after the birth of her
first child, when she grew frustrated with the quality of baby gear.
The playpen she had bought was too large to be rolled through
doorways from room to room. Her stroller didn't hold up to frequent use; the wheels snapped out of alignment. Her colicky son
would only be placated by a swing, but the swing had a manual
crank that would wake him whenever Scott geared it up. She
bought two diaper bags, neither of which had adequate compart-
mentalization; everything plunged to the bottom and disappeared
against the dark interior lining. After her second son was born,
Scott was dusting off what she had considered her "intelligent"
purchases for reuse, when she realized, What was I *thinking*? She
ended up keeping only a small pile of things for her second child
and carted off $1,200 worth of useless gear to the Salvation Army.

"A lightbulb went off," she recalled. "Here I thought I was such
a smart consumer, and yet I made a fairly expensive mistake." She
returned to Kraft but found herself working seventy hours a week
while dreaming about starting her own business. She sent a product questionnaire to 250 parents, their names culled from birth
announcements in local papers. Eighty percent of the parents
filled it out—an astonishing response for a direct-mail piece, for
which a 5 percent response rate is considered a triumph—and
they were scribbling notes in the margins about their purchasing
mistakes and lessons.

Scott's goal was to provide "solution-based" products to parents. She designed a diaper bag with built-in ergonomic elements
to lighten the load on Mom's slumping shoulders. The strap had

mesh on the back so her back wouldn't get sweaty. A light-colored lining so that it was easy to see rattles rolling around on the bottom. A one-handed release buckle so that a mom could maneuver the bag while carrying a baby. She developed twenty criteria for new products to meet before being deemed worthy of the catalog and pulled together a panel of 250 parents to judge which made the cut. The first year Scott sent out One Step Ahead, twenty pages of products she scouted herself, she made $130,000 in sales. By 1993, she was mailing 2.5 million catalogs with revenues of $25 million. As of 2006, she was mailing 20 million catalogs a year and approaching $75 million in revenue. (Her revenue per catalog, it is interesting to note, seems to have maxed out, most likely a sign of the Internet's impact on the mail-order business.)

Occasionally One Step Ahead makes a serious misstep. About five years ago, it offered the Diaper Check, a device with an LED readout that would alert parents to a soggy diaper, thus freeing parents from the task of swishing in a finger to check. "I thought it was pretty nifty because I had a personal experience where I wished I had a thing like that," Scott told me, without providing the gritty details. But the product met with widespread ridicule. About two dozen radio hosts caught wind of the Diaper Check and mocked it mercilessly on the airwaves. "We thought about it afterward and realized that there are certain times when a hand works well enough." Scott admitted. The inside of a wrist can ascertain whether a bottle's milk is too warm. Dunking a hand in the bathwater can do the trick just as easily as a custom thermometer. "You *can* overgadget."

BUT FOR THE MOST PART, PRODUCTS SOLD BY BUSINESSES LIKE One Step Ahead Baby catch on, perhaps because, according to researchers, mothers are more positive about and open to advertising. On the whole, moms are less likely than other women to dislike advertising, think advertisements are a waste of time, or find them annoying. Mothers are less likely to believe that ads patronize women. Indeed, moms are more likely than both other women and men to say that TV commercials are interesting, and more likely to enjoy reading magazine advertisements.[11] When the Sampling Corporation of America surveyed mothers who received its GiftPax of samples and information, it found that 98 percent tried the sample products and 89 percent read *all or most* of the literature.[12] Mothers are especially open to marketing messages when it comes to their kids.

All parents care about their children, and always have; it's just that parents today appear to be particularly fervent in their devotion insofar as it translates into purchasing patterns. Part of this is generational. Today's parents are primarily members of the so-called Generation X, children of World War II and Depression-era parents who were often quite strict and parsimonious when it came to child rearing. Born between the years 1964 and 1978, Gen Xers came of age during a time of high inflation and recession, and in a period that wasn't particularly child-friendly. They were the latchkey kids and the children of divorce. They grew up in a pre–*Lion King*, pre-Pixar age, when Disney movies—*Herbie Goes to Monte Carlo, The Cat from Outer Space*—were virtually unwatchable. Instead they sat through *Kramer vs. Kramer* and *Terms of Endearment*, films in which the kids on screen were grimly shuttled back and forth or consigned to the sidelines. When Drew Barrymore took her stand in *Irreconcilable Differences,* she stood for a generation. Having grown up with less, this crop of parents is inclined to give more to their own children, in parts to make up for what they wish they themselves had as kids.

Further, "competition very much distinguishes this generation of parents," according to Stephanie Azzarone, president of Child's Play, a marketing communications firm. "Not that we weren't competitive a generation ago, but it's very much more the case these days. Everyone has to get their child the most expensive outfit at school and have them take Chinese classes when they're six years old. It's predominant in Los Angeles and New York, but it's expanding everywhere." With so much pressure to have one's children excel and thereby to excel as parents, many parents do what now seems natural: whatever it takes to maximize their chances of success. This is where Gloria DeGaetano and the budding "parent coach" movement have stepped in.

In the late 1990s, after the Columbine school shooting, De-Gaetano, a classroom teacher and reading specialist turned speaker-for-hire on issues of media and violence, had what she called "a dark night of the soul." Having worked with parents for years, DeGaetano came to the realization that while parents, as she put it, were the CEOs of their families, "in an age of information, many well-intentioned parents were still not getting the kinds of information and support they needed." What they needed was a resource to help them navigate the "overwhelming and aggravating" aspects of parenthood. That would motivate them to become the best parents they could possibly be. That would validate— even embolden and inspire—them. She came up with the idea for the Parent Coaching Institute, a graduate-level academic program, run in conjunction with Seattle Pacific University, that would train special coaches for parents. In its first year, 2001, six people enrolled in the yearlong distance-learning program, which is primarily taught online and by telephone with several onsite workshops in Washington State. The second year, nine made it to graduation and went to work as parent coaches. By 2007, ninety-five graduates had shared their services with about five thousand clients across the country.

The Parent Coaching Institute follows a nationwide trend toward quick-fix expertise. Coaching—the off-the-playing-field variety—took off during the 1990s. First, executive coaches became the must-have perk in corporate America; by 2004, according to the *Harvard Business Review*, it was a $1-billion industry. Then coaching filtered into people's personal lives, with life coaches replacing therapists as the personal growth tool-du-jour,

helping individuals maximize their potential at the dinner table, in
the bedroom, on the telephone. In 1999, 2,100 people belonged to
the International Coach Federation, the industry's main creden-
tialing organization; by the end of 2006, membership had leaped
to 11,000.

In the past decade, life coaching has developed into niches:
diet coaches, dating coaches, retirement coaches, and, of course,
parent coaches. According to Daniel Martinage, the former executive director of the International Coach Federation, a nonprofit
organization that offers accreditation to coach training programs,
parent coaching is one of the fastest-growing areas in the industry.[13] DeGaetano already has several competitors. Coaching University trains general coaches who go on to self-specialize in
parenting, and smaller courses also "certify" parent coaches; other
practitioners simply set up shop with no formal preparation. One
Massachusetts-based parent coach I interviewed had no training
beyond a few vague courses in "nurturing" and "building better
communication," and claimed to set parents on the right path with
only three $75 sessions.

While the field is still in its infancy—all the coaches I spoke with
had been practicing for less than two years—DeGaetano and other
proponents have major ambitions. Not only do parent coaches* promote themselves locally by distributing brochures to neighborhood
hospitals, pediatricians, counselors, day-care centers, and other
mom-centric venues, they also broadcast their services via the Internet. There are even coaches who deal exclusively online, communicating with parents by e-mail. For $29.95 a month, a parent can
send as many e-mails as she needs to the For the Love of Kids Online Parent Center in Anderson Township, Ohio, and receive a response within twenty-four hours.[14] Rival Aboutmykids.com, out of
Cincinnati, offers similar services.

---

*They may have won a significant publicity coup when Britney Spears was publicly
court-ordered to see a parenting coach in order to learn the basics of raising young boys.

Parent coaches point out that only a few decades ago, counseling and the idea of psychological support wasn't even in our collective social consciousness. As DeGaetano sees it, "Counseling has had its long run, and while it's still needed, we're evolving as a human race and another form of reaching our full potential has emerged." Many coaches view their mission this way. Nearly all have Web sites with names like Parent Energy and Positive Parenting. "Are you in touch with your parent identity?" one site asks, and goes on to exclaim:

> You have the power to impact your child's future success! The future of our society depends on the type of parenting our children receive. Imagine what a world it would be if all parents had a strategy to maximize their child's contribution to society! [A parent coach] can help you develop just such a plan—a plan in which you use your positive influence to guide your child toward reaching his or her greatest potential.

"People aren't given instructions on how to be a parent," explained Cathy Cassini Adams, a former child and family therapist, who, with a bachelor's degree in elementary education and a master's in social work, was one of the best-trained coaches I spoke with. "Obviously, that's always been true. But today, mothers feel very alone in the struggle. They tend not to talk about the challenging times they experience, and often, with coaches, they just want someone to validate that yes, this is a challenge." One of the biggest problems, according to Cassini Adams, is consumerism. "It's never the reason why parents come to see me, but after we talk, they begin to see the connections. One woman's son watched TV and played with his Game Boy all the time. He was having trouble in school; they thought he had ADHD [attention deficit hyperactivity disorder]. But after his mom started having him spend his time more productively and spend more time with her, his whole demeanor toned down. Of course, it's hard to pull back once kids have all that stuff. It's easier to turn on the TV than to give them Play-Doh and create activities and deal with cleanup."

DeGaetano too blamed the larger consumer culture for many of parents' current woes: "We're in such a complex, media-driven culture that parents are never totally in control of what their children see, read, and do. The influence of all these things is staggering, yet we don't really understand how to be a parent in such a culture. We need relationships with experts who are compassionate and nonjudgmental to help figure it all out—even just to know what's normal these days. Between the baby DVDs, the cell phones for eight-year-olds, all this hype that's created over *things*. It's too easy to give your child over to the third parent, which is this industry-generated culture."

INTO THIS FRAY STEPS A NEW KIND OF PARENT, WHO APPROACHES modern parenthood with the full-on professionalism of ambitious managers at a corporate summit. Often, parents are raising only children, either by choice or by circumstance, and are heavily invested in them. We have children at an older age and, having waited a long time to start a family, throw ourselves into the undertaking. The average age of American mothers rose from 24.6 years to 27.2 years over the past three decades,[15] and women are giving birth between the ages of 35 and 39 at the highest rate since the mid-1960s—which was before widespread birth control, when families were larger and most of the children born to women in this age group were joining older siblings.[16] Some parents choose to take time off from work during a child's early years and are devoted full-force to the "parenting process"—just as they did with careers in their twenties and early thirties.

Generally beleaguered, overwhelmed by a particular parenting snafu, or simply with an eye to improving their parenting skills, more people are paying strangers to chat with them about intimate child-rearing problems. Why shouldn't personal coaches help to

master the task? As befits the price tag for their services—usually
between $50 and $100 an hour (and not covered by insurance)—
parent-coaching clients tend to be older (in their thirties or forties) and upper middle class. With more people delaying
childbirth until they are more advanced in their careers, many
parents earn a lot more. Despite small increases in the number of
women temporarily staying home with young children, more families are dual income than in earlier generations. Some of that
money goes to higher housing costs and to childcare, but it also
means greater disposable income. Finally, the education level of
moms in America is on the rise; in 2003, eight out of ten mothers
giving birth had at least a high school education.[17] Older parents
are more likely to undergo fertility treatments and give birth to
premature babies and multiples (doubling or even tripling their
expenditures and thereby the opportunities for the companies
who cater to them). Parents who went through a long process of
trying to conceive are also likely to be intensely involved and high-
spending parents. The day after my initial interview with DeGaetano, she was slated to begin work with a new couple who typified
those seeking a coach: together for eight years, both in their thirties, both professionals. "They're very intentional and conscious
about what they want to do as parents," DeGaetano told me. Over
twelve sessions, she planned to guide their entry into parenthood,
supporting their values and helping them figure out the best way
to start a family.

So we're older, wealthier, smarter (or at least better educated),
and ready to manage and spend on our children. We also have
more information about parenthood to apply our research skills to
than ever before. In addition to Dr. Spock, we've got Drs. Sears,
Weissbluth, and Brazelton. There's John Rosemond on the right
and Penelope Leach on the left. Online, we've got iVillage and
Babycenter and Babble.com; we've got specialized local parenting forums and message boards like MainLineMommy in the
Philadelphia suburbs and Park Slope Parents in Brooklyn. There

are television shows, DVDs, workshops, and conferences devoted to the pursuit of parenthood. If we want to know when and precisely how to wean, we can access detailed descriptions of at least seven different approaches via magazines, books, breakfast show interviews, prime-time specials, breastfeeding DVDs, La Leche League brochures, websites and chat rooms, each one overturning and obviating the other. We have so much information in our arsenal, justifying each and every spending decision. A newspaper clipping detailing the importance of tummy time in encouraging crawling? Exactly why we need to prompt the purchase of that black-and-white interactive playmat. A magazine article claiming that toddlers can self-feed as early as twelve months can lead to the acquisition of six varieties of toddler cutlery. For any given moment, stage, whim, passion, urge, or urgency, there are products to service our needs and our children's needs. Whatever it may take to make our lives more convenient and our children's lives more contented.

According to practicing parent coaches, we're none the better for it. Holly Schiffrin, a developmental psychologist turned parent coach based in Stafford, Virginia, thinks parents suffer from information and consumption overload. What we've gained in terms of information, it seems we've lost in terms of wisdom or even basic knowledge. "Parents didn't used to have all these resources, so you just went with your gut or how you were raised—or the opposite of how you were raised," she said. "Between books and magazines and the Internet, parents today are overwhelmed. They don't know how to sort through it. They don't have the expertise. Unfortunately, rather than empowering them, the glut of information ends up undermining their confidence."

Still, its practitioners emphasize, parent coaching is not therapy. It's not about early childhood memories and mishaps, deep-seated bitterness, or hand-me-down resentment. It's about replacing absent family wisdom with expertise. Today, parents live across the state or across the country from their own parents.

"One of the key reasons these [baby product] marketing programs work is so many mothers no longer have grandma around to give advice," said Tony Hart, chief strategist at RTCdirect, a Washington-based "relationship marketing" firm that designs direct-mail programs for the baby formula company Enfamil.[18] The isolation is not simply geographic; it's psychological too. New parents are less likely to heed the advice of previous generations. Having children later, we have developed our own identities and approaches to life much more so than a parent in her early twenties would have. Many of us haven't asked our parents for advice in a long time. Moreover, many parents dismiss earlier generations' approaches as outdated. *They didn't have as much information then. There was so little research done on children, so few resources. They favored formula, for God's sake! They had no idea what they were talking about.*

And parent coaches promise to give parents the right tools *quickly*. Without the time to go through the competing theories, advice, and expertise themselves, parents can turn to coaches for a time-saving solution. Working by telephone because busy parents don't have the time to attend workshops or travel to a weekly session, coaches do in weeks what therapists would want to do in months or years. While psychiatrists and counselors work with "patients" on long-standing issues, coaches work with "clients" on a short-term collaborative basis, addressing immediate concerns through the use of positive thinking and practical behavioral strategies. It's more pep talk than talk therapy.

"Parents are damn well exhausted," said Gloria DeGaetano. "They have no resources left. Our coaching model was developed to help energize them again. It's about getting rid of the extraneous stuff that's draining them, like keeping up with the Joneses' kids." Often that *Stuff* substitutes for time. Studies show that parents who spend less time with their children are prone to spend more money on them. In research for her book, *Born to Buy: The Commercialized Child and the New Consumer Culture*, Juliet

Schor found that parents who spent more hours working bought more videos, books, and especially toys for their children—an increase that could not be attributed solely to added income. Moreover, higher-income parents were even more inclined to spend more money when they spent less time with their kids.[19] Propelled by guilt and insecurity, many parents try to chase away their out-of-control angst by buying an extra Gymini playmat or iPod. Treating a child to private soccer coaching or enrolling her in music class. Giving her that green ketchup she's throwing a fit over, no matter how revolting. A lot of the time, we can't help it, and our vulnerability is ripe for exploitation. It's "the guilt factor," a powerful motivator to purchase. As the U.K. firm Research and Markets explains, "Companies that understand the underlying fears, hopes and motivations of parents will be more successful in marketing to this massive demographic in the U.S. population."[20]

Guilty, time-starved parents, unable to maintain firsthand control of their children's day-to-day, minute-to-minute lives themselves, are the first to purchase the right DVD, the best educational toy, or a top-of-the-line nanny, all in the hopes that their absence won't be missed too much, or will in any case be replaced with something of well-intentioned quality. Jeanie Caggiano, a vice president at advertising agency Leo Burnett and creative director of its LeoShe division, which specializes in the women's and mothers' markets, said companies try to tap into the struggles of what she calls "Tug of War" moms—working mothers who feel guilty, harried, and stressed-out. Not surprisingly, Caggiano said, they spend more than other moms, especially on brand names. "The guilt definitely comes out and marketers, whether they are playing to that or not, know that these mothers are using products to try to provide mothering that their lack of time won't allow them to do."[21]

"I think a lot of what parents struggle with today is that they're very invested in goals for their children and making sure that their kids get all the right things and get all the right experiences and get into all the right classes," said Cathy Cassini Adams. "While some of it can be valuable, a lot of parents lose track of what's in the higher good for their individual child or what's best for their particular family. They're just doing what everyone else is doing." And that's been turned into a profitable opportunity: "Parenting has become a business, just like weddings. Companies are preying on parents' fears. For anything that a parent could possibly worry about, there's now some marketing tool that purports to make that worry go away. Buy this toy, and he'll learn this skill. Take this class, and he'll be that much smarter. And when we feel out of control as parents, we unfortunately buy into it."

Many parents consult coaches precisely because they're afraid of revealing their fears and insecurities to fellow parents, of showing them that Hannah has not yet learned to share or that Zach may be hyperactive. "I would so much rather talk to someone who doesn't know me, doesn't know my husband, so I can say things and not have them be judgmental, like, 'Oh, that kid of hers is so bad,'" one parent-coaching client told NPR's *Marketplace*.[22] Linda Stiles, a forty-one-year-old mother of two in Marin County, California, told me she didn't bother asking other parent friends for advice before hiring a parent coach. "I disliked asking for help from others because it meant that I couldn't handle it."

There is enormous social pressure on parents for their kids not just to be the best they can be, but to be on a par with, if not demonstrably better than, their peers. "Child enrichment has replaced the yuppie trends of the late 1980s and early 1990s, when it was important to own a BMW and Rolex watch," explains a trade magazine in a feature on "Selling to Moms." "Today, the children of this same generation have become the vital signs of success . . . Messages that speak to mothers about bettering the lives of their children, enriching their experiences, and creating more intelligent students can be seen in print and electronic ads." Stephanie Azzarone, president of Child's Play Communications, a marketing communications agency specializing in products and services targeted to kids and moms, stressed the importance of using messages that create solutions. "Regardless of the age of their children, the key message that influences Mom is 'this is good for your child.' The two most effective selling points are: One, this will keep your child safe and healthy, and two, this will make him smarter and more successful."

Parent coaches hear about the resulting pressure from their clients. "Parents naturally want their children to do well in school but are given mixed messages about what is the best way to help kids learn," notes Kris Meyers on her website. Meyers is a former nursery school teacher and reading specialist who is now a parent coach. "In the last decade the number of 'educational' toys, videos and computer games has increased greatly, and expensive phonics and tutoring programs have become common." When Meyers herself was in a new mothers' group in Phoenix, an instructor came in and told them, "You know, you don't have to buy your babies every toy." Everyone in the group nodded and agreed. But when she visited the other women's homes for playdates, she saw that they all had the latest toys scattered around their homes. "I think people hear the message that it's not necessary, but then they get to the store and there's this pressure that you've got to have this toy and this new version is better and the next thing you know, you're buying it."

Rather than experiencing buyer's remorse, parents are plagued with the fear of abstainer's remorse. We are scared *not* to spend on our kids. "In the effort to do the very best for their children right from the start, [parents] are not only being taken advantage of but being set up for disappointment," Cambridge, Massachusetts–based pediatrician Deborah James told the *New York Times*. "If things don't turn out perfectly, they will blame themselves for not providing the right educational toy, book, video or music for their infant." In many ways, parent coaching is both a symptom of, and an attempted antidote to, the parenting business boom.

. . .

BUT, IT'S IMPORTANT TO REMEMBER (AND REALLY, HOW CAN parents forget?), shopping for children is also a lot of fun. The multitude of products geared toward parents, babies, toddlers, and young children are better designed and more attractively merchandised than ever before. We also have more places to drool over the latest trappings of parenthood.

Beyond the product announcements in our real and virtual mail, we can turn to parent magazines to bring us up to speed. Once a relatively staid category in the media, the number of these magazines has exploded in recent years. Traditional titles like *Parents, Parenting, American Baby,* and *Baby Talk* have been joined by ad-rich magazines such as *FitPregnancy Mom and Baby, ePregnancy, Martha Stewart Kids, Violet, Cookie, Plum, Twins, Working Mother, Family Fun, Time Out New York Kids, Parent & Child, Baby Talk, Wondertime, Brain,Child, Mom-to-Be,* and *Bundle,* a short-lived but alarming *Lucky*-like magazine that promised, "Shopping for you and baby from pre-to-three." These magazines see one of their key roles as helping parents sift through it all. "In a sea of products festooned in pink and blue bunnies, it takes time to seek out what's truly worthwhile, well-designed and, frankly, up to your standards," reads one of *Cookie* magazine's subscriber solicitations. "Want to dress your little ones in classic style? Surround them with great design? Stimulate their young minds with quality toys, books, music and art? . . . We'll do what you don't have time to do. We'll rate, review, and whittle down the choices to bring you the best—and only the best—of everything you want for bringing up baby." At the same time, of course, these magazines provide an essential venue for advertising all the new wares on the market. Advertising pages across the category were up 5.7 percent in 2005, and *Parents, Child,* and *Parenting's* ad pages grew 20 percent between 2002 and 2005.[23] Upon the announcement of Disney's new *Wondertime* magazine, the *New York Times* noted,

"If a company is going to start a new magazine, the parenting category is the place to do it."

Parents who wouldn't dream of buying themselves a new fall outfit just because it's August dote over editors' and advertisers' layouts of children's fashion and scarcely hesitate before purchasing an entire wardrobe for their kindergartner's back-to-school debut. Seventy percent of parents feel guiltier about buying expensive clothes for themselves than they do about buying pricey clothing for their children, according to a 2007 online poll.[24] Parents who haven't redecorated their own rooms in a decade leap at the chance to upgrade their daughter's nursery following the design on a glossy two-page spread as soon as she's tottered out of the crib. Organic products can often cost three times as much as conventional ones. According to a 2006 survey by manufacturer PBM Products, women are particularly likely to choose organic products for their children, even in cases where they wouldn't spend the extra money on organic for themselves.[25] The extra cost for organic groceries for one child through age seventeen: $50,000.[26] In a story on the high-spending myopia of "Yoga Mamas," *BusinessWeek* magazine put it this way: "Yes to a $150 diaper bag. But she's apt to pass on a plasma TV or Mercedes."[27]

Lisa Hazen, a thirty-four-year-old Web designer from Oakland, California, is not, generally speaking, a big spender. "I tend to be thrifty by nature," she said. "I really don't need a lot." She doesn't buy designer jeans. She doesn't consider herself materialistic. She is, she believes, a smart shopper—relatively impervious to consumerism, advertising, and the relentless march of trends. But all that changed when she gave birth to Finn. "To my complete surprise, I've gotten suckered into buying things that are really cute for my darling little boy. I fall for all of it. Like that special bouncy seat and the cute onesie." With an embarrassed laugh, she confessed, "I really wanted a fancy stroller. Let's face it: I wanted the [$800] Bugaboo. I *love* that stroller." And though her husband ultimately talked her out of that one ("He was totally right"), Lisa still overspent on things like fancy crib bedding and a nursery rug, despite all good intentions to economize.

Marketing to moms was once the musty province of detergent advertisers, but innovative entrepreneurs and savvy executives have taken notice of how embarrassingly easy it is for parents to be seduced. Take Steve Granville, an MBA in global consumer product marketing who worked with brands like Nokia and AT&T before getting into the parenting business with his wife, Catherine. "When we became parents and began to seek out products that we both needed and wanted, we discovered that most brands in the market were filling a need and not creating a want," Granville explained to *Children's Business* magazine. His openness about the ways in which marketers generate consumer needs where none naturally exist is almost refreshing, as is his opportunistic view of his target. "The people who are now having babies have been exposed to more brands than any population in history. With that exposure comes sophistication and discernment." In response to this upgraded parenting taste, the Granvilles started Fleurville— "Essential products for modern parenting."

Essential? Unlike the old-fashioned catalogs, Fleurville doesn't pretend that its designer diaper bags and haute high chairs bring extra benefits to babies. Instead, the appeal is to parents' consumer tastes—a strategy that's increasingly effective. "We feel that we are suppliers to the *parenting* market, not the baby market, and that there is a difference," Granville said. "We contend that much of the industry uses colors that they believe are more traditional baby. We ask the question 'who is buying the product; the baby or the parent?' "[28] As the Granvilles explain on their website, "A brand and its products, by design, should make users feel good."

Not only has shopping for babies become more appealing; it's more convenient. In addition to the dedicated superstores, elegant boutiques, and online companies catering to parents' every whim, newsletter services like Daily Candy and Urbanbaby send out e-mails plugging recommended products and services; with 32 million moms online, the Internet is fast becoming one of the best places to dip into parental wallets. Virtual communities such as Peachhead, a Web site visited by three thousand women which began as a Yahoo! group for fifteen mom friends in Los Angeles, have blossomed into vehicles for marketers. While Peachhead doesn't accept advertising (unlike nearly all other parenting message boards), local businesses descend like Mary Poppins on its annual Peachhead Day get-together to peddle their wares. Clay Shirky, a prominent Internet analyst, said he first became aware of the trend of moms convening online at a board meeting for MeetUp, the social-networking site that helps users organize offline events. Executives at the company reported that stay-at-home moms were the most active group on the site; more than fifty thousand mothers had joined groups since its launch. "We just all sat bolt upright," Shirky said.[29]

Eyes set firmly on this target, Child's Play, a New York–based marketing communications and public relations firm, offers the Web Mom Directory service to clients such as CVS, Gund, and *Parents* Magazine Toys. The directory consists of approximately five hundred "mommy" sites and blogs, to whose members Child's Play mails out product samples, hoping to generate buzz among Internet moms. Its offline venture, the Insider Mom Network, consists of established mom groups, each with at least thirty members and regular formal meetings, across the country. More than five hundred moms belong; they also receive products from Child's Play clients. "Companies are much more cognizant these days of the need to reach moms on a grassroots level," Stephanie Azzarone, president of Child's Play, explained to me. "They're all going to where moms are in an effort to get through."

Many of these moms are fueling the growth in the parenting business themselves. In 1998, at the age of thirty-two, Laurie Mc-Cartney, a Harvard MBA and Disney marketing alum, launched her company, BabyStyle, because, she complained, "I had to go to five or ten stores just to outfit my nursery."[30] McCartney decided busy moms needed a one-stop shopping experience to make things easier. One of a new breed of *mompreneurs*—women who start their own parent-related businesses after the birth of their children—McCartney began the company as a website; she now sends out direct-mail catalogs and operates nineteen retail stores nationwide.

The Internet has spawned dozens of sites offering tips and networking opportunities for such women. Mompreneursonline.com attracts 7 million visitors a month;[31] there's even a book, *Mompreneurs: A Mother's Practical Step-by-Step Guide to Work-at-Home Success*. Some mompreneurs are professionals who decide not to return to the workplace, but want or need to continue working in some form, and choose the flexibility of self-employment. Others say that as new parents, they discovered a need that wasn't being served. While no statistics specifically track mompreneurs, according to the Center for Women's Business Research, women are starting new businesses at twice the rate of men and own a 50 percent or larger stake in 10.6 million U.S. businesses.[32]

"I think the mompreneur trend is being fueled by Gen Xers who like to do things on their own terms," said Maria Bailey, author of *Trillion Dollar Moms*. "They're trying to lead an integrated lifestyle, rather than endlessly trying to 'balance' work and life the way boomers did. They want it all, but at their own pace, having grown up with the mentality of customization and personalization. They're tailoring their own lifestyles as mothers and starting their own businesses to help them do it." Bailey is a mompreneur herself; it was while running a small marketing company that she had three children under two and her "professional and personal lives collided." The result was BSM Media, a Pompano Beach, Florida–based firm that specializes in the mom market. Founded in 1999 with four employees, today it has a staff of nine, who handle such clients as Disney, the Cartoon Network, AOL, Chuck E. Cheese, and Microsoft. Along the way, Bailey has written two business books on marketing to mothers.

In the beginning, it was a struggle for Bailey to get businesses to pay attention. "For the first three years, I had to convince companies that women with kids were different from women without kids," she recalled. "Now, of course, it's a really big thing, and our business has grown fourfold annually for the past few years." She thinks corporate America still has a lot to learn. In order to reach mothers successfully, companies need to understand that not all moms are alike. "They're trying to personalize their experience of being a mother and are creating these subcultures," she said. There's the homeschooling mom. The granola mom. The scrapbooking mom. Bailey's specialty is segmenting the market into subgroups and describing their quirks, habits, and priorities to paying clients. "We segment moms in thirty-four ways," she informed me.

Bailey's baseline segmentation divides moms into three generational groups. "The baby boomers were the yuppies of the eighties, with their BMWs and Rolexes," said Bailey. "Then, in the 1990s, they shifted their spending to their children. Children became their status symbol." Discretionary dollars switched from diamond bracelets to private violin instructors and university sports camps located seven states away. "A lot of companies have seized the opportunity," she said. "They realized, Oh, wow, these women will do *anything* to better the minds of their children. And it's just grown from there. So now you have Kumon offering tutoring for preschoolers. In fact, the fastest-growing segment in tutoring is for pre-k."

According to Bailey, the next generation of parents, Generation Xers, "find their values in the happiness of their children and the emotional security of their families," she said. The following generation, the Millennials or Generation Y, who are entering their late twenties, is also poised for all-consuming parenthood, with near-zero resistance to consumerism. "This generation isn't rejecting their mothers and the way they were mothered," explained Marta Loeb, president of Silver Stork, a Hingham, Massachusetts–based company that also specializes in marketing to moms. "Instead they're saying, I'm going to do as good a job and even better. That means add-ons to strollers, even more interesting colors in children's fashions—ones that are consistent with mothers' tastes. This is a consumer-centric generation, impacted by over a million marketing messages a year, and they *love* products." They also happen to be a generation in love with credit cards, who will shop no matter how burdened by debt.

There's a new generation of fathers to consider as well. Like women, they are older when they have children; the average age of the first-time father is now twenty-nine, and men between the ages of thirty-five and forty-four are becoming new fathers much more often than men in their twenties.[33] Not only are dads older, wealthier, and better educated; they aspire to become more "momlike" in their relationships with their children. One in five fathers of preschoolers takes care of the children for more time than other child-care providers while the mother is at work (often in the morning or evening, around their own work schedules). In a 2005 nationwide survey of fathers, nearly one-fourth said their current work or family situation left them desiring more play time, family vacation time, and involvement in school-related activities like plays and teacher conferences.[34]

Despite competing demands, fathers are already more involved in their children's lives than those of a generation ago. Dads claim to spend more time than their wives doing certain activities with their children. One-fourth say they exercise more with their kids, 15 percent say they are more involved with mealtime, and 13 percent give the kids their baths more often than Mom does. More fathers also say they share parenting responsibilities equally with their wives. A majority play games, watch TV, participate in homework and bedtime, and read books with their children along with their partners.[35] As Silver Stork Research explains in its 2005 Dad Report, "Advertising success relies on the advertiser's ability to keep their finger on the consumer's HOT

BUTTONS." The modern father's top hot buttons: time, involvement, and family.

Not surprisingly, this translates into active in shopping habits as well. Eight in ten say they are involved in some way in everyday purchasing decisions. Half are "very involved" in buying electronics and 43 percent in buying recreational memberships, stereotypically male-dominated categories. They tend to purchase bicycles, sporting goods, computer equipment, home safety equipment, and televisions for their kids. Still, 26 percent say they are very involved in buying board games or card games for their children, and 21 percent and 16 percent are involved in buying kids' books and clothing, respectively. In fact, one in ten dads says he does *all* the shopping for his children's clothes. Not only are fathers shopping more overall; they may spend more money than mothers do. When it comes to purchasing for their children, dads are much less sensitive to price. Only 50 percent care about a brand's cost, compared with 83 percent of moms.[36]

Grandparents, always prone to spoiling the wee ones, are spending more money than ever, too. Today, a record 70 million Americans—about one-third of all adults—are grandparents; that number is expected to rise to 80 million by 2010, according to the AARP. Grandparents now spend an average of $500 a year on their grandchildren, up from $320 in 1992, constituting an annual $35-billion market.[37] "I would say 30 percent of my business today is moms buying for their kids, 20 percent is family and friends and the other 50 percent is grandmas and grandpas because the grandparents have more discretionary income to throw around," an owner of upscale children's stores in Wayne, Pennsylvania, and Greenville, Delaware, told *Children's Business* magazine.[38] According to the GrandParent Marketing Group, grandparents buy one of every four toys, four of every ten baby books, and one in five video games. Buying is on the upswing across every category: In 2002, 87 percent of grandparents bought their grandchildren clothing, compared with 74 percent in 1999; 76 percent bought toys, compared with 38 percent in 1999; and 28 percent bought computer software, up from 18 percent in 1999.[39]

In response, research firms are now studying the grandparent population to figure out why they're spending so prolifically, and enticing them to spend even more. SRI Consulting, a marketing services firm based in Menlo Park, California, first segmented the grandparent population in 2001, coining three behavior categories to describe grandparents. The first, "traditionalists," tend to be cautious, moralistic, and patriotic, and account for the largest group of today's grandparents (54 percent), but they're on the wane. As consumers, traditionalists are home-oriented, and prefer tried-and-true brands. The second group, "makers," (15 percent) is much more active than the first group, and is more likely to be independent and anti-authority. The third, "achievers," (9 percent) is more status-oriented, valuing interpersonal relationships and their buying behavior often relies on peer influence. Now, as baby boomers are entering grandparenthood, SRI sees a fourth group on the rise, which they've dubbed *thinkers*. Currently 16 percent of the grandparent population, they are intellectually curious, active, and globally oriented, and will start to replace the other three groups as boomers begin to dominate grandparenting. According to SRI, this new group is driven by principle. "The primary difference with the new wave of grandparents is they'll have a lot more resources—not just education and money, but also self-confidence, intellectualism, and global awareness—that will make them more open-minded and expressive in the marketplace," explained SRI's senior consultant, Kathy Whitehouse. Whereas in the past, a grandparent might buy a toy based on functionality or durability, she said, the new grandparent will research the toy's comparative merits and purchase it based on its perceived educational value, environmental quality, and ability to engage.[40]

Step into any children's store, and you can see this new grandparent in action. While shopping recently at Planet Kids on New York's Upper East Side, I observed a sixtyish woman enter the store and hold a toy truck aloft. She inspected it from various angles, poking and prodding its appendages and wheels. "What does this do?" she finally asked a store clerk, a note of confused annoyance slipping into her voice. "It's a truck," the clerk replied. The woman humphed and set the toy aside. "I don't want to buy something that doesn't do anything," she replied, as if plastic trucks couldn't vroom along the way they always have in the hands of an energetic toddler. "Where are the toys that *do* something? I want to give my grandson something that has more *value*."

Other marketers call these new customers the grand boomers. "This is the group that put those Baby-On-Board stickers all over their minivans in the 1980s," said Matt Thornhill, president and founder of the Boomer Project, a marketing consultancy in Richmond, Virginia. "They were so proud of having babies. What do you think they're going to do with their grandbabies? They're boomers—they're consumers."[41] And companies are going after them. Babies "R" Us hosts free seminars for grandparents on baby safety and baby care and recently partnered with Fisher-Price to sell a sixty-page guide called *Loving Your Grandbaby*.

THESE READY-TO-CONSUME TARGETS SOUND VERY PROMISING to corporate America. Several marketing and advertising agencies have cropped up in recent years to help companies pinpoint their messages. Silver Stork Research, founded in 2003, promises companies that its "Mom-focused research services enable businesses to be prepared to meet the challenges of a new generation of Moms." Its methods include a national panel of fifteen-hundred-plus moms and an "elite pre-screened panel of articulate, creative, talented, and forward-thinking Moms" dubbed Super Moms. The firm offers product play groups, informal focus groups where moms see, touch, and feel products; Mom Makeovers, in which mothers reinvigorate drab brands into "power-house Mom brands;" and the Incubator, facilitated sessions in which brands or categories are presented to mothers and new products or service concepts are born. "Never before has motherhood been celebrated as it is today," said its president, Marta Loeb. "A new generation of self-sufficient, successful, and family-focused women is reinventing motherhood, and we're seeing the impact of this change everywhere."

Loeb should know. After all, she started thinking about the mom market while pregnant with her first son, Max, in 2000, and issued her first Silver Stork Research report in 2003. "In those three years, I saw a dramatic change in maternity products and products for new mothers," she noted. In 1999, Loeb had to order from a pile of catalogs to decorate her son's nursery; today a mom can go online and buy exactly what Angelina and Brad scooped up for baby Shiloh. "Moms have always wanted the same thing for their children: health, happiness, education, and prosperity," she said. "We all want the best for our children, and that cuts across geography, age, socioeconomic background. The difference is in the way moms consume products and services, and in particular, the way they respond to marketing in order to achieve that goal."

Corporate parenting is intent on becoming that much more omnipresent, infiltrating every aspect of parents' lives. Megaconferences like Chicago's M2Moms: The Marketing to Moms Conference, founded in 2005, have created forums for companies like General Mills, Nickelodeon, Kodak, Kimberly Clark, and Hasbro to "get access, information, knowledge, resource and connections" in the parent market. Businesspeople attend lectures on subjects such as How Mom-Friendly Brand Experiences Can Work for You, Why Mothers Make the Best Brand Advocates, and How Parent Bloggers Are Defining Social Media and Online Marketing.

The parenting market is as big as it's been in a long time; not since 1962 have there been so many newborns in America.[42] There are nearly 4 million families in America that are home to children under two, and an additional 9 million families with children between the ages of two and five. Hundreds of companies are trying their best to get these families spending more money than ever before. For every single worry or wish, frustration or fear, anxious twinge or momentary longing, an answer has been developed by some entrepreneur or marketing executive.

"Across the market, a huge shift has taken place from a product perspective and a marketing perspective," Loeb explained. Once functional items have been hyped into consumer "experiences." The stakes have gotten higher as the marketing experts have descended on the parenting business, and whole categories have been invented and grown competitive. A company can't just pump out jugs of petroleum jelly anymore; baby salves needed to be dressed up with cartoon characters, cutesy designs, high-concept campaigns. "Every brand has had to take notice," Loeb emphasized. "Johnson & Johnson, for example, responded to the increase in boutique and organic products by creating its Naturals line. Companies are grasping that the new mother has come to expect the same consumer goods for her child as she expects for herself: 'If I put moisturizer on my face, then my child should have a facial moisturizer too.'"

3

Trouble in Toyland

Every parent can tell at least one Bad Toy Story. Here is one of mine: When my daughter Beatrice was eight months old, she went bonkers for a battery-powered puppet, one of the many samples that had been sent to me for review. The puppet (a monkey? a bear? a dog?) would sing "Head, Shoulders, Knees, and Toes" when one foot was pressed. The other foot, when squeezed, would intone, "Find your head. Touch your shoulders. Find your knees . . ." Though Beatrice fell within the professed target age range for the toy, she was absolutely content to repeatedly press the latter button so as to hear a continual loop of "Find your head . . . Find your he . . . Find your . . . Find your . . . Find your . . . ." without making a single corresponding gesture.

It didn't surprise me that Beatrice was unable to master the sucker. After all, it demanded understanding a fairly complex concept for a baby: that an object should talk, always saying the same thing, without eye contact or gestures or intonation, and expect that its listener should obey its "commands." As far as I was concerned, the thing didn't even resemble a puppet, that is, a toy that a parent or child could manipulate to say whatever he wants, in whatever voice he wants, to reflect any idea or emotion of the moment. Be that as it may, Beatrice adored it.

One day, amid the chaos of an afternoon playdate, the toy broke. Whether someone stomped on it, threw it in frustration, or twisted it the wrong way was unclear, but the result was unambiguous. Beatrice would press the feet expectantly, then stare, dumbfounded, when the puppet failed to reply. She looked at me, perplexed and disappointed.

That night, I asked my husband if he could break open the puppet and rewire its insides so it would once again sing on demand.

"*Are you kidding?*" he replied. "Let's leave it. We hate this stupid toy anyway, and it will be much better if it doesn't bleat the same song over and over." He had already insisted on hiding a singing, jabbering Learn n' Play Puppy in the closet because it wouldn't shut up.

"I know," I conceded, somewhat abashed. "But Beatrice *expects* the toy to sing and talk. When it doesn't, she finds it disturbing. Something that was once predictable no longer is. How should she interpret that?" I was aware of how ridiculous I sounded, but felt trapped. I had come to believe that we had to fix the toy or throw it away entirely, so my husband agreed to fix it, soldering the wires back together. Of course, Beatrice soon lost all interest in the puppet. I didn't blame her. It was nearly impossible to manipulate without setting off the blasted song, and the puppet never said anything other than its programmed chart, making it very much a one-note wonder. Like so many other toys on the market today, it didn't last long.

PAULINE AMELL NASH, A THIRTY-FIVE-YEAR-OLD MOTHER FROM Claremont, California, tries to be careful about how many toys— and what kinds—she lets into the house. Despite her intentions, and the fact that she makes many of her one-year-old daughter's toys from scratch, her living room seems filled to capacity with playthings. "We've probably spent more money than I realize because every time I go out, I see something that I want to bring home. Even if it seems small, like a bottle of bubbles or another toy car." Nash's objective is understandable. "I want to give her the best start possible, and that makes me constantly on the lookout for toys that are very interactive so that she's not just watching TV and being passive. Working at a college, I'm really aware of what it takes to succeed. I want her to hit the ground running."

When I was the manager of a book club at the children's publishing company Scholastic more than a decade ago, I would often present a graph depicting the level of parental anxiety about their children's development measured against Scholastic's distribution model. Scholastic sells the majority of its children's products in schools through book clubs, via a kind of minicatalog, that teachers distribute to students. Because orders are placed through teachers and are shipped to the classroom, parents see their purchases as contributing to their kids' education; based on the number of orders in their classrooms, teachers win points toward free teaching materials, so it's a winning formula all around. In the book club I managed, rather than sell *Goosebumps*, we featured parent- and-child activity books, educational toys and manipulatives, and a few nonfiction books for parents to read with their children. But the core business was parenting books: books about discipline, sibling rivalry, encouraging learning. The club's challenge was capitalizing on parents' fears at their height, during the first few years of a child's life, when many children aren't in school, early childhood centers, or educational day care and thus don't receive the catalogs from instructors. At that time, in the mid-1990s, Scholastic's access to the parent market peaked while children were at school, and our products were most desired by parents whose children were at home; my stark graph illustrated the marketing mismatch.

Today, that graph would be obsolete. Home has merged with school and vice versa, smacking the parental wallet in both directions. Once kids go to school, parents are expected to foot the bill for basic school expenses—participating in fundraising events and paying for school supplies—as well as subsidizing extracurricular activities. But well before the children get there, the home is meant to function as an outpost for education, with parents expected to foster learning at earlier ages on their second shift or to find someone else to do the job. Increasingly, this is accomplished through the purchase of toys that purport to teach. In a 2004 Kaiser Family Foundation survey, nearly two-thirds (62 percent) of parents said educational toys are "very important to children's intellectual development." In a 2002 *Parents* magazine survey, 42 percent said they felt pressure to raise smarter kids, and 69 percent were inclined to purchase a brain-boosting video or toy as a consequence.[1]

Of course, it's understandable that many parents want toys that promote child development in some way—be it social, emotional, or intellectual. All parents want their children to learn, but most parents also understand that in order for babies and toddlers to learn, they need to have fun. So while the toy market for older children has struggled—with children as young as eight spending far more time on video games and the Internet than playing with the board games of yore, for young children, the business has boomed, amounting to $4.6 billion a year in sales. A large chunk of that growth has come as the target age for educational toys has been pushed down. Between 2003 and 2004, the learning toy category ballooned from $496 million to $694 million.[2] In 2005, 14.6 million American households purchased toys or games for infants,[3] and according to a study conducted in 2006, one in four parents purchased an electronic teaching toy, spending an average of $146 a year on toys and games.[4] A 2005 market report notes, "As American parenting continues to become more and more sophisticated, the demand for educational ITP [infant, toddler, preschool] toys will only become greater and greater."[5]

Parental anxiety about children's academic readiness and performance pervades our culture, from our obsession with the dismal state of public education (and the lunacy of private school admissions and fees for those who can afford it) to the books lining the walls of the parenting section in bookstores. Of the spate of books intended to help parents boost their children's brain capacity, the trade magazine *Publishers Weekly* noted:

> A robust economy, demographics that have schools across the country bursting at the seams, parental anxiety about setting their offspring on the right track to succeed in a competitive world and concern about societal threats to their kids' well-being—these are some of the forces fueling today's sizzling market for books on childcare and parents . . . [T]he amount of money people are now willing to spend to help themselves be better parents has never been greater.[6]

Titles such as *How to Raise a Smarter Child by Kindergarten, Smart Baby, Clever Child: Brain-Building Games, Activities, and Ideas to Stimulate Your Baby's Mind,* and *Baby Minds: Brain-Building Games Your Baby Will Love* bombard parents with the message that it's their duty to get their children Ivy League–ready before they've left the crib.

Or even earlier. Those bent on zipping ahead can start their fetus on the BabyPlus Prenatal Education System, which teaches "sound lessons" in utero via a device that looks like a fanny pack. BabyPlus babies allegedly demonstrate earlier milestones, improved school readiness and intellectual abilities, and longer attention spans. Go ahead—ridicule the idea! But to Lisa Jarrett, president and founder of the Indianapolis-based company, BabyPlus is entirely logical. "A mother who takes a prenatal vitamin while pregnant would never be accused of trying to create a bodybuilder," she pointed out. "We're not saying that we're promoting geniuses. That's not our mission. We're about having moms think about long-term cognitive development at a time when you *should* be thinking about it." Pity the benighted parent who waits until a child is out of the womb before contemplating his cognitive future.

Here's how it works: A pregnant mother straps on the BabyPlus twice a day starting anytime after her eighteenth week of pregnancy. Her fetus can "listen" to lessons while Mom is carpooling or relaxing at home. The "curriculum" consists of sixteen lessons, each a heartbeat-like thumping sound at differing speeds and intervals. Lesson Two, which Jarrett played for me, sounds like the stethoscope-magnified heartbeat of a person reclining in an armchair. Lesson Four is like listening to a jogger hit his stride. While competitors advocate playing music or introducing words in utero, Jarrett, who worked as a laboratory biologist prior to starting BabyPlus, cautioned against the expectations built into such products. "Prenatally, that's *a lot* for a baby to know." She clarified: "In order to be called a curriculum, lessons have to build on what babies *already* know. Our sounds basically mimic variations of the child's prenatal language." The theory behind BabyPlus is that by listening to the contrast between the mother's internal biological soundtrack (heartbeat, digestive groans, inhalations, and other bodily functions) and the lesson of the day, the fetus will improve his auditory discrimination skills. That is, he will learn to compare and contrast the two sets of sounds. "Postnatally, that's called learning," said Jarrett, who is convinced that when babies learn this stuff extra-early, they have "stronger learning" later.

Her proof is entirely anecdotal; after all, how can you prove that a particular baby was smarter after following the curriculum than she would have been had she been left to mull over the old glub-blub of her mother's digestion? It's not exactly something that can be tested. But for Jarrett, the abilities of her own Baby-Plused children—now fifteen, thirteen, eleven, and three—provide ample evidence. "I can honestly say that my children at delivery were so alert. They tended to nurse very readily, right after delivery. They were calm, happy infants," she told me. "Of course, that's sort of subjective. But most BabyPlus parents say the same thing." Just like the parents in Lake Wobegon, where all the children are above average, Jarrett's clients tell her that their chil-

dren hit their pediatric milestones strongly and early. Their attention spans are longer than those of other toddlers. Rather than
play for minutes at a time, they stay engaged and interactive for
forty-five-minute stretches. Still, it's impossible to parse what
would have occurred without BabyPlus. "I think my children
would have been smart genetically," she admitted. "But it's not just
their intelligence. I really believe that I have strengthened their
long-term cognitive ability. We're not saying genetics don't matter;
we're saying, enrich the in-utero auditory component too."

Explaining the product's promise and delivery to prospective
customers has been a challenge, though Jarrett said it has grown
easier over time. "Independently, without any reference to our
product, almost all developmental specialists are saying that the
key to brain development is *prenatal* to three, not just birth to
three." She's right that the environment in utero matters. Research has demonstrated the importance of a mother taking folic
acid, for example, to prevent neural tube defects such as spinal
bifida. Omega-3s, the fatty acids in fish, and particularly DHA are
similarly important structural components of the nerve cells in the
brain. Conversely, if a mother consumes mercury, which is also
present in many fish, it can lead to brain damage and developmental delays, and alcohol consumption puts fetuses at risk for low
birth weight and other health problems. Yet no research shows auditory discrimination lessons in utero improve cognitive skills. No
matter. Jarrett and her colleagues are passionate about their product, doing everything to get the word out. Their latest effort re-
cruits prenatal educators to hand out brochures for BabyPlus
during childbirth-education and newborn-care classes.

In business since 1998, BabyPlus is growing between 15 percent and 25 percent each year, and in 2006, it sold about eight
thousand devices in sixty countries worldwide. Different markets
have different priorities. "Asian countries really understand this,
as you can imagine," Jarrett said. In the United Kingdom, moms
are sold on the fact that BabyPlus leads to better nursing. In the

United States, the biggest selling point is that it helps babies self-soothe. "The minute moms hear about our product and our mission, it's like an 'A-ha moment.' Parents intuitively are trying to do the best they can for their child from the moment they know they've conceived. They are very aware they can impact their child's long-term development. And when they hear about this particular curriculum, they understand our message."

THE INFANT, TODDLER, AND PRESCHOOL TOY INDUSTRY SPENDS $221 million a year sending such messages to parents,[7] and for good reason. "More than thirty percent of babies born in the U.S. are to affluent moms aged twenty-five-plus, who consider education a number one priority for their children," said Reyne Rice of the Toy Industry Association, by way of explaining the rise in educational toy sales. These families "are willing to do whatever it takes to give their kids a head start in life."[8] We read advertisements like the one for Tiny Love toys, which assure us that "proven developmental benefits" are sewn by experts into each wee plaything. We fall for items like the Chicco Bilingual Talking Cube and the LeapFrog Roll & Rhyme Learning Lion with their pledges of linguistic glory. Ever-present is the disquieting thought that if we *don't* buy these toys for our own children, other parents will. *Their* kids will learn shapes and sizes before our kids do. *Their* kids will have every opportunity. Our children will fall irredeemably behind. And it will all be because we were neglectful, irresponsible, and not sufficiently involved. Or just too cheap.

The clamor for educational toys has grown so fervid that any toy engineered for amusement alone has to reconsider its prospects. Market research firm Packaged Facts notes that companies have begun to "reposition" plain old standbys as primarily educational or developmental with shout-outs that appeal to education-minded parents. Heaven forbid a kid play Sorry! without a higher goal in mind. As observed in a 2005 report, "Educational and developmental value may in some cases continue to help boost price-points, especially if the toy in question employs sophisticated electronics, as do many of LeapFrog's toys. Handcrafted or imported educational toys, of the type purchased by Yoga Mommies in upscale boutiques, also command higher prices." But it's not just so-called yoga moms succumbing to the call. While the households that purchase infant and toddler toys tend to be headed by older parents with high levels of education and high incomes, grandparents and stay-at-home moms factor heavily among them, and the people most likely to buy infant toys hail from the Midwest.[9]

The latest toys for children are dubbed "smart toys"—not just because they claim to boost a child's cognitive development, but because they contain technological enhancements that enable a child to form, as the lingo goes, "dynamic, emotional relationships." Smart toys incorporate microchips, voice recognition systems, and wireless capability, allowing for features like real-time chat and interactive games so that toy and child can spend "quality time" together. Perhaps the first and most influential smart toy to enter the market was Tickle Me Elmo, a plush doll that burst into laughter when tickled on its belly.* A simple concept, but it was a sensation. Launched in 1996, Tickle Me Elmo became a megaseller, generating more than $22 million in revenue during its first Christmas season.[10] Ever since, other toys have been angling to catch up and their progress has been swift. At the 1999 trade show Toy Fair, about 30 percent of new toys contained some sort of "smart" element; by the next year, two-thirds of the toys on display were smart.[11] The once traditional Fisher-Price, which captures as much as 40 percent of the infant, toddler, and preschool toy market,[12] embedded microchips in two-thirds of its toy

---

*There may be no greater symbol of the electronic toy genre's inherent absence of creativity than the fact that in 2007, the T.M.X. Elmo, essentially a turbo update of the original, was named "Toy of the Year" at the annual trade show, Toy Fair. The prize ostensibly goes to a toy praised for its innovation and ability to generate buzz.

lineup in 2000. By 2003, 75 percent of Fisher-Price toys had an electronic component. In 2006, the company's big "toy" launches at Toy Fair were a digital music player and a digital camera for children as young as three.

In part, Fisher-Price has been trying to keep pace with smart-toy juggernaut LeapFrog, which was founded in 1995 specifically to develop electronic and interactive educational toys. The company adopted Tickle Me Elmo's technological mantle and added an educational bent, thereby setting the standard for the industry. At the time, the market for "learning" toys was considered limited. Who wanted a toy that was *ecch*, educational? Boring! But in its first year, LeapFrog stunned detractors, earning $3 million. By 2000, its LeapPad, an interactive "learning system" that resembles an electronic book, had become the country's bestselling toy—a first for a so-called educational toy. When the company went public in 2002, it was the year's most successful IPO, according to *BusinessWeek* magazine. With $640.3 million in sales in 2004, the company became one of the country's biggest and most influential toy manufacturers.[13]

"We all want to be parents of the next Einstein," opens an advertisement for Fisher-Price toys, going on to explain, with regard to items like kitchen playsets, that "the right toys at the right time will enrich the play experience of your little genius." Competitor Neurosmith describes its products as "innovative, open-ended, electronic learning toys that combine the latest child development research with fun, interactive play patterns, sounds and music." The promotional copy leaves no buzzword behind: "These musical toys utilize the highest available sound quality to stimulate key areas of the brain and actually help teach your child how to learn."[14] Similarly, IQ Baby offers "infant toys that invite exploration, encourage discovery and reward development in the critical years from birth through toddlerhood."[15]

But not all of these toys live up to their marketing claims. A two-year government-funded study by the University of Stirling, in Scotland, found that educational electronic toys such as the LeapPad and the Vtech V (a similar smart toy) provide no discernible benefits to children. "In terms of basic literary and number skills, I don't think they are more efficient than the more traditional approaches," explained researcher Lydia Plowman, summarizing the report's findings.[16]

For the past twenty-five years, Diane Levin, the Wheelock College child development specialist, has taken prospective teachers to a local mass-market toy store to pick out good and bad toys for children, according to what they've learned in their education studies. "They used to have a hard time finding bad toys for infants and toddlers," she recalled. "But about six or seven years ago, there was suddenly this whole range of what educators consider bad toys. Toys with batteries and buttons. Toys that tell children what to do. Toys that program children's play." These "educational" toys, Levin said, not only fail to teach children but make raising infants and toddlers "harder, more confusing, and more insecurity producing." Levin doesn't blame parents. "Parents are on the receiving end of a barrage of marketing messages that exploit both them and their children. When they're told that this toy will make their child smarter, they're understandably ripe to buy," she said. "Parents have always wanted to think that their kids are smart, and that's something the industry exploits viciously."

FOUNDED IN 1946, CHICCO IS A VENERABLE EUROPEAN COMpany based in Como, Italy. Chicco (pronounced "keekoh") claims to be "wherever there is a baby," and indeed a parent can easily outfit an entire household in Chicco and be perfectly satisfied. The company manufactures strollers, car seats, feeding paraphernalia, and all the other manner of accoutrement for a baby-friendly home. It's also one of the most successful manufacturers of young children's toys in the United States.

Though the company has long made dolls, toy strollers, and

dump trucks, in recent years it has pumped out an increasing number of talking, remote-controlled toys and ride-ons outfitted with electronic voices and buttons that respond on command. Bilingual toys took off in 2002, when the company introduced its Talking Farm, a toy barn populated by plastic animal shapes. According to Chicco, playing with the farm "improves children's language, thinking, and musical skills in both English and Spanish," "teaches children how to listen, recognize, and speak by teaching them to count to 10 and by helping them learn 11 animals' names, colors, and sounds," and "improves children's abilities to listen and sing along with its 8 nursery songs that are accompanied by electronic flashing lights." Propelled by such promises, Talking Farm became a huge hit. The company went on to launch the Bilingual Talking Cube and the Bilingual Talking Videophone, which retail at $29.99 and up.

"My viewpoint is that with so many dual working parents, the guilt factor steps in," said Rick Muraski, executive vice president of Chicco's toy division, explaining the products' success. "They're looking for toys that make them feel good. They think, if I'm not around enough, something can fill in that void for me, maybe if the toy teaches them something. I think that's what grew the category."

According to Muraski, "When it says 'educational' and 'award-winning,' it can only help the item be sold." Driving sales the most are the *Today Show* awards that televise children playing with the contenders, showing parents which ones hold a child's attention for more than a nanosecond and which are left behind. Citations from parenting magazines; are also valuable. "New parents are reading all those magazines it's like the bible to them," Muraski said. And companies make sure to keep parents apprised of the results. Most organizations that bequeath awards allow manufacturers to put stickers on the products advertising their wins. Many products boast multiple award stickers in an attempt to grab parents' attention. There are also "awards" that can simply be purchased; a manufacturer pays the "accrediting" organization a fee to carry a sticker boasting its endorsement.

It's as if by purchasing award-winning toys, we can ensure award-winning children.

Doesn't everyone want a Lake Wobegon child? That's the business-model assumption of Brainy Baby, whose tagline is "a little genius in the making." The Brainy Baby Number Bug, a heavy plastic caterpillar with colored number buttons and antennae that light up in conjunction with electronic music, asks babies three months and up to identify numbers and shapes by pressing buttons when asked. If the baby presses the appropriate button (fat chance for a three-month-old or even for an eighteen-month-old, unless my daughter and her friends are especially dim), a childlike voice cheers, "Very good. You're a *brainy* baby!" Lynn Scarborough, a spokesperson for Brainy Baby, boasted to me that unlike other companies, "Brainy Baby is educational stimulation first, and *that's* what's entertaining to babies. All Brainy Baby products have to have some type of educational value, be it teaching object permanence or encouraging cognitive development." Bulleted lists of skills adorn each Brainy Baby package. "We're not just slapping the Brainy Baby logo on a blanket," confirmed the company's senior producer, Marcia Grimsley.

Calvin Trillin once said that the famously arrogant John Sununu, former chief of staff to George H. W. Bush, was the perfect example of the perils of telling your child he has a high IQ. Whether or not you question the wisdom of telling your child he's a genius just because he can bang on the right button, there's the question of *how* such toys purport to teach. Brainy Baby's founder, Dennis Fedoruk, a cinematographer who created corporate videos for companies like Coca-Cola and Delta, started the company in 1995 with two videos, *Brainy Baby Right Brain* and *Brainy Baby Left Brain* ($17.95, each). His idea was that children needed to develop both right-brain creative thinking and left-brain logical thinking in order to mature into well-rounded adults. Translating that concept into marketable educational toys led to the *Brainy Baby My Right Brain Book*, which opens with a spread of a child gazing at clouds that are shaped like fish, butterflies, and bunny rabbits. "What shapes can you find in the clouds?" the text asks, though the images are so clearly defined and straightforward they don't exactly "inspire creative thinking." A similarly misguided product, an electronic cloth book featuring large plastic buttons that light up and make noises, inquires, "I wonder how I'll feel today?" when you turn on the power. If the child touches the first button, a yellow sun, the voice crows, "Yellow makes me feel hap-hap-happy!" Green "makes me feel big and strong," and red "makes me feel *loved.*" Allowing a child to decide for herself how different colors affect her doesn't factor into Brainy Baby's packaged prescription for creativity and self-expression.

As with so many smart-toy companies, Brainy Baby can cite no research that relates specifically to its products; it neither conducted nor commissioned any studies in developing them. In fact, a study by the Infant Laboratory at Temple University and the Erikson Institute in Chicago found that parents who discuss the content of traditional books while reading to their children promoted early literacy, while electronic books encouraged a "slightly coercive parent-child interaction" and were not as effective. The researchers described parents and children reading electronic books together as a "severely truncated" experience. "We're not neurolinguistic scientists," admitted Marcia Grimsley. "We went out and researched other people's work—scientists, neurologists, psychologists—and applied that knowledge to our products so they could be fun and beneficial to parents and children." For a company dedicated to stimulating genius, its methods are surprisingly laid-back. "We're very good at thinking like children," she said of the Brainy Baby development team. "Most of us are parents." Grimsley explained that a lot of what they do in creating new toys is "common sense."

BUT IS WHAT PARENTS ARE TRYING TO TEACH CHILDREN through these toys all that sensible? The very idea that play needs to be productive and purposeful, that there should be a prescriptive goal for a baby's free time, is self-contradicting. Consider the textbook meaning of *play*. According to Catherine Garvey of the University of Maine and Kenneth Rubin of the University of Maryland, play has five necessary elements. First, play is pleasurable and enjoyable. Second, play should have no extrinsic objectives. Third, play is spontaneous and voluntary. Fourth, play involves active engagement. Fifth, play incorporates some form of make-believe.[17] A plaything is not meant to teach anything at all; it is by definition *not* purposeful. Toys, in short, are *supposed* to be "just" for fun.

Yet many contemporary toys ask children to execute tasks, turning play into performance. The acclaimed Tufts University child psychologist David Elkind, who has spent years studying the effects of parental pressure on children, says making children believe they need to perform to gain a parent's acceptance dampens natural curiosity. In their pitches, companies urge parents to push and prod their babies and toddlers down an assembly line to academic achievement. Consider the emergence of flash cards for one-year-olds, often playfully named "discovery cards." Subjecting a baby or preschooler to academic drill techniques suited to SAT-cramming high schoolers is not play just because it's packaged that way.

Even far-from-flashcard toys that look potentially enjoyable are embedded with weighty expectations and laden with elaborate pedagogical claims. We've become convinced, for example, that all toys should be *interactive*. Interactive *sounds* good—the child must be *doing* something with the toy. Companies have picked up on the buzzword to counteract the dreaded "passive" entertainment that seems to dominate the culture (to parents' dismay). According to one market report, a toy designer's three watchwords should be *motion, sound,* and/or *interactivity*.

Interactivity, plus onboard electronics that teach music, the ABCs, numbers, animal names, or enhance coordination, is evident everywhere in the ITP toy industry. New examples range from LeapFrog's sophisticated laptop-like learning pads; to Hasbro's and Cranium's respective updates of Candy Land and Hullabaloo board games that now incorporate DVDs and one's whole living room in the games' design; to stuffed animals that talk. Even non-electronic toys are being positioned on their interactive, educational, developmental or coordination-enhancing attributes.

Once mute, stuffed animals now sing and twitch. After holding out for years, in 2007, the 109-year-old family-owned Gund, maker of good old-fashioned stuffed animals, finally capitulated to the trend, offering animated bears for the first time.[18] Blocks are embellished with sounds, flaps, doors, and bells. IQ Baby ("bright minds, bright futures") blocks assure parents that "surprise jingles, rattles and crinkles teach cause and effect." A tag affixed to the product notes, "IQ Baby products nurture the whole child—body, mind and spirit—through vibrant engaging toys designed to reward infant development and encourage social interaction."

By singing, talking, moving, and dancing, interactive toys are made to resemble live animals and human beings, as if to make up for the absence of a parent, caregiver, or playmate. Chuck Nelson, a neuroscientist and professor of pediatrics at Harvard Medical School, is concerned that parents will assume that if their babies have enough toys, parents won't need to play with them as much. "We know that babies thrive on interaction with a caregiver, and that's often what's absent from a lot of these enrichment products," Nelson said. "There's no biological reason why a child being reared in a normal home would benefit from these things."

Many toys on the market today may as well have a sticker on them that says, "Imagination Not Included." Rather than teach a child how to come up with his own answers, too many of the toys on the shelves dictate a right way to play, one that leads to *the* correct answer, in the correct direction. As with the phrase "learning through play," the ascension of "interactivity" rests on a fundamental misconception of how children should play with toys. What educators do recommend is not that *toys* be interactive—but that children *interact with* toys. When a baby cuddles a teddy bear and then throws it out of her crib, she is interacting with it; when a child picks up a plain wooden block and puts it on the table, he is interacting with it. The block does not need to light up and sing. And not surprisingly the teddy bear that doesn't get up and do the hula is, of course, less expensive than its dramatic, electronic counterpart.

It's easy to trace the origins of parental confusion over which kind of toys are best. First there was a widely promoted 1987 study showing that premature babies exposed to music, massage, and pictures were more likely to develop normally than those who weren't. Then in 1994, the Carnegie Corporation published a 134-page report describing a crisis among American children, who it said were suffering from the failing school system and the absence of their dual-career parents. The study noted that schoolkids weren't the only ones in trouble; babies' brains were extremely vulnerable to early influences, and the right (or wrong) development could seriously impact their futures.[19] Finally, the Romanian orphan scandal of 1990 barraged parents with images of crying infants crowded into bleak wards, wallowing in dirty sheets and diapers with no one to answer their pleas for attention. "Everyone heard about the orphans in Romania who were deprived of stimulation as babies, then had learning and emotional problems later," said Pat Levitt, director of the Vanderbilt Kennedy Center for Research on Human Development. "Yet there's a disconnect: People mistake comparing a deprived environment to a normal one, and believe that an enriched environment is therefore better than a normal one. There is *no* evidence that says you can drive the baby's system to ever greater heights."

As so often happens with child-rearing and pedagogical trends, today's parents have dispensed with the prevailing wisdom of the previous generation, when those who sought to raise smart, creative children eschewed battery-operated toys; now, many well-intentioned parents have been convinced that the more gizmos attached to a plaything, the more likely it is to foster cognitive development. Sarah,[20] a thirty-three-year-old stay-at-home mother from Wayne, Pennsylvania, found herself buying way too many toys for her baby. "I would see him enjoying toys at other kids' houses and would think, 'I should get that at home.' And that's what I do." Most of the toys her son plays with are new to her. "I didn't have these things when I was a child. A lot of them didn't exist. I don't think that generation believed in even half the toys we've gotten [our son]. It was more about toys that you found in the home—pots and pans, wooden spoons." By the time her son was a year old, Sarah regretted much of what she had bought. "Kids probably don't need as much color and textures and features as we think they need. I think they're just as happy with the spoon as they are with the multicolored ball that spins and plays music."

The smartest toys, according to the experts, are the ones children have played with for generations. Susan Linn, associate director of the Media Center at Judge Baker Children's Center and an instructor in psychiatry at Harvard Medical School, states that the best toys are 90 percent child, 10 percent toy. A good rule of thumb: the simpler, the better because the more open-ended and generic a toy is, the more opportunities for varied play experiences. Blocks, building materials, art supplies, balls, pretend play props, and puppets (the old-fashioned kind) trump toys with buttons any day. "Books should be books," Linn says, "not padded with electronic buttons or noises or accompanying CD-ROMs, all of which train children to expect gimmicks from reading, rather than storylines and characters." Unfortunately, finding a good toy now carries its own financial demands: With electronic toys and cheap, dispensable plastic toys clogging up the superstores, some of the best toys for children, hand-carved out of wood and other natural materials, are only custom crafted in small batches for an upscale market—with correspondingly lofty price tags. A pair of fox and crow puppets made of cotton and wood retail at $44, while a battery-powered, blabbing SpongeBob sells for less than $5 at the local drugstore. Parents pay a premium as well for items that are made, usually with more regulation and oversight, in Europe and the United States, rather than cheaply constructed in China.

Whether parents are tyrannized by the high cost of better-quality cotton and wood toys or by the incessant upgrades of the latest smart-toy technology, the truth is, babies don't really need so many toys. Most childhood milestones can be (and routinely are) reached through interaction with parents and immersion in a child's home and natural environment. As Child psychologists Sandra Scarr and Judith Dunn put it, "the baby who needs to be taught and stimulated is, in our opinion, a creation of salesmen who profit from making parents feel that they are not doing enough for their children."[21]

That sales pitch has infiltrated the way we raise our children. "Americans—though increasingly other Western countries as well—are exceptional among cultures in their obsession with making babies smarter. But there's a growing thought that maybe Americans are overstimulating their babies—or stimulating them in the wrong ways," said Meredith Small, a pediatric anthropologist and the author of *Our Babies, Ourselves: How Biology and Culture Shape the Way We Parent*. When babies are overstimulated, they get frustrated or upset. Other times, they simply tune out. In his research at Harvard, Chuck Nelson puts between 64 and 128 tiny little sensors on babies to monitor what's going on inside their heads. "There is almost certainly a limit to how much can be absorbed and processed by an infant brain," he explained. "A lot of products assume babies will soak it all up like a sponge, but babies have built-in filters. They just screen a lot of it out."

WHAT THEY DON'T SCREEN OUT CAN ACTUALLY MAKE THINGS worse. Once a baby becomes accustomed to overprocessed toys, spontaneously lighting up and emitting noises, toys that "do nothing" seem boring by comparison. The child never learns that *he's* the one who's supposed to provide the action. Allen Kanner, a child psychologist at the Wright Institute in Berkeley, California, says that about ten years ago, children began tiring of the puppets, stuffed animals, board games, and fairy-tale figures strewn around his waiting area. One child outright refused to play with them. "This is all old stuff," he told his doctor, requesting Transformers instead. One educator relayed the story of a two-year-old who searched for the batteries in every toy she picked up. Another shared the story of a four-year-old boy who rushed into her office, picked up a stuffed animal, and asked, "What does it do?"

We are phasing out the impetus for children to *create* something out of their playthings. Another category of pricey yet problematic toys are those that are "all-inclusive," which sounds good in theory—at least it means fewer components to buy, right? Not quite. A 2005 market research report on the toy market explains, "Modern American social pressures often mandate a more expensive, more substantial gift than a simple old-fashioned doll or toy truck—one has to provide the doll's whole castle, or the truck's whole repair shop." This not only drives *up* the price but has unintended consequences for children's development. With everything included, packaged kits instruct kids on how to make a specific project, be it a necklace or a vase, leaving nothing to the imagination. Such predetermined parameters don't allow for tinkering and deprive children of the opportunity for invention.

In 2006, the Alliance for Childhood, a national nonprofit organization devoted to the value of play in children's lives, conducted a study of kindergarten teachers in Atlanta. The goal was to investigate the apparent disappearance of imagination from early childhood classrooms. Kindergarten teachers described how when they gave children time for free play, the children no longer knew what to do. They had no ideas of their own, the teachers complained. Joan Almon, a coordinator for the Alliance for childhood, believes that in an era of microchip toys, children's creativity atrophies.

"The imagination is like an internal muscle that needs to be exercised," she said. With an overreliance on structured activities, and overly predictable play, children are losing a sense of adventurousness and risk-taking. The world in which sales of educational toys are expected to hit $5.5 billion by 2010 is one that, for children, is becoming increasingly restrictive, rigidly contained, and defined by consumption.[22]

Furthermore, though many parents are preoccupied with household safety gadgets, it turns out that toys may be the most dangerous things in our homes. In pursuit of greater profit margins and to suit the habits of children who churn through toys each week, manufacturers cheaply fabricate many toys in China or other countries where safety standards are lax. Current laws make it tricky to regulate toys, particularly imports, and the Consumer Products Safety Commission encounters daunting hurdles in enforcing product recalls.[23] Even when a product has been shown to cause thousands of injuries, it can take years for it to be properly relabeled, to have warnings attached or recommended ages adjusted, or for the product to be completely withdrawn. Take a few of the many egregious cases: Beginning in 2004, records show that MEGA Brands and its subsidiary, Rose Art, had received 1,500 reports that magnets on its Magnetix toys came loose from their casings. Yet it wasn't until 2006 that the company changed the recommended age from three and up to over age six, and in 2007, children were still being hospitalized, for an average of 8.7 days, after swallowing the magnets. In 2007, the toys generated an estimated $100 million for MEGA Brands, accounting for more than half its pretax earnings, which might have had something to do with the company's reluctance to take further action.[24] Easily swallowed "rare earth magnets," so strong they can tear up a child's intestines and even kill him, are still used in some toys. In 2007, lead paint was discovered on Thomas the Tank Engine trains, Dora the Explorer toys, Barbie merchandise, Fisher-Price playthings, and millions of Mattel-branded toys for preschoolers and babies. Those were just the major scandals and recalls. Meanwhile, hundreds of chewable, mouthable baby toys, from rubber ducks to bath books, contain phthalates, an endocrine disruptor, and bisphenol-A, an estrogen receptor, both of which have been linked to the "feminization" of boys, with symptoms including smaller penises and undescended testes,[25] low sperm count, infertile sperm, cellular resistance to insulin (a precursor to diabetes), cancer, and obesity. Other than a controversial ban of such products in San Francisco, no action has been taken.

Even when toys are safe and cheap, children need to cycle through more and more of them, faster than ever. The average child in America gets seventy new toys a year,[26] and the United States, with 4 percent of the world's children, consumes 40 percent of the world's toys.[27] Rather than bulldozing their way through dozens of one-note, breakable, and possibly harmful toys, children benefit from repetitive use of old favorites, finding new ways to play with them as their minds mature and expand. Lab studies show that when a child doesn't understand how a toy works, she'll play with it more and experiment with it in different ways. "If they actually *understand* the causal relationship [which is what happens when a child pushes a button on electronic toys], they'll move on," said Laura Schulz, a professor of brain and cognitive sciences at MIT. Instead of developing resourcefulness, children with loads of "smart" toys become passive absorbers; instead of honing their ability to focus, they develop impatience; instead of learning creativity, they learn how to behave like unskilled workers on a factory line.

Those who consider a child's development of creativity an inconsequential pursuit might consider research showing that high school seniors and college students who score high in creativity are also more likely to perform well academically. "We tend to think of creativity in a narrow sense—the ability to write a story or draw a picture—but it's also about flexibility," explained Robert J. Sternberg, dean of Tufts's School of Arts and Sciences and lead

author of the study. "Imaginative children can adapt to new situations and challenges."[28] Susan Linn at Judge Baker Children's
Center links the death of creativity directly to the explosion in
smart toys and media. "The erosion of creative play is the most
troubling aspect of this business," she told me. "Creative play is
the foundation of critical thinking, of making life meaningful. It is
essential to child growth and development, and we're interfering
with it in ways that are incredibly worrisome. In a democratic society, we need people who don't just accept what's put in front of
their faces, but those who wrestle with it and find ways of taking
action. It may sound like a leap to go from baby [toys] to the death
of democracy, but it's a valid concern. A democratic populace relies on people who know how to think critically, who are willing
and able to take action."

THERE'S MORE TO WORRY ABOUT. EDUCATORS AND CHILD DE-
velopment experts are concerned that by focusing prematurely on
reading and math, parents aren't giving children the opportunity
to learn what they *should* be learning before preschool: problem-
solving, imaginative play, resourcefulness, and conflict resolution.

"There seems to be a common assumption, in thinking about
children's development, that earlier is better," explained Elizabeth
Spelke, a cognitive scientist who specializes in young children at
Harvard University's Laboratory for Developmental Studies. "The
reasoning goes, if it's good for a four-year-old to understand counting, it would be even better if a two-year-old could be induced to
understand counting. But there's no evidence to support this assumption and some reason to be skeptical of it. Two-year-olds are
already engaged in the task of mastering much of the encyclope-
dic knowledge about objects, events, places, and people that we
adults take for granted. Diverting them from this task by introducing other tasks, like learning to read or work with numbers, seems
useless at best and possibly harmful."[29] Companies capitalize on

parents' anxiety that toddlers need to learn the alphabet and numbers before they enter preschool. Education professor Diane Levin thinks parents are sold a bill of goods. "They think that a child who knows his alphabet at age three is smart, and that's another belief that these companies exploit," she said. "These toys can actually hurt children's development of the very skills they purport to teach." It might do well to bear in mind the words of Henry David Thoreau:

> I am struck by the fact that the more slowly trees grow at first, the sounder they are at the core, and I think the same is true of human beings. We do not wish to see children precocious, making great strides in their early years like sprouts, producing soft, perishable timber, but better if they expand slowly at first, as if contending with difficulties, and so are solidified and perfected. Such trees continue to expand with nearly equal rapidity to extreme old age.

While we seem to realize that some babies get their teeth earlier (and that this has nothing to do with later eating habits, appetite, or body mass index), we seem not to accept that babies develop cognitively at different rates. Nor do we seem to recognize that cognitive development cannot be teased out and isolated from other aspects of human development. A nationwide study by the nonprofit research and advocacy organization Zero to Three, titled *What Grown-Ups Understand About Child Development,* found that parents place too much emphasis on less valuable forms of play, such as flash cards, educational television, and computer activities, and not enough attention to the connection between physical play—such as running down slides and mastering the monkey bars—and intellectual development.[30] Experts agree that cognitive development not only goes hand in hand with physical, emotional, and social development, but is utterly *dependent* on and in some ways secondary to the growth of those skills.

The role of social and emotional development in aiding cognitive and linguistic development has been captured in laboratory experiments. A study of ninety-six babies conducted by Andrew Meltzoff and Rochelle Brooks at the Institute for Learning and Brain Sciences shows that emotional intelligence (EQ) is just as important as IQ. Before babies learn to talk, they form emotional connections with their parents and caregivers by looking into their eyes. It's a big leap from looking at a person to seeing what another person is looking at—following a person's gaze. By tracking at what age babies learn to follow an adult's gaze and thereby see what an adult is referring to, Meltzoff and Brooks have been able to establish an early indicator of language ability. It turns out that the earlier a baby follows the gaze of an adult (generally between nine and eleven months old), the more advanced his language skills will be when he reaches two years of age. "Babies read their mother's faces," explained Meltzoff, coauthor of *The Scientist in the Crib: What Early Learning Tells Us About the Mind.* "Being able to read other people and their intentions and to know what they're thinking about is key to language development." Tickle Me Elmo's expression is always the same and never responds to that of its owner.

For the past twenty years, developmental psychologist Catherine Tamis-LeMonda has been observing babies interact with their parents in "naturalistic" environments—at home, running errands, going about their everyday lives—to see how parent involvement affects language acquisition. Through longitudinal studies, she has documented that the more mothers and fathers respond emotionally and verbally to babies' cries, expressions, and articulations, the earlier they talk and the more advanced their language skills are at age five. Parents who respond to babies' cues—reacting to grimaces and giggles, mimicking their sounds, extrapolating from *bababa* to *bottle,* labeling things they touch—help their children acquire language. Of course, emotional responsiveness shouldn't be forced. "If you're not enjoying yourself while labeling and playing with that baby, it's not going to do any good," Tamis-LeMonda cautioned.

"The infant brain craves novel stimulation, but that can be found in ordinary nonstructured, nonmarketed things around the house," said Ross Thompson, one of the founders of the National Scientific Council on the Developing Child, a research organization of scientists. "If a baby is flipping through a magazine, playing with a cat, banging around pots and pans, a parent can encourage that activity by talking to the child about what the cat is doing and sensitively responding to whatever has captured the baby's attention. And doing so in a relaxed, unhurried way." A baby will grab the same object over and over, replicating experiences, testing them out, conducting its own experiments. *If I smile, will Mommy smile back?* "Babies are very good at tracking statistical information in their environment," explained MIT's Laura Schulz. "They're incredibly sensitive to human action and to intentional acts in the world. They watch what people are doing to learn causal connections."

Providing a baby with consistent actions and reactions helps her make sense of her world and the people in it better than any toy can. "When a nine-month-old raises his arms to be picked up by Daddy, that demonstrates an incredibly complex chain of learning," said Claire Lerner, director of parent education at Zero to Three. "First the child has to have an emotional connection to his father. Then he has to form an idea: I want to be picked up. Then he has to know to raise his arms. In this tiny vignette, you can see how complicated a baby's development is." And how uncomplicated—and utterly cost-free—it is to reinforce that learning by picking up and cuddling the baby.

4

Let Us Edutain You

The camera is fixed on one-year-old Jacob, who is sitting on the floor, looking up expectantly. Next to him is his father, Christopher, who holds up big pieces of cardboard with words written in bold black type in front of his son. "Jacob, what does this say?" his father asks. "Haaih," Jacob replies, grabbing the card. "Hair," Christopher repeats affirmatively. The scene has been videotaped by Jacob's parents; there's a cut in the tape, and then Christopher proffers another card. "What does this say?" he asks. "Animas," Jacob says, grabbing the card. "Animals, good," his father confirms, pride and pleasure palpable.

Fast forward to Jacob at eighteen months. He is again seated on the floor, and his mother flashes a large Etch-a-Sketch–style writing pad to the camera with the words "Boats float in the ocean" on it. She turns the pad toward Jacob and asks him what it says. "Bost float in da ocean," he answers with a satisfied smile. Another cut to a board inscribed "Birds fly in the sky." Once again, Jacob recites the words with a smile as he fingers alphabet flash cards strewn across the floor. He then starts playing with plastic letters, spelling out his name on the beige carpet. He has done his part.

The camera switches now to his parents, Kathy and Christopher Ujhazy, seated on a sofa. Kathy tells us how their son started watching Dr. Robert Titzer's *Your Baby Can Read!* videos at the age of six months. "We followed Dr. Titzer's protocol," she explains on the video, used as a promotional tool for the video series, "and by twelve months, he was reading many, many words." Her husband, cradling an infant girl, chimes in, "At eighteen months, his vocabulary just exploded. He was reading books, signs, menus, newspapers, anything he could get his hands on." By Jacob's second birthday, he was testing at a second- and third-grade reading level. "And it's not like it's a chore or a task for him to read," Christopher asserts. "You can see the sense of accomplishment in his eyes when he figures out a word. He's excited . . . it's one of his favorite activities."

The Ujhazys are thrilled with their purchase. Christopher, a thirty-five-year-old airline pilot from Hopewell, Pennsylvania, learned about the series from a coworker. "My daughter used it, and she's way ahead in preschool," a colleague boasted. Since Jacob was already talking at four months, Christopher thought it sounded like a good idea. He and Kathy, a thirty-six-year-old stay-at-home mom, added *Your Baby Can Read!* to Jacob's video mix (he had already been watching *Baby Mozart* for months) when he was six months old. They diligently scheduled *Your Baby Can Read!* showings every day. Jacob's attention apparently never wandered, and after six months of solid viewing, the Ujhazys told me, he could read. He started by reading things outside, such as stop signs on the street corner. Christopher and Kathy decided to test him, writing words like *ball* on a piece of paper to see what Jacob could handle. "You could juggle them any which way, and he knew them all," Kathy claimed.

Jacob was reading Dr. Seuss by eighteen months. His parents worry that his apparent genius will set them back more than the cost of a few videos. "We're in a panic," Kathy told me. "We hope we can afford this kid!" The Ujhazys had Jacob's IQ tested, and he scored at the "very gifted/genius" level. Floored by the results, they began even earlier with their daughter, Clare. At two months, she was started on *Your Baby Can Read!* watching the videos back-to-back. "We really believe that at this young age, she is starting to read also," Kathy said.

Such parental testimony is the promotional bread and butter of Bob Titzer, president of the Infant Learning Company, which he founded in 1997 to sell his homemade videos and DVDs. According to Titzer, babies should learn the written form of language at the same time they learn the spoken language, rather than waiting for school to teach them to read and write. He cites a series of ominous facts: "Longitudinal research shows that the earlier a child is taught to read, the better the child reads, even when you control for IQ and socioeconomic status. Children who are taught to read earlier read better than children who are not taught until age five or six. Children who are not taught until seven or eight are even farther behind." Titzer compares learning to read with learning foreign languages, noting that "the older we get, the harder it is to learn language skills at a high level." What he calls the "natural window of opportunity" begins to close by age four. As Titzer explained to me when I interviewed him for *Time* magazine, "I'm suggesting that instead of waiting until kids are five years old, we teach reading in a more natural way, so that they learn the written language along with the spoken language."

Titzer's "natural way" is achieved through watching his home-grown series, which he sells everywhere from Amazon to Target. Titzer developed the series by himself; he holds a doctorate in human performance from Indiana University, a degree offered by the Health, Physical Education, and Recreation Department that combines kinesiology and psychology. The videos are low-tech, showing a series of simple words and phrases on-screen (e.g., *clap, arms up*), accompanied by a voice saying each word, followed by images of the objects or actions. At various points, Titzer and his young daughter Aleka, Titzer's prime subject, provide narration and guidance. Now fourteen, Aleka began watching her father's videos at three months and learned to read in about six months, which Titzer said is the average amount of time required in his program. "I didn't want her watching television," he confided. "So she learned in large part by watching the videos over and over at the sitter's house." By age four, according to Titzer, Aleka had the phonetic ability of an eighteen-year-old. "Aleka reads *Harry Potter* in about two hours and retains the information. She remembers sentences from it verbatim."

Titzer considers himself "very anti-TV" and says children shouldn't watch television in general. "But [my program] is to help parents out when they're busy so they can entertain their child in an appropriate and helpful way." He claimed that unlike other videos for children, his series uses a "multisensory approach" that teaches babies more effectively, and suggested that babies view his videos for an hour a day, "instead of watching mindless baby videos that just entertain babies with shapes floating around the screen," which he called a "complete waste of time." Like many in the edutainment business, Titzer implied that there's no choice between allowing a baby to watch videos or not; it's simply a question of *which* programs to allow. Every baby, in Bob Titzer's world, is ready to watch.

THERE IS LITTLE DOUBT THAT THE "MINDLESS VIDEOS" TITZER referred to are those from Baby Einstein, the mother of baby "smart videos." By far the top-selling brand, Baby Einstein has been viewed by one in three babies in America. It's surprising, given the numbers, to realize just how humble Baby Einstein's origins are: the brain-child of a former teacher staying at home with her infant baby. In 1996, Julie Aigner-Clark began to search for a video suitable for her newborn daughter, Sierra. Frustrated that most videos were aimed toward older children, Aigner-Clark, then thirty, and her husband, Bill, forty-five, decided to videotape some of Sierra's favorite toys to the tune of animal noises, mothers counting in different languages, nursery rhyme chanting, and music. Eschewing animation, they videotaped "real-world images" in their basement and hired foreign-language speakers from the International Language School in Atlanta, where they were living at the time. Instead of lullabies, they chose classical music as the soundtrack. Together, they assembled the footage using Adobe software on a budget of $8,000, withdrawn from their personal savings. Aigner-Clark finally had a video worthy of Sierra's time and attention.

And everyone else's. The videos, which hit the market in 1997, were an instant hit, selling close to two hundred thousand copies in the first two years.[1] By 2006, more than one billion copies had been sold.[2] Why shouldn't they have sold like hotcakes? Aigner-Clark promised that the videos "will stimulate your child in a way that even the most caring parent probably cannot duplicate."[3] The company's early website told parents that listening to foreign languages would create "dedicated neurons in the auditory cortex, resulting in greater brain capacity," while warning that "by the age of 12 months, the brains' 'receptiveness' to all phonemes disappears and the unconnected neurons die off. A great opportunity has been lost." Once people got the message, they were afraid *not* to show the videos to their babies.

In 2001, the godfather of children's entertainment, the Walt Disney Company, purchased Baby Einstein for a reported $25 million and vaulted it to even loftier profits. Under Disney's stewardship, Baby Einstein's business grew 91 percent. By 2005, the company was generating $200 million in sales a year, selling in thirty countries around the world with products in more than twenty-five languages.[4] Baby Einstein ballooned into an infant edutainment empire, producing branded music, books, toys, juvenile products, baby gear, party supplies, bibs, and soft bath items in addition to its videos and DVDs, though each product claims to embody the learning philosophy of the original videos. Infant clothing includes finger puppets tucked into pocket sweaters, mirrors tagged on booties, noise-making features attached to hats, and characters from the videos festooning onesies. (Remember, this *is* Disney.) There are even "Sip & Discover" plates with "stimulating designs" to "encourage the tri-lingual development of language, colors and shapes." In 2005, Baby Einstein entered the older preschool market with a Discovery Channel TV program, *Little Einsteins*,[5] and a companion set of home videos.

Videos from Baby Einstein and *Your Baby Can Read!* fall into what's called the *infant developmental media category*, which promises to transform "passive entertainment" into lessons on everything from the basics (ABCs, numbers, shapes, colors) to the artistic (painting, music) to the scientific (animals, seasons, nature), just as smart toys claim to reinvent the teddy bear. According to the Kaiser Family Foundation, three-quarters of the one hundred top-selling DVDs for babies from birth to two years make educational claims, whether they're from PBS or Nick Jr. There are even videos to encourage religious faith among the zero-to-twenty-four-month set. Baby Faith promises "developmentally appropriate" videos like *God Made Animals* and *God Made Me* will "lay a solid foundation for babies to thrive developmentally and spiritually." Created by the multimedia powerhouse Sony Wonder, the videos feature the voice of Disney's "Little Mermaid" and teach tiny babies the story of David and the Psalms with "stimulating, inspiring and nurturing programs."

Between 2002 and 2004, sales of baby developmental videos tripled to $100 million, according to industry executives. By 2004, the children's video and DVD market was an estimated $4.8 billion. It has been steadily increasing since.[6] Today, a Baby Einstein DVD retails for $19.99, and those aimed at children under two account for $1 billion in sales.[7] Parents are bound to stumble across a lot of junk given the sheer numbers involved. In 2003, there were 140 educational videos or DVDs for kids aged two and younger for sale on Amazon; in 2007, there were 750. With a leery eye to his emboldened competition, Dennis Fedoruk, founder of Brainy Baby, noted, "Consumers are becoming more discerning about entertainment with a so-called educational theme. A lot of studios are jumping in to cash in without a lot of thought or foresight."

Seemingly, much thought goes into what constitutes educational baby programming. Most baby videos eschew cartoons in order to better fit what many parents think of us as more appropriately educational: puppets, photographs, live animals, outdoor scenes, and classical music. "Music makes a difference," Baby Genius DVDs and CDs tell us. Indeed, classical music is a common component, based on the idea that it improves a baby's ability to reason. This theory gained popularity following the publication of a 1993 study that showed college students performed better on a paper-folding-and-cutting test after listening to twenty minutes of Mozart, heralded as the *Mozart Effect.* With visions of Yo-Yo Ma and mathematical Nobel winners, parents began snapping up classical music albums, which were increasingly hawked to help babies. (Titles like *In Utero—Music for My Baby* even offered the Mozart Effect for fetuses.) The music was sometimes remixed at higher registers, with bells and other childlike flourishes added and with darker, more dramatic notes minimized or eliminated. In 1998, then Georgia governor Zell Miller (he who famously declared on *Hardball,* "I wish we lived back in the days when we could challenge men to a duel") allocated over $100,000 in his state budget to give every newborn a classical CD or cassette. "Listening to music at a very early age affects the spatial-temporal reasoning that underlies math and engineering and even chess," Miller said at the time.[8]

Zell's zeal was misplaced. The original Mozart study, conducted by Gordon Shaw and Frances Rauscher, made no claims about six-month-olds. Moreover, in repeated follow-up studies, researchers were unable to replicate the results of the original experiment, even with college students. "The Mozart Effect is just so much nonsense," said Christopher Chabris, a Harvard Medical School researcher whose 1999 article in *Nature* debunked the hypothesis. "It's just not supported by neuroscience. It's hype, and it gives a false impression of what's supported by scientific research."[9]

Music isn't the only area in which academic research is twisted to support baby media claims. Another hyped subject is foreign-language instruction. Parents can purchase videos with the explicit purpose of teaching a foreign language, be it Spanish or Chinese, or buy DVDs with multiple language settings so that an infant can flip from English to French while watching a program about the changing seasons. The idea is that babies need to learn languages fast—before their innate capacity for language acquisition fades away. Julie Aigner-Clark wrote in her original liner notes for Baby Einstein, "Research has shown that infants have a natural ability to distinguish and assimilate the sounds of all languages but that the ability begins to fade at approximately six months. During the subsequent 12 months, *areas of the brain actually shut down and no longer respond.*"

What Aigner-Clark didn't note in her ad copy is that there is no evidence that buying CDs or DVDs to teach a baby Spanish is actually useful. Patricia Kuhl, who studies language acquisition at the University of Washington, conducted an experiment in which a native Mandarin speaker played with a group of babies for an hour a day while speaking Chinese. Through laboratory testing, she found that babies were subsequently able to recognize Mandarin sounds. But *not one* of the three control groups—a set of babies who saw the Chinese speaker play with babies on a video, another group who listened to an audio recording of the Chinese woman playing, and a third group who had no exposure to the Chinese speaker—were able to distinguish Mandarin sounds from English ones. It turns out that in order for a baby to learn a foreign language, a foreign-language-speaking human being needs to be present. Furthermore, the idea that a child must be exposed to a foreign language during some kind of "critical period" before the age of three simply isn't true. While it's easier to learn a language at a young age, people can learn another language well into adulthood.

Even in the face of such research, many parents have a hard time saying no to edutainment, which comes packed with an emotional wallop. For a parent, checking out a Baby Einstein video for the first time is both oddly soothing and anxiety-provoking. The videos project a safe, comfortable, coddled environment, far from the hectic chaos of working parents. There are the murmurs of soft, friendly voices, cows mooing, and chiming Bachian bells. Lavender blooms abundantly in undulated fields under sunny skies. Words float across the screen, pointing baby viewers to their eyes, hands, and toes and showing them the differences between cats and chickens, spring and fall, yellow and green. This all seems pleasant enough. The anxiety, though, is furtively built in. If your child *isn't* watching these videos—and every other baby you know is—where will your child be without them? Parents with colicky babies recount the miracle calming effects and those with babies born premature, deaf, or with developmental delays proclaim Baby Einstein's unique healing abilities. Even parents suspicious of the benefits might buy one "just in case"; the rationale being, "It can't hurt" or "At least I'm giving my child the opportunity."

Even if you aren't worried about a particular ailment, both *Your Baby Can Read!* and Baby Einstein (along with competitors like Brainy Baby and Baby Genius) tell parents directly or indirectly that watching their videos will beef up a child's brain. That might explain why nearly one in five babies under the age of two watches at least one DVD or video *every day*. The Baby Einstein website includes testimonials such as, "James was mesmerized by the music and images . . . A couple of weeks ago, I purchased 'Baby Shakespeare,' he said 'apple' the next day!" The proud mom goes on to say, "He is usually very active, but while watching the videos, he is always glued to the images. He dances and talks back to them, but in a quiet way." A captive toddler playing nice and learning all by himself? How handy! "We never wanted our son to be a big TV watcher. If we are going to let him watch it we wanted it to be good for him," writes one Amazon reviewer of the *Brainy Baby Right Brain* video. The fact that videos are essentially the same as television programs doesn't seem to register.

The fundamental problem with edutainment is that there is absolutely no proof that it works. According to a 2005 Kaiser Family Foundation study, "A Teacher in the Living Room?," baby media companies do essentially no research on their products. "There is just an enormous market of educational media products for young children," said Vicky Rideout, vice president of the foundation. "Lots of claims are being made, and right now, the research to document the accuracy of those claims is lagging way behind." Moreover, considerable research shows watching such videos not only is developmentally inappropriate for young children—but could very well be harmful. A 2005 study in the *American Behavioral Scientist* concluded, "Although the experimental studies are still few, they are remarkably consistent in indicating a video deficit for children 24 months and younger. Although there is some learning indicated by some of the studies, the learning is dramatically less than found for equivalent live displays."[10] A human companion beats a DVD any day.

"From what I have seen of the science, there isn't a tape in the world that can teach a nine-month-old baby how to read," according to Andrew Meltzoff, codirector of the Institute for Learning and Brain Sciences at the University of Washington. "It goes against everything we know about the evolution of language in human beings." To claim that it's unnatural to learn spoken language separate from written language, Meltzoff said, is incontrovertibly disproved by human history. After all, spoken language came well before written language. This doesn't mean that the children in Bob Titzer's videos aren't responding to their lessons. "Babies are very smart," Meltzoff explained. "But there's a difference in being trained to touch your foot when you see the word *foot* and reading. They're making an association between a visual pattern and a motor response. Is that reading, or is that just training?" And is it desirable? Babies are human beings, after all, not dogs.

When asked to back up his claims for *Your Baby Can Read!*, Titzer relied on his own anecdotal data; no scholarly journal has published the results. Nor has any independent or longitudinal research demonstrated the efficacy of his program. Instead Titzer turned to "thousands of letters from parents, calls, e-mails" in which parents have told him how well their children are reading. He showed me e-mails stating, "Ashton is now fifteen months old and knows all his body parts, he was an early talker and can READ!!!" and "I love to tell other parents that my son can read! You should see the look on their faces!" Viki and Kevin from Fremont, California, reported that their daughter Cori watched *Your Baby Can Read!* twice a day from the age of four months ("It's her favorite video") and that at age five, she tested at a fifth-grade reading level.

Getting your child ahead of other children seems to be the primary motivator for many such purchases—or at the very least, ensuring your child doesn't fall behind. Kayvan Farzin, a forty-two-year-old father who lives in San Diego, told me he started showing his five-year-old daughter the videos when she was two and a half months old because he wanted her to be an accelerated learner. "I don't want her to follow the normal path," he explained. "If she can grab more from what's surrounding her, great. If there's a chance she can read at twelve months old, I want her to do that . . . Education is very important to me. My plan is to get her into a good college." As far as Farzin was concerned, the tapes worked. "I'm positive that they have helped her in kindergarten," he said. "Kids her age cannot read a book the way she can."

Children's brains do develop rapidly during the first few years, and children deprived of a normal level of stimulation (that is, talking, holding, and playing) during these crucial years do suffer subsequently in terms of their social, emotional, and cognitive development. Early childhood education beginning at age three positively impacts later academic performance. But as in the case of smart toys, it does *not* follow that because children's brains develop quickly during the first few years, there needs to be extra learning stuffed into those years. Nor should that learning come via a TV screen. There is no data showing that academic programs for babies under the age of three are helpful in the long run. Needless to say, none of the anecdotal evidence proffered by Bob Titzer and his competitors suggests that babies watch TV—though that's precisely what watching a DVD or video amounts to.

"The story with these products is quite clear," said Alison Gopnik, a professor of psychology at Berkeley who studies early childhood, cognition, and language development. "There's no FDA for children's products. You can say whatever you want about how something will make your baby smarter, and nobody reviews it or asks if there's research to back this up." Universal opinion among cognitive scientists and developmental psychologists holds that a toy *might* be able to teach a baby to associate a word and a sound—*with* a parent's assistance. But the truth is, babies learn much more important, complicated things by crawling around and interacting with people around them. As Gopnik put it, "The best you can say about most edutainment is that it's a waste of money."

THAT'S NOT WHAT PARENTS BELIEVE. IN A 2004 SURVEY BY THE nonprofit Zero to Three, 82 percent of parents were comfortable or very comfortable with children under two watching television, and 89 percent were satisfied with the quality of available videos.[11] By the age of twenty-four months, 90 percent of babies are regularly watching TV, DVDs, and videos, for an average of an hour and a half per day. When asked in a nationwide study why they exposed their babies to media under the age of two, despite explicit warnings against it from the medical profession, parents said "education."[12]

Imagine a different scenario. Suppose that when Julie Aigner-Clark was dreaming up her business, she dubbed it "Video Baby" instead. Suppose the advertising copy had read, "These videos will introduce young babies to the exciting entertainment and viewing pleasures of television! You no longer have to worry about her not being entertained or interested by content that's too 'old'—here are images and sounds that are *just* right for her. Now your baby can begin to enjoy TV at as young as three months. Get *your* baby going on a lifetime of television viewing today!" Of course, that copy, though it accurately describes Baby Einstein, wouldn't have lured in nearly as many parents as the company's blather about learning and discovery. But perhaps we wouldn't have a world in which showing infants DVDs is considered absolutely normal. It isn't that hard to conceive of a baby-video-free world. After all, *not* showing videos to a baby was the norm for so long. Programs for children under age three didn't even exist before *Teletubbies* launched in the United States in 1998.

"Oh, the Baby Einsteins!" groaned Elisa Sherona , a sixty-three-year-old grandmother. "That stuff is taking the place of mothers interacting with their babies and babies learning language from their mother's intimate contact." When Sherona was raising her five children in Pennsylvania in the 1960s and 1970s, force-feeding babies to "learn" was unthinkable. "You don't need to have a baby that knows the encyclopedia! We're putting more pressure on kids by pushing information on them. I'm no expert, but I think when you push a baby that early to learn all those colors and numbers and letters . . ." Sherona broke off and sighed. "I think the way we're raising our children now is changing the way they're going to think as adults. You see kids on the computer all day long, playing video games, using MySpace as a way to socialize. That's *not* socially interactive."

Consumer advocates, pediatricians, and early childhood educators are hoping that the aggressive marketing of baby videos may soon come to an end. In 2006, a major child advocacy group affiliated with Harvard Medical School and Boston Children's

Hospital, the Campaign for a Commercial-Free Childhood, filed a complaint with the Federal Trade Commission charging Baby Einstein and Brainy Baby with false and deceptive advertising. (This didn't stop George W. Bush from inviting Aigner-Clark as a special guest to his State of the Union speech in 2007, calling her a "talented business entrepreneur and generous social entrepreneur.") "There is no research to show that watching a screen is beneficial to a baby in any way, educational or otherwise. If anything, it may be putting babies at risk," said CCFC member Alvin Poussaint, a child psychiatrist and director of the Media Center of Judge Baker's Children Center in Boston. "A two-dimensional screen can never replace a real environment, rich in all five senses. Holistic play is what develops all the pathways to the brain."[13] Susan Linn, cofounder of the CCFC, cites studies linking early TV viewing to diminished deductive reasoning and childhood obesity. Additional research links television viewing with sleep irregularity in babies (a prospect sure to set off alarm bells in any sane parent). Behavioral scientists point out that the "calm" observed in children while watching TV often backlashes later when children's cooped-up energies surge into hyperactive bursts of activity.

While companies know that playing on parents' fears and ambitions can send them running to the cash register, they are also aware of another reason why videos like Baby Einstein are "one of the fastest-growing, most lucrative and competitive business segments." As Sean McGowan, an industry analyst from Harris Nesbitt, explained, a company's success "hinges on whether or not they create products that fit the day-to-day needs of today's parents and caregivers." He's talking, of course, about parents' time. Time free from chasing a toddler. Time free from making silly faces at a cranky infant. Time free from teaching a baby the difference between her nose and her toes. In other words, Baby Einstein's great selling point is time *off*.

Back in 1999, Baby Einstein's website was forthright about the product's babysitting capacities, saying the videos will "stimulate your baby in your absence, allowing you time to take a shower, make a phone call or do other brief chores baby-free." That message has since been wiped clean from its promotional material. These days, the company says its videos are for babies and parents to watch *together*, its mission to "expose little ones to the world around them and encourage parent-child interaction in ways that are relevant to today's rapidly changing lifestyles."[14] According to Rashmi Turner, vice president of marketing communications for Baby Einstein, "Moms are looking for a way to keep their hands free and interact with their babies." So rather than have to pick up a flower and show it to their babies, they can point to a flower on the TV screen. "Our philosophy is all about creating moments for parent-child interaction," she told me. "Babies are naturally curious and fascinated by the sights and sounds around them, so by exposing them to real-world images, brightly colored items, and simple language, we create more ways for parents to interact with the child."

But let's not kid ourselves. The *last* thing most parents want to do is watch Baby Einstein. In a 2006 survey of parents with children under two, only 32 percent of parents said they always watch a video or television alongside their baby. Many set the machine to repeat mode so that their children can watch in endless loops until the baby passes out or balks or until they have finished whatever it is they set out to do in their "free" time. Sticking a baby in the bouncy seat or exersaucer in front of the TV set while Elmo or Dora do their thing is the modern equivalent of the once-ubiquitous, now verboten playpen. It's just that today's edutainment allows parents to believe that while they carry out the mundane chores of household management, their child is learning about the animals in Noah's Ark.

It's a comforting thought, but it's not reality either. No matter how "real life" edutainment images may seem, they are *not* real life. Take Baby Einstein's *A Day at the Farm* DVD. In a twenty-second segment, the scene changes six times. It's about the most wearying day on a farm imaginable. In real life, you can't take your child to the farm and zip from pigsty to chicken coop in nanoseconds—and that's not a bad thing. According to Dimitri Christakis, the director of the Child Health Institute at the University of Washington, overstimulation is damaging to the developing mind. The brain's orienting reflex, first described by Ivan Pavlov (of the famous dog), is triggered when a baby hears a strange sight or sound: He can't help but focus. Rapidly changing colors, sounds, and motions force a baby's brain to stay at attention. Each time her gaze might wander, action rivets her back to the screen. *Attennnn-tion!* Kind of like the gruesome scene in *A Clockwork Orange* in which the protagonist is locked into a chair with his eyeballs peeled open by metal calipers and forced to watch violent movies.

"Parents say, 'My child can't stop looking at it! She loves it!'" Christakis said. "Well, true, she can't stop looking at it, but that does *not* mean she loves it." A baby's attentional system is almost obligatory, explained Chuck Nelson, the Harvard Medical School neuroscientist. Unlike an adult who can choose to look away from a disturbing accident, for example, if something is moving and colorful, babies are going to look. "They can't help themselves," Nelson says. "Babies don't have the emotional or cognitive control to say, 'I'm going to look away' even when they want to." Not only might the baby not really be enjoying the program, Christakis said, but "based on the research I've done, there's reason to believe these products have deleterious effects on the developing mind." Studies show that high levels of television viewing before age three are associated with subsequent bullying, and impaired reading and mathematical proficiency.[15] A 2006 study in *Pediatrics* found that the more television children under five watch, the less likely they are to engage in creative play.[16]

Fears over the effects of television aren't new. Back in the 1970s, teachers complained that children were arriving in kindergarten with shorter and shorter attention spans, though the evidence was anecdotal. To establish hard, scientific data to help teachers and parents understand why, Christakis developed a longitudinal study that looked at 1,400 children before age three and then tested them again at age seven. At the beginning of the study, parents were asked how much TV their one- to two-year-olds watched. The average was 2.2 hours a day; three- and four-year-olds watched 3.4 hours a day, consistent with national studies. To put these numbers in perspective, the average three-year-old is awake 12 hours a day, which means they are spending 30 percent of their waking time in front of the TV. When the children in the study reached age seven, parents were asked how well their children were able to concentrate, as well as questions such as, Is your child impulsive? They found that for each additional hour of daily TV viewing before age three, the chances of having attentional problems increased 10 percent; a child who watched two hours a day on average was 20 percent more likely to have attention problems. "The more TV babies watch, the more likely they are to have attentional problems later in life," said Christakis. Interestingly, by 2007 these results were already outdated. After all, the study predated the advent of *Teletubbies* and Baby Einstein.

Christakis believes that early exposure to TV and video games conditions the developing brain to expect a very high—an unnatural—level of input. Real life by comparison becomes boring. Moreover, numerous studies have shown than when compared with real-life lessons, videos and DVDs are poor teachers. For example, in one study of two-and-a-half-year-olds, it took six viewings of a video to accomplish what a single live demonstration could do with simple-step operations like removing a mitten or playing with a puppet, a gap that has come to be known as the *video deficit*. Research has also suggested that while children can learn new words from watching TV, videos are less effective than live experiences, particularly for viewers under two.[17] A 2005 study of 1,200 children published in *Archives of Pediatrics* found that children who watch TV before age three have lower cognitive scores at age seven.[18] (Keep in mind that the average newborn brain, which weighs 333 grams, triples in size over the first three years of life, reaching 90 percent of adult size by age seven.)

Christakis is adamant about the worthlessness of videos like Baby Einstein and Brainy Baby. "It's clear that parents are going out of their way to show these programs to children, much more than they ever did before, in part because they have been led to believe that these videos will make their child smarter. They're being very aggressively marketed." The cover of a Brainy Baby DVD, for example, shows an infant with a bubble coming out of his head that says "2 + 2 = 4," though most children don't even begin to understand counting until they are at least three. The increasing directedness of children's play is evident in DVD programs like Preschool Prep, which attempts to teach babies and toddlers letters, numbers, and shapes at the earliest ages. The founder of Preschool Prep, Kathy Oxley, was quoted in a company press release as saying, "Our philosophy is that early alphabet instruction is crucial for getting children on the path to literacy . . . We need to make sure they have the tools they need to be successful. By waiting until late preschool or kindergarten, *other interests emerge making it hard for a child to focus on learning letters and numbers.*"[19] Isn't having a child develop his own interests something to be encouraged, not avoided?

Worse, early television viewing is actually associated with behavior problems and even cognitive delays.[20] A 2007 study by Christakis, Meltzoff, and their colleague Frederick Zimmerman found that for every hour per day spent watching baby DVDs and videos, infants understand an average of six to eight fewer words than infants who did not watch them. Not surprisingly, the American Academy of Pediatrics recommends no television viewing before age two—a fact of which only 6 percent of parents are aware, even though the warning was established in 1999.[21] When asked what they think about the AAP advisory, company executives demur, differentiating the medium of television from that of videos and DVDs, or explaining how their products differ from other programming out there. As Marcia Grimsley, the executive producer at Baby Brainy, put it, "We respectfully beg to differ from the AAP. If you choose carefully, videos can be extremely helpful."

While certain types of media exposure can be beneficial to three- and four-year-olds—the best example is *Sesame Street*, which has been shown in reliable studies to help some preschoolers with learning skills—there is no evidence that exposure before age three is a good idea and plenty to suggest that it's harmful. In fact, even watching *Sesame Street* before age two is associated with delayed language,[22] which is one of the reasons why Sesame Workshop's decision in 2006 to launch a line of videos targeted to children as young as six months met with shock and dismay among child development experts like T. Berry Brazelton and David Elkind. "I absolutely support the American Academy of Pediatrics' recommendation that children under two be kept away from screen media," wrote Brazelton in a protest letter. "It's too expensive for them physically as well as psychologically."

The controversial videos, "Sesame Beginnings," were created in conjunction with Zero to Three, the widely respected nonprofit group, further befuddling and angering those who have studied the effects of media on babies and toddlers. As Susan Linn noted, "It's a shame to see a prominent public health organization get involved. People trust Sesame Workshop so much. To have the combination of that and Zero to Three, I think it's very likely that parents who have been hesitant will jump right in."[23] According to Sesame Workshop, the decision to enter the baby video market was based on their belief that they could create effective ways to promote interaction between parents and babies, something they thought other video programs failed to do. Another rationale was that babies under two were being exposed to videos anyway— better that they at least be as developmentally appropriate as possible. "What we're trying to do is meet parents in their daily reality," explained Matthew Melmed, Zero to Three's executive director.

"The reality is there's TV in ninety-eight percent of all homes, and parents feel comfortable with it," added Rosemarie Truglio, vice president of education and research at Sesame Workshop. "The key is moderation. We're not advocating just plopping kids in front of a TV screen."[23]

Of course, no parent plunks a kid down in front of a television intending to corrupt his mind or erode his brain cells. Quite the contrary. Parents do so in the effort to expand little Max's and Madison's mental capacity and broaden their horizons. It's one of our top goals as parents, one we take seriously. In an experiment conducted by a Georgetown University researcher, parents were *explicitly* told that videos were to be shown to their babies in order to determine whether or not babies could learn from TV and videos. Many of the parents then told the researcher that they had already read research supporting the videos' educational value. But they couldn't have—no such research exists.[24] Parents have clearly absorbed the advertising and marketing messages implying educational value and assumed there was proof behind the promises. One thirty-three-year-old stay-at-home mom told me she tried to get her son to watch educational television, but he just didn't seem interested, and she would try out Baby Einstein DVDs instead if they weren't so expensive. "I personally think it helps them with speech, learning to say words, and the alphabet," she said.

It's hard to find fault with parents for such assumptions. "The parents who buy these products are usually very ambitious for their children and want the very best," explained psychologist Allen Kanner. "It makes a surface kind of sense, exposing the kids to culture. After all, here's Disney, for example, a reputable corporation, selling it and making the claim that it's educational, and most parents don't think past that. The fact that it's hooking your child on television and probably not doing much more than entertaining at best is something most people don't want to think about."

• • •

WATCHING VIDEOS IS JUST THE BEGINNING FOR OUR EARLIEST
techies and those who cater to them. Now several computer software series start with programs for babies as young as nine
months. Giggles Computer Funtime for Baby goes even younger,
aiming at six-month-olds. "My son had been whacking at the keyboard for several months while I was working from home," recalled Tim Leverett, founder of Giggles and a former creative
director in advertising. "When he was ten months old, I decided it
was time to find some kind of software for him to play with, something that would enable him to touch keys and see something happen on-screen." Leverett searched the software available online
and in stores but found that everything was geared to children
over two. "Some claimed to be for one and up, but they weren't.
They were just programs where the parent sits and does everything while the baby watches. They really didn't involve the baby
at all."

"Everyone I knew was having this problem," Leverett told me.
"With computers as ubiquitous as toasters, any household with a
computer was faced with a dilemma: The baby would see the parent on the computer and want to pretend to be like them, just as
they did with telephones. There was a huge hole in the marketplace that nobody was addressing."

Leverett got to work. It took two years to develop his first line
of baby software, mostly because of technical issues. For a product to be successful, the baby had to be able to touch any key on
the keyboard—or combination of keys—without affecting the
computer; the keyboard had to be completely locked out so that,
on the freak chance that a baby managed to hit Control-Alt-
Delete simultaneously, the computer wouldn't shut down and re-
boot. It requires a lot of guts to let your ten-month-old go wild
on your home office computer. At the very least, parents had to
be assured that their files wouldn't be accidentally renamed or

disappear. For Leverett, lacking that confidence in the product would be a deal breaker.

Once he resolved the technical issues, there was considerable work to be done on the creative side. "I really got into making the program engaging and appropriate for babies." It was a task Leverett took on himself. "I found that trying to work with psychologists and professionals, I ran into a brick wall, because there's a huge stigma right off the bat. The AAP put out a big report saying that children shouldn't be exposed to media under two. I just don't completely believe it. I mean, obviously you don't want a baby in front of the TV for twelve hours a day, but I just don't believe that exposure for twenty or thirty minutes a day is bad. And I would challenge anyone to show me research that it is." Rather than have consultants work with him, Leverett worked with babies. "They're the best experts," he said. "Until you put a product down in front of thirty babies, the theories don't mean anything."

The testing phase was useful in flagging problems with the program. For example, left to their own devices, babies would press down on a key and not let go, which would cause the action associated with that key to repeat, rapid-fire. Leaning down on the *A*, *aaaaaaaaaaaaaaaaaaaaaaaaa*, resulted in a hyperspeed screen image that was like a strobe light pulsating into the baby's eyes. Leverett had to tinker with the software so that when a baby leaned on a key, the action would repeat, but at a much slower rate.

Shortly before Leverett officially unleashed Giggles Computer Funtime for Baby, he made the rounds of consumer trade shows. Paying for a booth at the American Baby Faire in cities across the country, he could easily get five hundred babies playing with his program, showing him in no uncertain terms whether they approved. It was one thing to sample the program with his friends' children, quite another to subject it to hundreds of strangers. "It's a completely uncontrolled atmosphere," he said. "Parents have no vested interest. They're going to tell you exactly what they think." Leverett was expecting a lot of pushback, at least at the beginning.

"But the immediate reaction was, 'Oh my god, I've been looking for something like this!'" Frankly, he was surprised. "It was cool to see the look on the parents' faces when their baby would play with it and just start laughing. I think *they* were surprised their baby loved it so much." Giggles was the bestselling product at Leverett's first Baby Faire in Chicago, in 2005. After that, he debuted the program, priced at a market- and profit-friendly $19.99, at Toy Fair in early 2006.

To his credit, Leverett doesn't claim that Giggles turns babies into geniuses. "That's not realistic," he said. "And it's unethical marketing." His goal, first and foremost, was to make something fun, and that won the program praise from institutions like the *New York Times* and the Association for Library Service to Children "I don't see anything wrong with letting them play and letting their imaginations go." He paused. "That said, there is a lot of residual learning. In shapes, for example, they learn shapes and color. With the very youngest users, what they're really learning is cause and effect, which is very important." Even babies as young as five or six months old can benefit, Leverett said. "It provides parents a way to let them touch keys without hurting the computer. And the more they play, the more they see the connection between their actions and what appears on-screen." Once babies start talking, they can discuss what they see and point to images on the screen. In one activity, the mouse cursor corresponds with the image of a dog's nose on-screen, and manipulating the cursor moves the dog's nose on and off the dog's face. The dog then chases his nose and puts it back on. "It really helps them get better at moving the mouse," Leverett pointed out.

"People do crazy things like put their kid in a high chair so he can play by himself, but it's really meant for the parent to be involved," he went on. As with other manufacturers in the growing baby software segment, Leverett calls his programs *lapware*, meaning that the child plays with them while sitting on a parent's lap. "This isn't Baby Einstein, where it's basically just babysitting, and believe me, I use plenty of those—I have every single one. This is meant to be a much more interactive experience," Leverett explained. By age five, Leverett's son TJ, who had played with them since he was a baby, was "very adept" at the computer. He laughed. "He goes to all different websites—the Cartoon Network, different Disney sites. He even plays games like World of Warcraft along with his eleven-year-old nephew who lives with us. On a game like that, TJ knows how to type in the user name and password himself because he can recognize the letters on the keyboard."

ACCORDING TO THE KAISER FAMILY FOUNDATION'S "A TEACHER in the Living Room?" study, two-thirds of parents believe computers help children under six with learning. It's no surprise then that most software purveyors tout their educational as much as their entertainment benefits. One of the more academic programs for babies and toddlers comes courtesy of Knowledge Adventures, a major producer of children's software that has been in the business since 1987. Its JumpStart series, which sell for $19.99 per program, starts with JumpStart Baby, geared to babies eighteen months to two years, then transitions to JumpStart Toddler (eighteen months to three years) and JumpStart Advanced Preschool (one to four years old).*[25] These programs, JumpStart tells parents, help "prepare your child for preschool and beyond." Indeed, JumpStart Advanced Preschool claims that babies learn more than fifty skills, from phonics to Japanese. "It's pretty hardcore here," said Barry Levenson, chief marketing officer at Knowledge Adventures. "Everything we do is academic, even for toddlers and babies. There's nothing in there that's just purely for fun."

Leslie House, senior vice president of product development, said JumpStart Baby is a way for parents who work on a computer

*Until the 1990s, the term *preschool* referred to four- and five-year-olds. Today, it usually means any child under kindergarten age.

at home to "appropriately" engage their child in what they are doing. "Every child wants to grab the steering wheel of the car when
they see Mom driving," she explained. "And that's what we saw
children doing with computers." House has been designing products at JumpStart for eighteen years, and over time she's seen the
changes wrought by technology on even its youngest users. "When
we first launched JumpStart Toddler, we brought in three-year-
olds and found that they had a really hard time controlling the
mouse or doing anything that involved clicking and dragging. But
we found that the more we tested the product, within a really
short time—six months—even the new kids we brought into the
lab had less and less trouble with mouse control. It seemed like
there was this strange gaining of skills, just by being surrounded
by technology." The toddlers' ability to control the mouse aston-
ished House and her team. Learning the relationship between a
mouse's movements on a tabletop surface and the cursor on the
screens involves a complex, not altogether obvious, thought process, as anyone who has watched a seventy-year-old try a mouse
for the first time can attest. Edutainment lapware has had to keep
up with these techno-toddlers. When Knowledge Adventures issued an upgraded version of JumpStart Toddler, it included a new
level that allowed parents to turn on mouse control to accommodate toddlers who were able to master it. "What's amazing is that
kids now take the mouse away and want less participation from
parents." Their parents are also increasingly open to allowing their
babies to explore the home computer. "They assign a great deal of
learning value to products played on the computer," House said.
According to House, the games guide children through a series of
tasks that get progressively more challenging and lead to an ultimate goal. "Kids have always learned with games," House noted.
"It's natural. This is just the new way to do it." Knowledge Adventures has what it calls the "kitchen test": A product passes the test
when Mom is walking into the kitchen and can hear her child from
the other room singing a JumpStart song or counting with the

JumpStart characters. That babies have fun is one of the most appealing attributes of lapware. "Parents want their children to get a jump start literally, but they don't want to feel like pushy parents," House explained. "So the kind of experiences kids have with these games makes them feel like good parents. It makes them feel safe and happy about their child's experience." Companies marketing software to toddlers are careful in their promotional copy to ease parental concerns about hooking babies up to computers. BabyWOW!—a computer program for babies nine months old and up—reassures parents, "There's no replacement for your baby's or toddler's discovery of the real world. However, unlike for most of us as children, their real world includes the computer." The copy goes on: "BabyWOW! 3.0 was created to reward a child's natural curiosity about the computer with an interactive experience based on early development research . . . It doesn't replace anything in your child's life. Instead, it creates a new opportunity for you and your child to learn and interact together." The same phrases that helped propel Baby Einstein to superstardom—"early development research," "interact together," and "discovery of the real world"—are all there.

Many parents consider the computer to be the lesser of two evils; rather than turn on the television, they perch their toddler in front of the keyboard. "I think they get more skills from the computer," one mother of a child under three told researchers from the Kaiser Family Foundation. "Our world is so computer-oriented. I certainly didn't know how to use a computer when I was three . . . If I had a choice of a computer or TV, I would definitely choose the computer." A mother of a five-year-old boy told me she was cautious about allowing her child to be exposed to technology, proudly pointing out that while her son's peers all have Game Boys, he doesn't, and that she avoided buying the Leapster LeapPad. Still, her son was an avid player of computer games, and she bought him Reader Rabbit, a software program often used in schools. "It has definitely helped," she told me. "It is without a doubt the reason he can spell and read. I wish I could claim the credit, but it was the program." Her son now ably navigates the Internet, going online every day to check baseball scores on MLB .com. "He even knows all about eBay. It's amazing to see how easy it is for him to get around." She considered her approach to be a careful, thoughtful one. "I think that there will be that line drawn between the overstimulated child, the 'over-computered' child . . . but that line is going to drop every day."

Even video games are being created for children as young as three, complete with expansive edutainment claims. TV commercials for the $60 V.Smile, created by Hong Kong–based VTech, carry the motto "Turn Game Time into Brain Time" and feature a mom admonishing her children for not playing enough. "You'll never get into college if you don't play your video games!" she nags, while the narrator informs viewers, "With V.Smile, your kids will learn letters, numbers and love learning almost as much as they love playing." V.Smile Baby (with "age appropriate Baby Smartridges") entices parents of babies as young as nine months to "get your child's mind running before he can even talk." As with smart toys, video games up the ante on what's considered entertaining to young children. "There's a shift in need in terms of what a child finds fun," said Jim Silver, the editor of the trade publication *Toy Wishes*. "A lot of that has to do with the computer age. If a three-year-old is entertained by software, the toys that might normally entertain him might not have the same value."[26]

Contemporary toddlers are certainly wired in a new way. Usage has risen dramatically in the last fifteen years. A nationally representative study from the 1990s found that only 17 percent of children under one were watching television and fewer than half of children between the ages of one and two watched. In a 2006 study of 1,009 parents, 40 percent of babies were watching TV or DVDs/videos by three months;[27] the average baby started watching videos at six months and regular television at ten months.[28] By age two, 40 percent of toddlers are able to change channels on the

TV themselves using a remote control, and 42 percent of two- and three-year-olds know how to put a DVD or video into the machine. It seems only logical then that in 2006, a twenty-four-hour channel aimed at babies under three, BabyFirstTV, hit satellite television, giving parents content to show their babies around the clock. "BabyFirstTV goes above and beyond traditional TV," promises the company's promotional material. "It is an educational tool that provides a positive learning environment and an engaging experience for both you and your baby." Another twenty-four-hour channel, PBS Kids Sprout, is ready for BabyFirstTV's graduates, with programming aimed for children two and up. And of course, there's Nickelodeon's Noggin, the home of Dora, Maisy, and *Blue's Clues* and wildly popular with children under three.

While many shows and channels geared toward viewers under three eschew advertising, this is mostly because commercials have been shown not to work for children that young. But that doesn't matter. The entire *program* is advertising—big, twenty- to thirty-minute-long commercials for branded baby and toddler products. The revenue is in the licensing—those hundreds of products featuring Elmo, Dora, and Little Einsteins, on everything from cereal bars to balloons to DVDs. Viacom's Nickelodeon unit generated $1.4 billion in sales of toys, backpacks, clothes, and other products featuring Dora in 2005.[29] Baby edutainment is very, very profitable. Lapping it all up are the one in five babies under one and the three in ten children ages two and three who have a TV in the nursery.

Knowing that television viewing by children under the age of three is associated with reduced scores on tests that measure reading recognition, reading comprehension, and memory makes these statistics all the more alarming.[30] Surveys show that children six and under spend three times more time in front of a TV, computer, or video game each day than they do reading.[31] Provoked by this radical transformation of children's leisure time, the Senate passed a bill in 2006 mandating further study of the effects of screen media on the social, cognitive, and physical development of young children.[32]

Ample data already suggests cause for concern. David Perlmutter, a neurologist and the author of *The Better Brain Book,* said that because babies eighteen months and younger can't distinguish between reality and what appears on a screen, media for young babies is particular inadvisable. "It's too much stimulation for a baby's brain. And all the high-tech stuff we give to our children these days is ineffective. It doesn't capitalize on what the brain is genetically designed to do, which is to learn through responses from other human beings." Rather than use a computer whose mechanics they have no prayer of understanding, they would be better served by playing with balls and ramps, shovels and sand. "We want to raise a child who is able to take chances, who is able to draw upon previous experiences in novel situations to create solutions. The more experiences a child has in learning how things work, the more tools he'll have to deal with when faced with a novel situation in the future. *That's* what creates a better student."

In its report on the role of technology in the lives of children, the Alliance for Childhood notes, "Children invariably love to imitate adults, and may well show an early interest in 'playing computer.' But we would not mistake a preschooler's fascination with fire trucks as evidence that it's time to sit her behind the wheel of a real hook and ladder. Curiosity about computers and other powerful technologies is not a sign that a child is developmentally ready to operate the real thing. We are far more likely to help children grow intellectually by letting them create their own 'pretend' computers, powered by their own imaginations, than worrying so much about how soon children need to operate these powerful machines themselves."[33] As psychologist David Elkind put it, "Computers are part of our environment, but so are microwaves and we don't put them in the crib."

5

Class Time

Though she is a thirty-six-year-old mother of a preschooler, Marni Konner has the chatty effervescence of an It Girl hosting the sweet sixteen party of the year. There is nothing momlike about her. Slim and attractive—she could place runner-up in a Sofia Coppola look-alike contest—Konner wears skinny jeans, kitten-heeled mules, and a slippy little T-shirt as she presides over the flagship location of her enormously successful Little Maestros class—"New York's Premier Infants and Toddler Music Program."

In the large basement of the First Magyar Reformed Church on a lovely tree-lined block on Manhattan's Upper East Side, a session for one- to two-year-olds is about to begin. "I'm here for every class," Konner told me as she hummed about, adjusting the position of puppets placed on mats around the room, dashing from parent to parent to answer urgent queries about sign-ups and reservations. "I'm a total control freak."

Children and caretakers stumble and weave into the room, some rushing from naps, others still swilling their midmorning milk, a few holding tight to sacred dolls and blankeys. Some of their parents may have been lured by the class's promise: "You and

your child will love our weekly musical story-time, show tune per-
formances, language development activities, fantastic weekly puppet show, and 'bubble music.'" Some may have heard that their
neighbor's daughter enrolled and learned her ABC's extraquick
and in time to swing music. Some may not trust a caregiver to adequately stimulate their children or, if they're caring for their children themselves, maybe just wanted to get out of the house.
Whatever their reasons, the class is packed.

At the back of the room, the band's five musicians warm up.
Each has been carefully recruited. Enid, the pianist and musical
director of Little Maestros ("An absolute musical genius," Konner
raved. "She's one in a billion. She wrote for *Fame*.") is standing by
her keyboard, setting up props. The saxophonist is from Prague;
he played stadiums in the former Czechoslovakia as a teenager. As
the Little Maestros website boasts, "Teaching staff all have qualified backgrounds, degrees, and careers and have been trained to
teach the Little Maestros curriculum."

The music begins. It is loud, too loud, at least to me. I can't
help wondering what it sounds like to the babies. Maybe they're
used to it, but I wince at the thought of their sensitive eardrums
rattled like this on a weekly basis. I look around the room to see if
any are noticeably wincing but the babies appear indifferent. One
girl is spinning around and around, oblivious to instructions. One
is lying in the middle of the giant mat gnawing at her toe. Another
sucks her thumb, deep in thought. Some of them are clapping;
others are crawling. Two band members take their places in front,
acting as group leaders/entertainers/encouragers. They ask the
children to jump to the music. Four enterprising tots take up the
challenge. Many of the parents lift less mobile tots aloft in response.

Then comes a song that will weave intermittently through my
head over the course of the next few weeks. "First little maestro's
name is Whitney," the female lead chants, going through all the
classmates' names in succession: Reid ... Sloane ... Jack ...

Sunny . . . Abby . . . Sydney . . . Dylan . . . Skylar . . . Ella . . . Maxwell . . . Several children have started sucking on their puppets. "We send these puppets out to be cleaned constantly," the male singer preemptively assures parents. A winded mother darts into the classroom in flip-flops, cotton still woven in and out of her toes from a pedicure. She plops herself down next to her daughter, and her Caribbean nanny moves aside and slightly behind. Baby classes everywhere, not just at Maestros and not just in New York City, seem to divide along mommy/nanny lines.

The next song starts: "Down on the Farm." Like each of the tunes that follow, it is catchy, upbeat, a little rock 'n' roll. At any given moment, about four children are actively engaged in the activity at hand while the others look like they may as well be home. Nearly all the songs involve props of one kind or another: A box filled with animal-shaped rattles. A white board and marker on which the singer writes the letter of the week, *C*. ("How did *you* get so smart?" the pedicure mom asks the child next to her when she meows in response to the picture of a cat.)

After about thirty minutes, a number of children have retreated to their parents' laps or made their way to the stroller park, where they fumble for loveys and snacks. During the next song, the babies are asked, "Who can show one finger?" Not a single baby responds. Other activities elicit more enthusiasm, especially the final song, during which a round of balls is released from boxes and the lead singer brandishes an industrial-strength blower to whiz out dozens of perfectly formed bubbles at a time. (The handheld manual bubble wand I occasionally wave during bath time at home is profoundly underwhelming by comparison.) Shrieks and laughter fill the room. Scuffles break out as some of the more robust toddlers tussle over the larger balls. There are bubbles everywhere.

Class ends with the male singer shouting over the din: "This class is full with a waitlist for fall. Please be sure to confirm your spot, or you risk losing it!" which unleashes a tense frisson among the mothers, some of whom whip their heads around, looking for where to sign up. As if to alleviate the pressure, the band shifts into "Funkytown" while the adults gather their charges, breaking the recalcitrant away from their balls and harnessing them into strollers.

Little Maestros' goal is not just entertainment. Konner periodically hosts what she calls a Maestro Summit for new teachers and employees where she fills them in on what the class is *really* about. "I show them studies and findings about the benefits of music, even in utero," she explained. "Like the whole Baby Einstein idea, which gave a lot of credibility to music instruction for this demographic." She informs them about the window during which babies' fine motor skills are developed enough to handle instruments. "Even though a lot of this stuff is camouflaged by entertainment, it's really educating and nurturing them," she said. "A lot of milestones happen here; it's really cool. In this location alone, every two weeks we have someone who takes his first step—he'll usually be walking toward the bouncing ball or the bubbles, something we're doing to get him involved. I think babies are really encouraged and inspired by the community and the props and the methods and the safety of the environment."

Babies aren't the only ones meant to reap Little Maestros' benefits. Mothers seem to relish the time to catch up with other parents and compare notes. Any stay-at-home mom can tell you of the acute need to escape the confines of the nursery and have some fun. "Everyone hangs out after class and bonds with friends and family," Konner said with pride. "Moms tell me that they're networking and talking about pediatricians and comparing strollers and exchanging information about if it's time for their toddlers to wear shoes." Parents seem to actually enjoy themselves. "They're so happy when they see their child responding and getting involved. They can sit and relax and have fun, and we're doing all the work. I think they really find themselves inspired, too. We're showing parents they can have fun, with their kids. We take a lot of parents out of their shells. It's 'C'mon, bounce your babies in the air!' It makes them realize, 'Wow, parenthood can be awesome!'"

That enthusiasm has propelled the company's phenomenal success. Though Little Maestros has garnered a fair amount of press, from the *New York Times* to the *Today Show,* most of its popularity has been achieved through what Konner calls "word of mom." After three months in business, in 2002 Little Maestros expanded from eight to nineteen classes. By 2006, Maestros offered 138 classes in eleven of New York's best venues, including the Scholastic Store, the Jewish Community Center, and the Reebok Sports Clubs. Packages run between eight and seventeen sessions, with an average cost of $40 per class. "We offer evening programs, and for a lot of working parents, those are the only ones they can go to. They're really grateful."

Konner understands where they're coming from. After working in marketing at Atlantic Records during the 1990s, she got married, had a daughter, and quit the music business. "I was going to be a stay-at-home mom!" she marveled with a laugh. Then, in an effort to introduce her daughter to music, she went to several trial classes around the city and, like other mompreneurs before her, was disappointed by what she found. "I was looking at my watch the whole time," she recalled. "I just felt like this was stuff that I could do in my living room." The music was outdated and uninspiring, and Konner feared her daughter would absorb her mother's boredom.

So she decided to get creative. She asked the church across the street if it could provide her space for an hour, put together a band for her playgroup, and hired a composer. "A lot of people underestimate kids and equate children's music with lullabies and nursery rhymes." She thought kids could handle more challenging genres—Motown, rock, disco, show tunes—and that they would appreciate the difference between recorded music and a live band. Seems she was right. In 2006, Little Maestros—represented by powerhouse talent agency William Morris—recorded its second CD. It hosts an annual musical at New York City's 675-seat Danny Kaye Theater and hopes to develop a TV show and tour around the country. Konner is constantly approached by people who want to be part of expanding the franchise. Two Japanese parents told her that Gymboree had launched in Japan and they thought she should do the same with Little Maestros. "I was like, 'Wow, the T-shirt alone would be so cool!'" She hired a business adviser to help take her company to the next level. "We all feel totally pumped and fired and honored by all the interest. I want to make Little Maestros as accessible as possible."

ONCE UPON A TIME, A PARENT'S AMBITIONS FOR A FOURTEEN-month-old's day were pretty straightforward. If all went smoothly, he would wake at a reasonable hour, eat and nap as expected, perhaps snooze a bit in the stroller or the car while his mother went about her errands. She might stop by a neighbor's for an impromptu playdate, or if the day were busy, she could hope that her baby wouldn't break down while she hurtled herself through the supermarket or made just one more stop at the dry cleaners. With luck, he would not need his diaper changed while they were trapped on the freeway. Perhaps he would even be able to roll with the punches if her schedule forced him to go to sleep a little earlier or later than usual, in order to accommodate other plans.

Today, instead of squeezing infants into our own schedules, we dash madly around their activities, our own responsibilities squeezed into rare moments off. With so many of us working and everyone absurdly busy, playdates must be plotted weeks in advance. We hardly ever attempt to stop by another mother's home on the spur of the moment; the chances of catching a free slot in another child's schedule are slim. Instead, we ferry our children around town to dedicated baby classes, from Gymboree to Music Together to Tumbling Tots. We arrange our lives around our children because we're told that it's never too early to begin a program of social and emotional learning, and music appreciation, and gross motor movement, and adaptation to structure, and a host of other required skills. We're told that if we don't give our baby all the opportunities available, we'll deprive him of the chance to develop alongside his peers. As a 2007 report by the nonprofit research organization Education Sector notes:

> Parents have been [hit] with a striking threat: The experiences you provide your child during the first three years hardwire the brain and forever set your child's intellectual potential. Fail to provide the right stimulation during early childhood and your child will suffer devastating consequences. Pass on baby water aerobics, in other words, and you can say goodbye to college.[1]

Encouraged by the baby instruction industry, many parents now operate under the assumption that classes give babies the edge needed to "make it"—in *preschool*. Entry into a high-quality preschool (and thereby, the theory goes, a good elementary school, high school, and college) has become cutthroat. Many schools in major cities require formal exams, and most require an "interview," which often consists of observing a three- or four-year-old playing with a group of similar toddlers under inspection. Unless children are accustomed to group classroom settings, parents fear, their children will fail to "perform" well enough to get in. "It's become a craze in the city to get into a mommy-and-me-class," one New York City mother of two told the *New York Times*. This pre-pre-education doesn't come without costs. Music classes alone cost between $1,290 and $5,745 for a yearlong program.[2] - In urban areas like New York, the most popular classes—Free to Be Under Three, Little Maestros, Take Me to the Water—have months-long waiting lists. It's either enroll your baby early or stew at home, seemingly wasting your child's time and trying not to go stir crazy or beat yourself up with guilt.

Karen Miller, a forty-nine-year-old mother from Sierra Madre, California, took her then-two-year-old daughter Georgia to Music Together because, as she put it, "I just felt like I didn't have enough to offer her on my own. I thought I wasn't clever, patient, or creative enough to reach her. I felt that as a mother, I'd never be able to introduce her to enough." For Miller, it was tough to surrender to Georgia's interests, which mostly meant sitting on the floor and making a mess. "I was looking for some kind of structure," she said. Like many moms, she also yearned for a way to escape the day yawning before her, and she felt a crushing sense of obligation. "You end up thinking that you've really got to *create* the child—to mold and direct and form and educate and manipulate and encourage—that the onus is on you." Though she longed to offer an educational opportunity to her daughter were other forces at work. "I think that there's a kind of deep need that propels us out of the house. We're desperately seeking something other than us . . . I was filled with such a sense of dread that I wasn't enough."

Guilt. Desire. Ambition. Insecurity. Expectation. Fear. Desperation. A prime marketing opportunity, and companies have met it. Since 2000, international behemoth Music Together has doubled the number of teacher-training sessions offered.[3] My Gym Children's Fitness Centers, another nationwide franchise, has grown almost 50 percent since 2002.[4] In major cities and upper-middle-class suburbs, parents can spend upwards of $3,000 on a year of classes for a child under three. Marketers are increasingly heightening expectations, hyping the promise of building crucial skills. "In our market research groups, people say they want their children to have a breadth of experiences," said Jill Johnston, senior vice president of Gymboree. "They want children better prepared for preschool or even help them get in."[5]

After more than thirty years in the business, Gymboree Play & Music has 533 branches in the United States and operates in twenty-five countries abroad, generating more than $11 million in annual revenue.[6] While earlier advertising campaigns developed in-house emphasized the theme of "play and music," in 2004 Gymboree hired the Hive, a hip San Francisco ad agency, which suggested a more heavy-handed sell. One of the subsequent print ads, dubbed "College Education," debuted in the February 2005 issue of *Parents* magazine, featuring a photo of a toddler accompanied by the text, "If a college education is in his future, then think of us as an under under undergrad degree." Another ad asked, "Percentage of brain developed at birth: 25%. Percentage of brain developed at 5 years: 90%. So what are you doing next Tuesday morning?" One brochure came with the heading "Kids don't come with instructions. That's why there's Gymboree."

DeAnn Budney, cofounder of the Hive, explained to *Adweek* magazine, "Our campaign for Gymboree Play & Music talks to parents adult to adult, with insight, humor, and an understanding of how hard it is to be a parent in 2005."[7] The Hive's website outlined the strategy further.

> [Gymboree] was having trouble in 2004 making their case to parents. They saw Gymboree as a place to play, but couldn't understand why they should pay $200 for a few playdates when they could play at home for free. Gymboree called The Hive to help refocus their message on the benefits of child development.

What parent could ward off a twinge of fear reading an advertisement that warns, "The nine months of getting him into the world are over. The eighteen years of getting him ready for it start now"?

Along with reconfiguring its advertising approach, Gymboree began offering more services with a developmental hook. On its website, it claims that classes for children under age five "build the intellectual, physical and social skills they need to be confident and successful learners." In 2005, it added the tagline "Growing young minds," and the following year, teamed with LeapFrog to create cobranded programs "designed to help children gain key skills in preparation for pre-kindergarten and kindergarten classes." These new classes incorporated LeapFrog's SchoolHouse products, such as the Imagination Desk learning centers, to introduce children to the alphabet, counting, shapes, and color identification. According to the company, the classes "build confidence, encourage curiosity, and promote independent learning and problem-solving skills."[8] In 2007, Gymboree revamped its curriculum to include a class, called Level 1, for babies zero to six months. The new class "caters to the early stage of a child's brain development [and] focuses on the right stimulation at the right time." Part of the program is parent education, with expert instructors showing parents how to conduct a baby massage and how "best" to show pictures and objects to their babies at home.

Whether such classes truly speak to babies is questionable. Sarah,[9] a thirty-three-year-old stay-at-home mother from Wayne, Pennsylvania, took her son William to a local Gymboree at five months. "I heard about it through friends who said it was a good place for kids to explore, to see songs and lights and parachutes and bubbles to stimulate their brains. And it's a great thing for moms who want to get out of the house." But while some of the older children appeared to be stimulated by the different sounds and sensations and by playing on the mats and looking in mirrors, William seemed less than riveted. "I don't think he was getting *anything* out of it," Sarah confessed. "It seems like he was bored. Maybe it was too early for him. I actually think a lot of it was over the kids' heads."

Andrea Kahl, thirty-two, a stay-at-home mother of two from Kings Park, New York, had a similar experience. When her colicky, clingy daughter Sabrinna was fourteen months, she enrolled her at Gymboree to get her used to being around other children. But Gymboree didn't allow much time for socialization. "I felt like they were expecting too much structure from kids that age," she told me. "They would move from thing to thing too quickly, and sometimes the classes were just too big so she wouldn't get a chance to try an activity unless she ran to it first. We would end up lagging behind so she could try something while the teacher moved on." Whenever children strayed from attention, the teacher acted impatient, and Andrea felt like she constantly had to chase after her daughter to bring her back in line. The teacher would read a story during each class and "look annoyed that the kids weren't enraptured by her reading." But, Andrea explained, "It would be a long, involved story that forced children that age to sit for too long." Compounding the problem were the other mothers. "So many of the moms there were looking for other moms to talk to, and they would just let their kids run wild while they chatted. I found myself having to reprimand some child for shoving mine, or helping a child climb something because nobody was supervising him."

Of course, not all baby classes are so fraught. Kahl found that Little Gym, an international franchise of baby class centers, worked well for her son Paul because, as she said, "They understand that kids at a certain age aren't necessarily going to be willing to try each and every thing the teacher has set on the curriculum." She believes Little Gym taught her son gross and fine motor skills, balance and coordination, in ways that saved her from hollering, "Get off the couch!" Tessa, a thirty-four-year-old stay-at-home mother from Nashville, said that when she enrolled her fifteen-month-old daughter Natalia in Gymboree, she became more adventuresome and improved her balance. "Gymboree really opened her up," she said. "She used to cry and cling to me if a new person was in front of her." At twenty months, Natalia was asking after her classmates and looking for her teacher when she passed the Gymboree at the local mall. Tessa considers Gymboree a "multisensory learning" experience that she wouldn't have been able to provide herself. "I'm not an expert in child development, so I probably would have just taught her things by talking to her rather than singing and using physical actions. I think it would have taken her longer to build those same skills."

• • •

GIVEN THE PREMISES AND PROMISES OF THE MYRIAD CLASSES
offered to children under five, many parents are left feeling ill-
equipped to adequately amuse and enlighten their offspring on
their own. In ten states, Little Scientists, for example, teaches children as young as three, "innovative educational techniques" by
"coupling interactive projects, entertaining demonstrations and
simple experiments with children's natural curiosity." New York
City's Mixing Bowl introduces children as young as two and a half
to the culinary arts. Founded in 2000, Super Soccer Stars, which
operates in forty locations, instructs children as young as two to
bend it like Beckham. Driven by the notion that early exposure to
foreign languages promotes language acquisition, in suburban areas from Boston to San Diego children are studying second and
even third languages at ages when they are just learning their first.
In Livingston, New Jersey, one-year-olds enroll in Bilingual Buds,
a Chinese-language preschool. According to the *New York Times*,
"In the past five years, foreign-language studies for the under-5 set
have become as common as art and music lessons."[10]

Many classes rely on elaborate entertainment to differentiate
themselves from one another and entice new customers. For $685
a semester, parents can enroll in Broadway Babies for infants under six months old:

> With a carefully written curriculum guided by highly accredited
> teachers and pediatricians, Broadway Babies weaves entertaining
> educational activities through the story and songs of each musical.
> These activities focus on pre-K development of language, motor
> skills, color and letter recognition, counting, socialization, and so
> much more.

Ailey Babies offers music and movement classes to two-year-olds
at the famed Ailey School of Dance. By age three, children have

plenty of opportunities and encouragement to start learning Suzuki-style violin, piano, painting, and art appreciation. All of these skills can be wonderful enhancements to a child's life. But we are racing to raise prodigies at younger and younger ages without necessarily considering the whys, benefits, and drawbacks to that goal.

One of the most astonishing baby class trends—at least to non-parents—is the surge in sign-language classes for babies who can hear.* Yet nearly every parent today is aware of the classes, which have cropped up in community centers, pre-preschools, and other mom-centric venues around the country. Dozens of books (including a *Complete Idiot's Guide to Baby Sign Language*), videos, DVDs, and workshops from companies like KinderSigns purport to teach the method to parents eager to foster early language skills in their infants. Baby signing has become so well established that it was featured in the 2004 film *Meet the Fockers*, in which Robert De Niro's character teaches his grandson to sign to comedic effect.

Yet the theory behind baby signing is quite serious. Because gross motor skills develop before the fine motor skills involved in phonetic and articulatory actions (moving tongues and mouths in the proper way to create speech), signing advocates say babies can be taught to communicate with their hands before they are physically capable of articulating thoughts. Any parent can vouch for the fact that her baby seems to understand more than he can say. Who doesn't want to know what's going on inside her often inscrutable infant's head?

The popularity of baby signing can be largely attributed to the efforts of the psychologists Linda Acredolo and Susan Goodwyn, cofounders of the Baby Signs Institute. In 1982, Acredolo taught

*When the star defensive end for the New York Giants, Michael Strahan, was going through a bitter divorce from his wife, he complained that among other extravagances, his wife spent $1,700 on sign-language classes for their twins—"even though neither daughter is hearing impaired," according to a front page in the Metro section of the *New York Times*.

her twelve-month-old daughter Katie how to sign, and together with Goodwyn, one of her graduate students at the time, she published a research paper on how they fostered Katie's burgeoning skills. "I should say that Katie taught us," Acredolo told me. "She was so frustrated that she couldn't talk, she started using gestures. She spontaneously started making up signs." Katie would point to a rose bush and sniff. She would rub her fingers together to indicate the word *spider.* And so on.

In 1996, Acredolo and Goodwyn published their first book, *Baby Signs: How to Talk with Your Baby Before Your Baby Can Talk,* which sold more than half a million copies. *Baby Signs* produced a burst of publicity as Acredolo and Goodwyn hit *Oprah,* the *Today Show, Dateline NBC, 20/20,* and *Good Morning America* and told their story to *Newsweek, U.S. News & World Report,* and *Parents* magazine. By 2005, the Baby Signs Institute had trained seven hundred teachers. A series of books, DVDs, baby sign charts, flash cards, and even a puppet dubbed "BeeBo the Baby Signs Bear" followed.

According to the Baby Signs Institute, teaching a baby to sign has remarkable emotional and social benefits: reducing tears, tantrums, and frustration; allowing babies to share their worlds; increasing respect for babies; strengthening the parent-infant bond; and boosting self-esteem and self-confidence—all things that parents, even those who aren't angling for a minigenius, are keen to encourage. Moreover, it purports that signing makes learning to talk easier and stimulates intellectual development. "When babies are using signs, they pay more attention to what's going on around them in terms of language," explained Susan Goodwyn. "They're stimulating the language portion of the brain." To back up these claims, Acredolo and Goodwyn conducted a long-term study, funded by the National Institutes of Health, of 140 families. The results were astonishing. Babies taught to sign at eleven months tested eleven months ahead of other babies in terms of vocabulary and linguistic ability by age three. At age eight, signing babies scored higher on IQ tests than the control group. "You can increase your baby's IQ score, that's for sure," Goodwyn assured me. "And you increase your child's verbal development, which pays off in school."

Gesturing has been proven to be a positive force for children who have developmental difficulties, and needless to say, it is crucial for hearing-impaired children. Still, that doesn't mean it benefits everyone. In 2005, researchers at the Universities of Ottawa and Waterloo published a paper titled "Teaching Gestural Signs to Infants to Advance Child Development: A Review of the Evidence," which examined the claims made by baby-signing advocates.[11] The scientists reviewed more than 1,200 studies and found that only ten actually measured objective outcomes in teaching signing as compared with groups of hearing babies. As for Acredolo and Goodwyn's celebrated research, the team uncovered several methodological problems. According to one of the paper's authors, Cyne Johnston, Acredolo and Goodwyn failed to explain the methodology used to select and group their study's children. It may be, for example, that the parents in the baby-signing group were volunteers who were already highly motivated, educated, and involved, and thus likely to foster language development in their babies with or without signing classes. In addition to the baby-signing test group, there were two control groups: one in which parents received training to encourage verbal language skills with their babies; the other in which there was no intervention at all. But Acredolo and Goodwyn followed up with only one of the control groups—the babies with no intervention—which means that no long-term comparisons can be made between the parents who were trained to encourage spoken language and the parents who were trained to use sign language. It is possible that the verbally trained babies did just as well with language acquisition and IQ as the signing children, but the research doesn't say. Furthermore, the attrition rate in the follow-up study was as high as 40 percent. "When there's a high attrition rate, you wonder what happened to the other children and whether they were intrinsically different from the subjects they could find," Johnston told me.

The results were also inconsistent. One early study measured an improvement in language at the very beginning of the training, but by the time the babies reached two years of age any advantages linked to signing had disappeared. The researchers were unable to establish any of the other benefits attributed to baby signing, finding no evidence of improved emotional development, cognitive development, or parent-child bonding; indeed, these areas weren't even explored in the studies. Moreover, the research focused on signing taught by Baby Signs–trained parents. Today, a slew of classes unaffiliated with the institute as well as piles of videos and DVDs claim to teach babies signing. No one has studied the effectiveness of these alternatives.

It's not that baby signing is necessarily *bad* for kids, Johnston explained; it simply may not be beneficial in the way parents are led to believe. Nor is it clear that the benefits correlated with signing are necessarily *caused* by signing. Parents who sign to their children are also talking to them—and no study can prove that talking alone didn't lead to later verbal advances. The 2005 report urged caution: "Parents can be stressed by the challenges of meeting demands of work, caring for a young child, and other family and personal obligations, and experience guilt if they feel they are not doing everything recommended by infancy specialists and the infancy industry," the authors wrote. "Secondly, the normal course of child development may be challenged by efforts towards earlier and greater developmental achievements. The short prelingual period of the child's life is concomitant with other naturally occurring milestones in gross motor and in nonverbal social development." In other words, training babies to communicate using signs may disturb or disrupt important routes and patterns of development for other skills and processes besides language. Humans are not, after all, designed to be on a fast-track singular path to speech.

For now, the evidence doesn't weigh definitively for or against. "Our final recommendation for parents was that they should find activities that they enjoy with their child and spend one-on-one time sharing language with their baby," the report notes. "If for one family, it's sign language that comes naturally to them and stimulates their language interactions then that's fine for that family. For other parents, the activity might be reading." The most reassuring thing you can say to parents about signing is that it's just not necessary. "What's with baby sign language?" Elisa Sherona, the grandmother from Glenmore, Pennsylvania, wondered aloud to me. "What's the matter with the old way of communicating with a baby—by touch? I believe in an individual connection with a mother or a father without following a set prescription someone else came up with." But in our consumer culture, parents have been told that buying into a package or program is smarter than what one could do on one's own, for free.

THE SHINY LOBBY OF MEGA–BABY CENTER KIDVILLE ON NEW York City's Upper East Side is enormously appealing. There are colorful displays of quality children's toys and upscale baby clothing adorning the walls. A café offers waiter service and plentiful seating with actual space dedicated for strollers, car seats, and high chairs. A desk in the lobby is fully staffed by cheery greeters. Glossy Kidville "magalogs" promote the club's services and outline class schedules by age and interest. There are indoor playgrounds and an outdoor rooftop playground at the club's second location, on the Upper West Side of Manhattan.

Kidville radiates Friendly, Happy, and Safe. Everything in the playrooms is padded and protected; ramps are made of foam and balls of supple plastic. A squad of employees hum about, spritzing, wiping, and sweeping away any traces of drool, dirty fingerprints, or spit-up. It's your fantasy playroom, if you had a mansion and a team of household help.

It all bears the imprint of Kidville's stellar pedigree, the creation of New York City power couple Shari Misher Stenzler, a successful public relations executive, and Andy Stenzler, an MBA and experienced entrepreneur. Backed with millions raised from investors like Andre Agassi and Steffi Graf, Laurie Tisch, the founder of the Children's Museum of Manhattan, and Emanuel Stern, the founder of the chic Soho Grand Hotel, Kidville launched in 2005 to a frenzy of publicity. The *New York Times* called it "a gleaming, charming, $3 million, four-story temple to the lengths Manhattan parents will go to slip the bonds of strollerdom."[12] A reporter from London's *Independent* touted "the genius of Kidville" and described "an almost limitless number of pastimes to choose from."[13] Before Kidville even opened, a thousand members had signed up. Within six months, the club's registry listed two thousand member families. Kidville University, the center's pre-preschool, filled its three hundred slots in lightning speed, and there are perpetually children standing by on its waiting list.

By 2006, when Kidville opened its Upper West Side branch, it counted five thousand member families and projected sales of $10 million. In 2007, branches opened in the family-trendy neighborhoods of Tribeca and Park Slope, Brooklyn. The Stenzlers plan to open a fifth on the outskirts of Las Vegas, one of the country's fastest-growing regions for young children, and another in Scarsdale, a suburb in New York's tony Westchester County. Eventually, they expect to target neighborhoods across the country with at least fifteen thousand families, with a goal of grabbing at least 20 percent of those families as members.

Bursting with energy, Andy Stenzler whizzed me around the club firing off explanations and statistics, before hurrying to his next appointment. Wiry and full of smiles, he is visibly giddy with Kidville's success. "We started the club in part because of Shari's experience taking our daughter to classes, which were always in dirty basements or up a flight of stairs," he said, bounding into an elevator full of toddlers. Shari wasn't the only one with complaints; their friends had expressed similar dissatisfaction with existing options. First, there was no place where they could go to different classes under a single roof. Instead, they were driving and taking buses and pushing strollers all over town, loitering in McDonald's while waiting for the next class to begin. Second, there was nowhere to meet a friend before or after class, nothing that took into account a parent's needs. Third, many places did not seem sufficiently safe, secure, or clean to meet an exacting parent's standards. Addressing these complaints and offering a unique and valuable program for children are, as Stenzler put it, "the reasons we're winning."

While Kidville focuses on safety and cleanliness to assuage parental fears, most of its sell is about the positive impact its classes can have on children: Instead of learning to make Duncan Hines in a run-down nursery school kitchen, kids enroll in Silver Spoons and Paper Plates, taught by professional chefs, and get their own recipe book at the end of each semester. In the Construction Junction course, two-year-olds "go beyond just blocks . . . This advanced art program lets children learn how to plan, build and construct their own 3-D art projects! Roads, towers, monuments and pyramids are just a sample of the structures to be introduced, imagined and created with wood, collage, cloth, clay and more." Each week in My Masterpiece, children complete a new project in painting and sculpture. At Kidville University, a keepsake portfolio is prepared for each student by the teachers to "document his or her experiences in each development area" so that parents will see "how their children are learning—not just what they've learned!"

At a cost of $695 and up per seventeen-week class, Kidville promises both process and results. Good, messy fun in a squeaky-clean environment. Progressive child development theory and get-ahead proof of achievement. It also offers services for grown-ups: Reclaim Your Abs classes, mani-pedis at its salon (which also offers grooming for children), and parenting lectures. Kidville started on the Upper East Side and Upper West Side of Manhattan because, as Stenzler explained, "the most prestigious, worldly, and discerning moms" live there. But, he said, the formula should work anywhere. "All parents want to give their children a head start."

Stenzler accompanied me to Fairy Princess Camp, one of Kidville's star programs, where we crouched in a corner watching a bevy of pink- and lavender-festooned girls flutter around an art table. In 2005, the center offered two of the $725 weeklong Princess Camp sessions; by 2006, it needed six sessions to meet the demand of princess-minded three-year-olds. "Little princesses begin their day dressing in costume, and then take a trip to the salon! Next, they travel to the theater and our dance studio for special art activities, songs and dances." On the first day of Princess Camp, girls come dressed however they want, Stenzler noted, but by the second day, all them are dressing up. Kidville provides wings and tiaras to top off their outfits. "We spend a *fortune* on this class," he told me, and it showed. The girls, fetching in their ensembles, were making flowerpots under the supervision of a teacher. At one point, a girl fretted that she didn't have any flowers at home to put in her pot. The teacher replied, "Well then, ask your parents to buy some for you."

Parents are certainly buying into classes—in droves. "You'll never grow broke, it seems, selling cutting edge educational techniques to Manhattan moms," the *New York Post* noted when in 2006 Little Maestros signed a $5-million licensing deal with Kidville, giving the expanding chain the exclusive right to operate and manage its classes. Marni Kanner's dreams of expansion were coming true. "The goal is to turn Little Maestros into the next Wiggles," Konner explained. Wiggles, an Australia-based, billion-dollar children's entertainment business, includes live world tours, licensed goods, CDs, DVDs, and television. "We want millions of the children to experience what New York children experience in the classes."

In large part, the popularity of places like Kidville and Apple
Seeds, another New York City megacenter for parents and babies,
is a matter of convenience. "I'll walk into Kidville to take my
daughter to a class, and I'll see strollers parked in the lot and families sitting in the café drinking coffee," said Shari Misher Stenzler.
"The kids are eating chicken fingers or fried rice while waiting for
class to begin. Mom will be looking at the toys for a birthday party
she has tomorrow. It's a relief instead of packing the stroller and
fitting into some non-kid-friendly pizza place. It's exactly as we envisioned it—as if on cue—everything we did to make life easier,
more enjoyable, more convenient."

Following a similar logic, companies across the country that
used to focus on one form of learning—Gymboree's physical play,
Music Together's songs—have expanded their curricula. Kindermusik, an international chain that trains educators to provide music classes at day-care centers, community centers, and storefronts,
now offers signing classes and summer camp. "The parent of ten
years ago would maybe choose one activity for their child and
would then stick with that until their kids aged out," said Lisa
Rowell, director of marketing for Kindermusik. "Now parents go
for a buffet of activities. They may dabble in music for a couple of
semesters and then want to try swimming or soccer, depending on
what's hot in the market." The challenge is to get parents to stick
to one venue. After all, as Rowell acknowledged, the world of
baby classes has "absolutely gotten more competitive . . . There's
an explosion of other opportunities out there, both homegrown
and corporate."

Kindermusik, with its stodgy-sounding name and dusty lineage,
has itself had to modernize to keep up. Founded in West Germany
in the 1960s and imported to the United States in the late 1970s,
Kindermusik likes to call itself "the General Motors of childhood
development" (an appellation it might consider rethinking these
days). Classes begin just after a child is born and continue through
age seven. But now Kindermusik sells DVDs, books, musical in-

struments, and other toys and props used in its classrooms. It tells parents on its website, "You're here because you love your child. You want to give them the best possible beginning in the world. And you'd love to know what's going on inside that wonderful little mind. You came to the right place." Its philosophy: "We teach children music so they can become better learners . . . Today music and the mind research is known as the 'most rapidly developing field of human study,' according to recent reports from the Royal Institute of Great Britain, home to 14 Nobel Prize scientists."

This direct sell to parents is relatively new for Kindermusik. For years, the company's strategy was to recruit potential educators to get them to sign up for training, then have them go out and recruit parents for their local classes. But there was a problem. The kinds of people who wanted to teach music to kids were typically music fans and children lovers. They knew how to romp around a room with toddlers, but they generally were not born businesspeople. The message wasn't getting through to the potential end customers.

In order to get its message directly to parents, Kindermusik shifted gears in 2002. "We realized, *we're* the ones skilled at marketing a business," Rowell explained. "If we could get them to go to a class, the educators can get them to stay there." The new strategy included a major effort online. Kindermusik paid for search engine optimization on Google, Yahoo! and MSN and bought advertisements on baby blogs and in e-mail newsletters. In 2006, it ran ads on parenting websites like BabyCenter. To increase brand awareness, Kindermusik also began forming strategic partnerships. In 2005, it teamed up with Babies "R" Us, offering class demonstrations in 194 stores nationwide, and began a series of events with *BabyTalk* magazine, such as "The World's Largest Playgroup," which included a Liz Lange maternity fashion show, vendors, and live musicians.

After a spike in growth, Kindermusik now teaches 250,000 to 300,000 children a year in the United States (in addition to operations in sixty-four other countries). Rowell emphasized that Kindermusik's philosophy isn't about testing and performance, but about process. Kindermusik, she said, gives the child the foundation for creativity, teaching children social, emotional, and cognitive skills with music as the vehicle. Still, she remarked, parents are increasingly ambitious. "I think that parents today seem very focused on setting their child up for success as early as possible," she said. "There's a lot of concern about will my child get into the right school? Will they test well? What can I do with my children that will give them a head start above everyone else?"

But to some people, like Don Burton, founder and CEO of A-Ha Learning Partners, a New York City–based center for young children, most classes for babies still seem like mere entertainment, gussied up as educational experiences. In Burton's view, babies are just listening to music and dancing—the way they would if their parents turned on the stereo at home, picked them up, and warbled aloud, no matter how badly out of tune. When his wife took their daughter to her first baby class, it was, Burton said disparagingly, "Now we're going to sing songs to your baby." He was amazed the classes were so packed with paying parents. "It seems like a very popular format, but what they were doing didn't take any research about child development and apply it," he continued, shaking his head. "I understand there's a need for entertainment— moms want to get out of the house, and I don't pooh-pooh that. If you do that just once a week, I don't think it's going to do serious damage to your child's brain. But it's certainly not the best thing to do for your child." Which kind of sounds like a parent has to choose between screwing up their kid or stewing at home, frantic with boredom.

That's why Burton, a Harvard Business School graduate, started A-Ha, which, he said, is "not about entertaining your child," but about "practicing intelligence in action." A-Ha considers its services more high-minded than its competitors. "We're not going to have a spa for parents. You can socialize with other parents, of course, but they'll be parents interested in child development. We're interested in informed and active parents who understand that there's an art and a science to raising kids."

Though the premise sounds weighty, the "art and science" behind A-Ha Learning Partners isn't a dreary mix of flash cards and phonics. In fact, the principles behind the program are grounded in an understanding that play is how children under three learn. Rather than offer adult-centered programs, as Burton believes too many baby classes do, A-Ha's program is devised to allow babies to take initiative and explore their own interests. The classes take place in "immersive play environments," filled with open-ended materials like blocks, sand, and buckets.

On the afternoon when I visited, four one-year-olds, all boys, showed up for the Balls & Ramps "play lab." The instructor, Meredith Olmstead, a former teacher with undergraduate and graduate degrees in education, knew what she was doing, gently guiding the children and parents into a variety of activities, but never dictating how any one child should or should not be playing. "We try not to force children into doing things," she explained. Instead, Olmstead tries to do for parents what she'd like for her own daughter. "If I'm paying someone else to help with her development, I'd want it to be done the right way," she told me. "I don't want her to be merely entertained; I want her to learn independence." At the end of class, Olmstead distributed a brief handout to the parents and nannies, explaining the pedagogy underlying the day's activities.

Yet A-Ha's class had only four participants, whereas the other classes I attended were jam-packed. "I have to compete with the wow factor and the entertainment factor of other classes," Burton explained. "I have to say to them, 'Hey, we have these great clay labs and ice labs, and the experience here is equally joyous and entertaining.'" After establishing that A-Ha's classes are just as fun as the competition's, the next challenge is "to get parents to see the more substantive stuff, on top of the cool play experience." Harder still is to get parents to view developmental progress in

ways that go beyond memorizing the ABCs and counting numbers. "Those are narrow, isolated skills that parents can measure
and compare to other kids," Burton said. "Other cognitive skills,
like the ability to sustain attention, are tougher to see and compare. They're broader and more diffuse, so parents don't notice
them as much. We want to get parents to see this kind of rich
thinking and value it more."

Finding the right way to sell all this to parents hasn't been as
easy as he expected. To establish the A-Ha formula, Burton ran
three trials—one in New York City, another in Princeton, New Jersey, and a third in Greenwich, Connecticut—prior to opening in
January 2005. In the first trial, he asked parents to come to the test
location and showed them how to play with everyday objects from
home in ways that encouraged learning. "Parents didn't like that
at all," Burton recalled. They basically said, "Why would I come to
your center if I can do all this stuff at home?" Burton's response
was, "But don't you want to learn to be a good parent?" The parents universally replied, "But I *am* a good parent." Telling parents
outright what they ought to be doing—especially when it seemed
so commonsensical—turned out to be bad marketing.

Burton realized the experience he offered to kids had to be
more "wow." "It's taken longer than I'd like," he confessed. "But
once I get out all the kinks, I'll scale it to different locations."
(When I checked back a year later, the curiculum had already
been revamped.) Burton is funding the project on his own. For
now, the center remains small-scale, especially compared to the
colossus that is Kidville. There are two play areas in use—one on
the ground floor at the storefront's entrance, and one downstairs,
used for classes—and an art room remains unfinished. At any
given time, Burton said, they have about two hundred clients.
A-Ha isn't dark and dingy, but the spanking-clean, whiz-bam
bustling atmosphere of clubs like Kidville is decidedly absent. The
whole thing feels a bit homey and down-to-earth, like a well-
intentioned day-care center in a progressive New England town.

Yet Burton is foremost a businessman and one with ambition. "I'm an ex-McKinsey, Goldman Sachs guy," he said. "I don't want to be pigeonholed into those leftist earthy granola-head type things like Montessori and Waldorf. I'm trying to take the best of what we know about child development and bring it to you, Mom and Dad. Yes, I care about academics, but I'm going to deliver results in a better way, so you don't feel like a teacher jamming flash cards down their throats. The research shows that your child is going to be better at math and the ABCs if you play with them the way I want you to play with them. They'll be better at school and at life."

EVERYONE WANTS A CHILD TO BE "BETTER AT SCHOOL AND AT life." Every parent has high hopes. But when did it become necessary to spend hundreds of dollars on classes to encourage our children's natural curiosity about themselves, animals, blocks, and the world around them? Imagine the comparative deprivations suffered by Benjamin Franklin and Thomas Jefferson when they were children, left to dawdle at home.

The much-debated idea of the overscheduled child is a familiar one. As far back as 1931, critic Ruth Frankel noted that "the modern child, with his days set into a patterned program, goes docilely from one prescribed class to another, takes up art and music and French and dancing . . . until there is hardly a minute left" and argued that overprogrammed children become jaded and bored.[14] But whether school-age children are increasingly shoehorned into activities or not, there's no doubt that the number of formal activities for babies and toddlers has grown dramatically in the last ten years. We're not talking about fourth-graders overburdened with extracurriculars; we're talking about parents feeling pressured to enroll their fourteen-month-olds in three classes a week.

In consumer parenting culture, the message sent to parents through learning centers, music classes, and gymnasiums, no matter how well-intentioned, is that parents aren't equipped to open the world up to our children by ourselves, with our extended families, in our neighborhoods and communities. That an ordinary adult, no matter how invested or caring, doesn't have the information or ability to fill her child's day with opportunities for enrichment. Our day-care centers, children's grandparents, or nannies aren't enough. Hundreds of companies have done their best to cement this suspicion into conviction. According to a 2006 *Parenting* magazine poll, half of moms think that mothers who take their infants to classes in subjects like music and art are normal, and a third think it's a wise decision to "nurture their children's potential so early on." Fewer than one in five thought that parents who take kids to classes are "a little neurotic" because "babies don't need lessons."

Many parents have come to believe that to do it themselves would require an art supply shop's worth of supplies and formal training. That in order to enhance our children's appreciation of music, turning on the stereo and dancing around isn't enough; we need a four-piece band, knowledge of music theory, and at least six soundtracks of lyrics memorized from beginning to end. Yet prior to Gymboree, children somehow learned to somersault and touch their toes without a cheering, trained instructor. They managed to learn socialization skills from their local play group or the children of their parents' friends or the kids on the block. Prior to classes like Sally's Music Circle in suburban Maryland and Pennsylvania, whose founder has a PhD in music education, kids learned to love Raffi and played with Fisher-Price turntables and bobbled around the living room. They managed to make it into nursery school without being tutored in object permanence and spatial reasoning. That fact is, though the marketing of baby classes creates the aura that learning only happens in the realm of the classroom, the skills these classes claim to teach are developmental milestones that all children surmount eventually—some faster than others—but with little impact on long-term well-being or success. We don't actually need to promote these skills; *they just happen.*

While there's a lot of solid science about early childhood development and the development of the brain, raising a healthy, confident child is much more art than science. "Young children don't need to be taught so much as they need to be provided opportunities in which to learn," said pediatrician Jack Shonkoff, chairman of the National Scientific Council of the Developing Child, a group of leading neuroscientists and child development researchers. And learning, he emphasized, is not being a passive recipient of teaching, but allowing kids to have some control over their experiences. "Children do *not* thrive when they are overprogrammed and every minute of every day is filled with stimulating learning opportunities. The danger is that learning can become associated with tension and pressure instead of pleasure and enjoyment. That's obviously something nobody would want imprinted on a young baby."

Though classes can be fun, and can be especially important for the development of social and emotional skills for children two and up, not everything being taught in today's baby classes is necessarily beneficial. In many art classes for children under five, projects are heavily directed by adults. In one class, whose location shall go unnamed, I observed two-year-olds being led through the steps of making fish out of paper plates. Each child was given an identical plate and identical cups of blue and green paint and told to paint with brushes onto the plates. Children who used their fingers or tried to paint elsewhere were admonished. Next, each was given glitter to sprinkle on the plates, and again, children who tried to do anything with the glitter other than the prescribed action were guided back to the glitter's intended destination. Finally, the teachers cut out a triangle from one end of the fish and attached it to the other, creating a mouth and fish tail. Near-identical finished projects were hung on the wall for visitors to admire and then distributed at the end of the week so that parents could see how much their child had "learned."

"With these kinds of classes, it's the *adult* making the artwork, not the child," explained Diane Levin, the Wheelock College education professor. "Children that age are interested in *process*. They would be happy scribbling with markers on paper." Not only do such classes run counter to toddlers' instincts; they inadvertantly teach children some unfortunate lessons. First, that there is one right way to create art, and that you do what you are told. Second, because they are not allowed to explore, experiment, or move the paints around, children do not make a connection between their own actions and what's happening on the paper. "The best thing that might come out of a class like this is learning how to follow instructions," said Joan Almon of the Alliance for Childhood, who spent years as a kindergarten teacher and is horrified by what some baby classes teach. "Unfortunately, they're learning that at too young an age. And while they're 'learning' that, they're losing the sense that they can express themselves freely through art materials. I can't imagine those kids growing up and feeling confident in their own expression."

Other classes simply go over their heads. Babies thrive on novelty—if you put on a new album at home, your baby is going to listen, perhaps bounce and move and perk up to the newness of the song; a change of album is enough newness to get a baby to pay attention. But in a class, *everything* is novel to a baby: Where am I? Who are these people? What are they doing? "Focusing on the intended goal of the class, whether it's music or gym, is probably one of fifty things they need to deal with at that moment," said Levin. "Babies are not programmed to be in these kinds of overwhelming situations. They may stop moving and look catatonic, so the parent might think, 'Ah, my baby is paying attention!' But you have to wonder, are they really paying attention? And if they are, what are they paying attention to?" Rather than listening to the music, they may be honing in on the bright colors of the padded mat beneath them. Or they may simply be overstimulated and have completely tuned out.

For instance, in a music class I attended, toddlers were seated with their parents around a parachute while a singer strummed the guitar and sang. Another instructor threw balls onto the parachute and barked orders at the parents to wave the edges of the parachute in the middle of the air. "Popcorn!" yelled the second instructor, as the balls flew in the air atop the undulating parachute. Several babies crawled onto the billowing parachute; others looked stunned. A number of them clung to their caretakers, and a few tried to wander off. "This kind of class makes no sense for children that age," Levin explained. "How many of them even know what popcorn is? Or how's it made? A baby's thinking is more like a slide than a movie until age four. They can't process these ideas." What seems like exciting amusement to an adult is more likely to look like utter chaos to an infant. And what if a ball hits a baby? A baby can't anticipate what a flying ball does and doesn't have the ability to retrace events to understand where it came from. Moreover, because children react differently to intense stimuli and are at a range of developmental stages even if they are all the same age, they usually require very different responses from instructors. But with such classes hosting a dozen babies or more, there's no way for the instructors—even if there are two of them, even if they *are* experts—to tailor the experience to each baby's needs.

We thrust our babies into this kind of commotion, yet are afraid to just let our kids do their own thing at home, in a safe and nurturing environment. We have allowed ourselves to be robbed of confidence as parents and to deprive ourselves of one of our most ordinary and—often quite easy—roles. It doesn't take a rocket scientist to allow a child to pick up a leaf in the backyard and learn to "explore the natural environment." Without any encouragement, a child will tear a leaf up and glean whatever he needs to know about crinkly noises, wind, and gravity as the little pieces float and fall away from his hands. Even if we're "only" running errands with our children in tow, kids learn about movement, things that go, and their neighborhood. In an era when so many of us lament the loss of community, toddlers could do worse than meet the local cobbler or babble at the cashier in the grocery store. A child who spends her days pursuing her own interests at a nearby playground or running through the aisles of the pharmacy is acquiring the same developmental skills as the child ferried off to gym class twice a week for directed play, and doing so in ways that are a lot less expensive.

For adults, busyness is so often equated with productivity, and productivity with advancement, that we tend to assume the world operates in the same linear, forward motion for our babies. If we don't keep pushing (or at least prodding) our children, we risk having them fall behind their peers. "We're seeing parents who want to fill up every waking moment," Marie-France Greer, founder of MiniMasters, a children's activity center in New York City, told the *New York Sun.* "Parents are trying to expose their kids to as much as possible, and you almost feel left out if you don't." One thirty-five-year-old mother of two explained, "Preschool is never going to be enough. Kids have so much energy and they're so curious. I don't want to hold them back just because some people think that kids are overscheduled. I don't want to limit their potential."[15]

The parenting industry wants us to feel that we have to maximize every moment, especially if the amount of time we have together is compromised by the demands of work and other obligations. That we need to cram as much as possible into those moments and control as best we can the quality of the time spent apart. And that if we fail to ensure our children's "engagement" in the world, our kids might lose interest in learning or veer off into less productive—even destructive—behaviors. Our children will be out of control, or at least, out of *our* control. Yet the laundromat is just as interesting to a two-year-old as the Museum of Fine Arts, and children need unstructured time to explore. When freed from entertaining environments and planned experiences, they are most likely to discover things on their own.

Educators are now urging parents to hold off on preschool prep. The Alliance for Childhood has issued guidelines for parents urging them to "curtail time spent in organized activities." In 2006, the American Academy of Pediatrics issued an unusual report for an association of medical doctors: "The Importance of Play in Promoting Healthy Child Development and Maintaining Strong Parent-Child Bonds," which laments the preponderance of structured activities and marketing-driven, adult-centered play, calling on doctors to help parents recognize the importance of free play to healthy brain development. "When play is controlled by adults, children acquiesce to adult rules and concerns and lose some of the benefits play offers them, particularly in developing creativity, leadership, and group skills," the report noted. No holds barred, the AAP condemned the role marketers play in depriving children of just that kind of free time:

> Parents are receiving carefully marketed messages that good parents expose their children to every opportunity to excel, buy a plethora of enrichment tools, and ensure that their children participate in a wide variety of activities . . . Specialized gyms and enrichment programs designed for children exist in many communities and there is an abundance of after-school enrichment activities. These tools and programs are heavily marketed, and many parents have grown to believe they are a requirement of good parenting and a necessity for appropriate development.

The result, according to the AAP, is that much of parent-child time is spent coordinating and transporting children from one activity to the next. The AAP suggested that "purveyors of these special programs should be encouraged to produce long-term evidence that define how their products/strategies produce more successful children" and that pediatricians help parents "evaluate the claims made by marketers and advertisers about the products or interventions designed to produce super-children."

Parents will often tell you that their children seem to flourish with an anticipated schedule of classes; they enjoy recognizing a familiar environment and appreciate a class's regularity. But while it is true that babies benefit from routines, creating and maintaining routines doesn't require hauling them to a half-dozen classes around town. "Having rituals, like bedtime and mealtime, brings order to babies' lives, which helps them organize their thinking," explained New York University's developmental psychologist Catherine Tamis-LeMonda. Being able to anticipate future events as well as remember and create memories of past patterns fosters cognitive development. As a child gets older, having her participate in creating and managing those routines develops cognitive skills.

There are additional benefits to children taking part in ordinary household routines—the very activities many parents dismiss as being less worthwhile than classes. Children take pride in a job well done. They learn to cooperate with parents, caretakers, and siblings. They learn an early version of the all-important work ethic. Perhaps most important, they learn the value of family obligation. In the 1976 edition of his child-rearing guide, Dr. Spock wrote, "How do children learn to perform various duties? By their very nature, they start out feeling that dressing themselves, brushing their teeth, sweeping and putting things away are exciting and grownup things to do. If their parents succeed in keeping on good terms with them as they grow older, they will enjoy going on errands, carrying packages, and raking the lawn, because they will want to have a part in important jobs and to please their mother and father." According to Spock, "Participation in the work of the home is good for the child's soul and provides a basis for the very soundest kind of companionship with parents.[16] The Alliance for Childhood similarly advises parents to "bring back the art of real work." According to its guidelines, "Adult activity—cooking, raking, cleaning, washing the car—actually inspires children to play. Children are likely to help for short periods and then engage in their own play." As an added benefit, children become accustomed to helping out around the house, something that is increasingly difficult to introduce as children get older.

There are other good reasons to keep kids at home, involved in the daily doings of maintaining the house. One 2003 study by sociologists Scott Coltrane and Michele Adams of the University of California, Riverside, found that when fathers participated in housework with their school-age children, the kids had more friends and were less likely to be depressed or have trouble at school; the researchers surmised that the children witnessed positive gender equality, cooperation, and democratic values. "Because fewer men do housework than women," said Adams, "when they share the work, it has more impact on children. By performing domestic service with their children, fathers model cooperative family partnerships."[17] Plus, think of the squeaky-clean future. A son who empties the dishwasher automatically will someday make a great husband; a girl who shares housework will grow into a woman who appreciates—and expects—her own family's help. Housework may seem boring to adults, but it's not to little kids. Ironically, the children who end up *most* likely to complain about being bored are the ones whose free time has been engineered into organized activities and entertainment, and don't know what to do when left to their own devices. For these children, "fun" becomes professionalized and commercialized, whether it means spending money or hiring someone to deliver elaborate birthday parties, extracurricular classes, or other forms of amusement.

Introducing a toddler to a class or two can be a much-needed reprieve, especially for stay-at-home parents who are desperate to break up their days with some kind of diversion, but it's important to understand what the money is being spent on. When a child is very young (under a year), the benefits—getting out of the house, meeting other parents—are more for the parent than for the child. For an older child, classes might expose him to something that you or your child-care provider don't have the time or resources to provide, such as interaction with animals, playing with sand, or running around in a spacious, safe indoor environment.

Classes can be wonderfully diverting, especially for older children who don't have siblings or playgroups or who have limited access to large spaces and art materials. But for babies, classes may simply be too much and truly unnecessary.

"Parents are bombarded with messages about what they need to buy and what class they need to go to," said Claire Lerner, director of parent education at Zero to Three. "They're understandably confused about what their role is and what it takes to help a baby thrive. But they need to know that they don't need to do anything extraordinary in terms of classes. Taking a class or two may turn out to be a wonderful experience for you and for your child, but if the point is trying to expedite your baby's development, it's important to remember that there is absolutely no research out there to support that it's useful."

6

Pampered

Perhaps it all started with the Bugaboo. In 2004, when *People* magazine showed a picture of maternal goddess Gwyneth Paltrow pushing baby Apple in a Bugaboo, those of us who were once content to putter along with Gracos and Kolcrafts suddenly felt like we were not the best parents we could be. We were has-beens. Cheapskates.

Soon, we were surrounded by other Bugaboo-pushing celebrities, high-fashion moms, and urban upscale couples. The Frog model's customers included Kate Hudson, Russell Crowe, Debra Messing, and David Letterman. Among fans of the pricier Cameleon model, we had Matt Damon, Courtney Cox, Liv Tyler, and Mark Wahlberg. (Like most children's luxury companies, though some deny it, Bugaboo compiles a list of its celebrity clients.) Everyone who was anyone maternity-wise suddenly had a Bugaboo. And then even those of us who weren't anyone in particular decided we needed one too. The Bugaboo wasn't just a business success; it was a social and cultural achievement. You had to have a Bug.

But the Bugaboo started off more as a joke than a marketing phenomenon. When Bugaboos first entered the U.S. market in

2003, people doubted anyone would cough up $700 for a baby carriage. After all, the average price of a stroller in America was $170. Bugaboos were a complete unknown and were selling at a price point never seen before. Only two renegade stores, one on the East Coast and one in California, would even commit to carrying them. "Nobody saw it happening," recalled Stellario D'Urso, vice president of the Italian stroller maker Ingelsina, who had been working in the U.S. market for twenty years. "Everyone laughed at them."

The naysayers turned out to be the fools. Sales of Bugaboos doubled between 2003 and 2004. The fat-wheeled Dutch turbostroller is now a commonplace sight in metropolitan areas. On New York City's Upper West Side, the old-fashioned independent store, Albee Baby Carriage, reports that Bugaboo is its bestselling stroller. "Bugaboo is the perfect example of the phenomenon that is family spending today," said Eva Dillon, the founding publisher of the new upscale parents' magazine *Cookie*. "Three years ago, you never saw one on the street. Now they are in every major city. The number of units they've sold in this country quantifies what's going on in the family arena today."

Credit for the new luxury baby ride goes largely to Kari Boiler, the thirty-six-year-old marketing director for Bugaboo North America. Boiler was an advertising executive expat in Amsterdam when she had her first child in 2001. Like many of the Dutch parents in her adopted city, she purchased a Bugaboo, which had been sold in the Netherlands since 1999 and become commonplace in Europe (where it costs considerably less). She gave the Bug little thought. But when she took a holiday in the states, people stormed her on the street to ask about her baby's stroller. With its boxy design and bright colors, it looked nothing like the traditional American or British versions. It had wheel suspension and pneumatic tires. It seemed high-tech yet user-friendly. Unusual, yet instantly comprehensible. It was also supercute, with a bouncy logo and a catchy name—the stroller equivalent of the Mini Cooper or the Volkswagen Bug.

Boiler had recently left the advertising agency to raise her daughter, but her marketing acumen was very much intact. When she returned to Amsterdam, she knew just what to do. She set up a meeting with Bugaboo's corporate office and asked to help develop a business plan for entering the U.S. market. In 2002, she moved to Los Angeles and established the infrastructure of what would become Bugaboo's North American operation, creating user guides geared to major American cities and setting up an office. Shortly thereafter, an executive from corporate headquarters came over to deal with logistics and sales so that Boiler could focus on marketing.

Then Boiler had a brilliant idea. HBO's *Sex and the City* was at the height of its cultural supremacy. She decided to call the producers. Bright, successful, and quirky Miranda, the only character to reproduce, was expecting a baby imminently, and naturally, Boiler realized, she would need a stroller. Boiler pitched the show on giving Miranda an exclusive European model, one that wasn't even available in the United States yet. In June 2002, the first episode featuring Miranda and her Bug aired, creating a frenzy of interest even though the strollers would not ship into the American market until January 2003. Everyone wanted Miranda's stroller, and tantalizingly, nobody could get their hands on one. By the time Bugaboo shipments hit American shores, the vaunted stroller had appeared in nearly every parenting magazine. Boiler had a six-month-long waiting list to handle the clamor.

The waiting list was part of her strategy. "We wanted to come in and really control branding and distribution," she recalled. "I know it seems like we grew really fast, but there were actually enormous opportunities earlier on that we could have taken advantage of." The company elected to stay out of mass retailers, allowing only a handful of regional chains—Baby Style, Right Start, buybuy BABY, and Neiman Marcus—to carry the Bug. Boiler spent what she said many companies might deem a ridiculous amount of money creating a thirty-two-page brochure for the Bugaboo Gecko. "It's not our goal to spend unnecessarily," she explained. "But we do want to invest in tools we believe in. That means taking a step above the rest and taking different measures from other companies in this category." Each decision positioned the Bugaboo as far superior to any ordinary stroller.

Before the Bug came along, $300 was widely considered to be the maximum anyone would shell out for a workaday item like a baby stroller. Upscale stroller makers such as MacLaren, Peg Perego, and Ingelsina had all kept in sight of the limit. Then Bugaboo turned the entire industry's pricing strategy upside down. "When you think about it, the market for a more expensive stroller was there all along," Ingelsina's Stellario D'Urso pointed out. "You spend 300 on a stroller where you put your little baby, the most precious thing in the world to you. That's how much you spend on a pair of shoes! There's *no comparison* between a stroller and shoes or anything else a woman buys for that amount of money. A stroller lasts for three or four years, it keeps your child safe and comfortable and mobile—and it only costs 300 bucks!" Bugaboo was the first company to perceive this opportunity. "The parents were always there, but nobody was exploiting them. Bugaboo was very persistent, they did a phenomenal marketing job, and they single-handedly changed the market."

According to Boiler, "In the past, the stroller was really a very ordinary object, but when the Bug came along it reinvented not only the product but the entire category. It opened up the possibilities to great design and increased functionality. Now people want more." That "more" includes being able to steer the stroller with one hand while carrying a cellphone, hanging any model of diaper bag on the handle, and having customized accessories like umbrellas, rain covers, and cozies. To Boiler's eye, the alternatives are no competition. "You get what you pay for. We all know when you buy the real thing, you get the real thing. If you go for affordable, inevitably something will be missing. And in the environment we're living in right now, our level of expectation as parents and our understanding of the possibilities means that we all want to be part of the well-designed world."

Just four years after the Bug's American debut, a swarm of designer strollers buzz around metropolitan areas and suburban enclaves. Stokke charges a gob smacking $1,000 for its Xplory, which looks a little like a Bug gone wild and is meant to make "baby and parent happy" by lifting the infant to a higher level, closer to the steering handle. Yummy mummies wheel their infants in $2,800 Silver Cross prams imported from England. Long-standing stroller manufacturers, now considered downscale, have scrambled to compete; Maclaren licensed new fabric designs for its strollers from Burberry, Kate Spade, and Lulu Guinness and commissioned the interior designer Philippe Starck to create a new line. Graco, the reliable standby, offered a limited-edition series designed by Cynthia Rowley. Even rock star Jon Bon Jovi has designed a stroller, the Rock Star Baby, retailing for a cool $499.

The race to sell parents on the latest luxury comfort has manufacturers redesigning their models each year, just like car companies. They refine old features and add new ones, like ergonomic wheel design, angled canopies, recline-adjusts, cup holders, additional storage space, comfort restraint systems, and removable or adjustable handles. They adorn them with features for jogging and bicycling parents. To appeal to parents' hankering for exclusivity, they release "limited editions" like the gold Mamas & Papas stroller, which only ten lucky parents (along with Gwen Stefani) get to own, for $860 each. Ingelsina updated and expanded its line of prams, which now sell for upwards of $730. "With its bassinets, Bugaboo was instrumental in convincing parents that it's better for babies to be lying down during the first few months," D'Urso explained. "Today, we do very well with our prams. It's become fashionable to push a pram." Ingelsina's latest models "address the fashions of the more upscale mother" with modern colors and finishing touches. The company is also contemplating offering a line with faux-fur trim, leather tailoring, and embroidery. Among the parenting set, strollers are the new luxury car. "If we were a car, we would probably be a Mercedes," D'Urso volunteered. "But not a BMW. We're traditional and elegant, not edgy and super-modern."

The emblem of contemporary parenthood, strollers broadcast to the world what kind of parent we are and how we'd like to be perceived. They encapsulate our approach to technology, our aesthetics, our commitment to outdoor life. The brochure for the Dutch-made Mutsy stroller, which retails for $699 and up, doesn't show a single image of a baby. Instead, it features fashion shots of a hipster couple, the man with long sideburns and funky sunglasses, the woman sporting dangly earrings and a high-tech hairstyle. For some parents, having the hot stroller marks them as a comfortable member of the local set—the Peg Perego on the west side of Los Angeles, the Stokke in San Francisco. People pride themselves on having a unique model that catches the attention of passersby. (In our household, we are particularly fond of our Canadian sports stroller, which attracts comments and queries as we whiz through Central Park.) One market research report puts it:

> Strollers are an image-complement when parents are out in the world. Yoga Mommies and those who aspire to be them can wield their choice of some high-tech, upscale stroller brand as a means of expression. Because the plethora of stroller marketers offers so many models finished in so many different fabrics, the would-be trendsetter may feel that her new stroller is virtually customized just for her . . . Oh, and for Baby, too.[1]

IT'S NOT JUST THE BUG, AND IT'S NOT ONLY STROLLERS. THE past ten years have seen an explosion of luxury offerings for the nation's crib consumers, and parents are susceptible to the pitch. When you live a luxury lifestyle before parenthood—as today's often older, wealthier parents often do—it's not easy to walk by a Bonpoint boutique without sighing over the French designer's delicate frocks or to resist impeccably designed, hand-carved European toys, each a little sculpture begging to perch charmingly on a toddler's bookshelf. Why not splurge on a nursery that complements the taste and effort that have gone into the rest of your home?

Popular culture extols the luxury baby life with its relentless coverage of celebrity offspring, Hollywood baby mania surpasses even the celebrity wedding craze. In the summer of 2006, *People* magazine issued a special summer-long newsstand edition called "Babies of the Year," which featured the progeny of Gwyneth, Brooke, Donald, and Denise on its baby-pink cover. When *Vanity Fair* published photographs of Suri Cruise, both the *CBS Evening News* and the *Today Show* gave the "event" extensive screen time. *People* magazine charged a dollar extra for its issue with Shiloh Jolie-Pitt, hallowed offspring of Angelina Jolie and Brad Pitt, on the cover. It still became a bestseller.

Celebrity coverage pays off for the parenting industry. When baby Shiloh appeared in *People,* the crumpled gray T-shirt she was wearing became an instant best seller, too. You could plug the words *Shiloh baby shirt* into Google and find dozens of outlets selling the $42 distressed "pots-and-pans band" sensation. The shirt's designer, Kingsley Aarons, told *USA Today*, "Everyone's claiming that they're responsible for sending them their 'gift package' because they want publicity."[2] Belly, a Denver boutique, claimed to have sent Jolie the shirt along with some maternity clothes several months earlier. Rivals sneered that it wasn't necessarily clear that Belly was responsible for the *actual* T-shirt adorning the infant Jolie-Pitt.

Manufacturers and their publicists are so eager to spread the word about which celebrities are using their products that they shower pregnant celebrities with free car seats and diaper bags, send breathless press releases to editors of parenting magazines, and then pray the celebrity tot in question will be photographed sporting their particular design. The products editor at *BabyTalk* magazine described how one stroller manufacturer accosted her at the ABC Kids Expo in Las Vegas to proclaim that Jennifer Garner had selected its model stroller in blue for her daughter, Violet, as yet unborn. "There have to be ten companies that have already sent her strollers, hoping that theirs will be photographed with her," the editor marveled. "I'm afraid mothers will think that it's the best, safest stroller because Jen is using it when, in reality, it's the one closest to the door when she walks out of the house."[3]

In 2005, trade magazine *Children's Business* cited the "Celebrity Baby Boom" as a major industry trend. With media focused squarely on the celebrity set, it's no wonder vendors of kidswear and gear are itching to get their product in the hands of a Hollywood mom. When the likes of Kate Hudson are spotted wielding a particular toy car, sales spike. As Fred Segal's resident celebrity expert Stacy Robinson put it, "Celebrity babymania is impacting the business in ways it never has before."[4] Copying celebrity baby purchases is relatively easy. While many of us admire celebrity living rooms in *InStyle* and long for the fashions shown on the red carpet, few can afford to hire an interior designer or drop thousands of dollars on couture. What we *can* do is spring for the somewhat less expensive (yet still pricey—who are we kidding?) items that celebrities give their babies. It's a lot easier to rationalize buying a $35 onesie (even though three-packs at Target cost less than ten bucks) than charging $2,000 for Kate Moss's handbag. After all, it's not for us, it's for our *child.*

When celebrities aren't scooping up items for free, they're giving things to other celebrities, upping the ante on gift giving as well. Kelly Ripa gave Suri Cruise a pair of Roberto Cavalli Ballerina Swarovski crib shoes ($114)! Gwyneth's baby Moses received knit baby overalls from designer Bella Bliss! On her popular talk show, Ellen DeGeneres presents custom-designed strollers to lucky celebrity guests. Suri Cruise's stroller carriage is decked out like a pink airplane in homage to Tom Cruise's flying hobby. The Trump heir received a golden carriage complete with marble bottom and crystal chandelier. Giving a best friend a little Baby Gap outfit at her shower has never seemed so insignificant.

. . .

WHEN THE WEALTHY GIVE MORE TO THEIR KIDS, IT DRIVES
everyone's costs up. "Any rational marketer can instantly see that
the demand for ultra-expensive kids' products . . . is necessarily limited; yet the same marketer will recognize that the niche is highly
important for its influence on a vast portion of the [baby] business,"
explains a market research report.[5] The *InStyle*-ization of parenthood means that the entire category of children's goods is influenced by a small number of luxury consumers. As Steve Granville,
cofounder of the luxury brand Fleurville, told *Time* magazine,
"Modern design may only represent 5% of the children's furniture
market, but it's a very influential segment of the market."[6]

Parents are increasingly cost-*in*sensitive when it comes to pam-
pering the little ones. *BusinessWeek* describes an emerging class of
middle- and upper-income mothers who, "no matter their income . . . spend like lottery winners on their babies and toddlers. In
the process, they're revolutionizing the baby-products market and
forcing manufacturers and retailers of all sizes to adjust." Said Tim-
othy Dowd, a senior analyst at the market research firm Packaged
Facts, "This group is influencing other moms who have money and
plenty of moms who don't. Yoga Mama is pumping up sales across
the board."[7] In a 2006 survey of parents with children under twelve,
65 percent admitted they often indulge their children with extras,
and 70 percent said they want to provide their children with things
they didn't have when they were children. The luxury segment of
the infant, toddler, and preschool market alone is worth $14.5 bil-
lion in apparel and $1.6 billion in shoes, according to consumer
strategist Michael Silverstein of the Boston Consulting Group.

Spending has increased on baby goods not only in expected markets, like New York and Los Angeles, but also in places like Bethesda,
Maryland, where parents spend an average of $300 on infant cloth-
ing, and Newton, Massachusetts, where they spend $282, compared
with the nationwide average of $136.[8] Alongside celebrity babies,

Children's Business named "luxe" one of its twenty big developments of 2005, reporting, "As a growing pocket of American consumers becomes more affluent, the consumer base for Luxe is no
longer concentrated in Beverly Hills, Palm Beach and Manhattan: it's
everywhere."[9] That trend has been captured in the subscription lists
for *Cookie* magazine, which has found 22 percent of its readers in
the Midwest, 28 percent in the South and Southwest, and only 10
percent and 13 percent in New York and California, respectively.[10]

At the 2006 M2Moms: Marketing to Moms conference,
Stephanie Ouyoumjian, a senior vice president of the marketing
firm Publicis USA, proclaimed, "What's happening in Wisteria Lane
[the setting of ABC's *Desperate Housewives*] really is happening in
middle America, in terms of demographics. Some of these women
have a tiger in them, and they talk about it with their friends." Ouyoumjian traveled the "fly-over states" to meet and interview women
she dubbed "Main Street moms," who she said are adopting luxury
baby goods just as quickly—if not more so—than moms in New
York and Los Angeles.[11] High-end baby retailers are proliferating
nationwide. In Miami Beach and Miami, the Genius Jones high-end
baby boutiques carry an exclusive miniversion of Mies van der
Rohe's celebrated lounge chair. "The idea behind Genius Jones was
so that parents who really care about design can bring design into all
aspects of their lives, including their life with children," co-owner
Daniel Kron explained on the Fine Living Television Network. He
and his wife, Geane Brito, started their business in 2003 as frustrated new parents who could not find sophisticated household
products for their children. "We had kids a bit later, so we had
money to spend. But the field is dominated by plastic and ply-
wood."[12] Lynne Gonsior, owner of the Minneapolis specialty shop
Über Baby, also stocks high-end designs for babies and toddlers.
"Parents who are looking for high-design in nurseries and even apparel are willing to spend more for their children to do so."[13]

Parents who can't quite afford the purchase of an $800 stroller
have many other opportunities to emulate the baby-styles of the

rich and famous. Everyday essentials have become infused with a designer aesthetic and prices to match. Witness the diaper bag revolution. In 1998, Kate Spade created a $200 diaper bag that became an unexpected bestseller. Since then, other leather goods companies have gotten in on the game. Louis Vuitton, for example, sells a $1,500 diaper bag; Burberry's retails for $495. In 2003, new parents Michael and Ellen Diamant founded the now-multimillion-dollar business Skip Hop on the premise that most diaper bags were still dowdy and unappealing. They have since expanded their line to baby bottle racks, diaper caddies, and baby food jar organizers. "We decided to take products that are under the radar and turn them into objects that are beautiful to look at," said Michael Diamant, one of a new set of "papapreneurs."[14] The most mundane objects of infancy are getting first-class upgrades. A company called Paci Posh sells rhinestone encrusted pacifiers, like the "Diva Bling" for $54.95. Christian Dior offers not only a $40 pacifier, but a $35 logo-covered bottle as well. The formerly functional high chair has gone high style, with a pistil-shaped foam and aluminum high chair in customized colors selling for $925.

Getting parents to upgrade from spend to splurge is a process marketers are tackling with a vengeance, even when it comes to basic supplies as diapers and baby powder. "Can Marketers Spur Demand for Higher-End Supplies?" asks a report geared toward baby-care suppliers. "How do marketers persuade more frazzled parents to 'go premium' when many still view babyhood as a brief stage in which commodity product versions will do?" is the key question. "Creative is the answer," the report explains.

> It is time to bank on the Hipster Baby, the Elegant Baby, to hit the same nerve in parents that the prestige and pop-prestige retail spheres (a la Sephora and Origins, etc.) hit. This will allow forward-thinking parents a bit of style, at the same time reassuring them of superior product formulations, at least according to their own perception.[15]

"What makes parents spend so much money on something that's going to be outgrown in a matter of months?" asked an analyst for NPD Group, a market research firm. "What's happening now is that people are recognizing that it's not about what they need—it's about buying for others. And there's a lot of aspirational spending on the family. We continue to see parents who don't have big incomes buying higher-end items."[16]

Of course, not everyone can afford or rationalize the expense of luxury baby gear. "The really affluent consumer at the top of the economic ladder can afford these things," said Betsy Taylor, cofounder of the New American Dream, a nonprofit organization devoted to responsible consumption, and author of *What Kids Really Want and Money Can't Buy*. "But their behavior affects people further down the socioeconomic ladder who then feel that they're not OK if they're not getting the silk blankets and the theme-driven bedroom."

WE'VE INFUSED THE ACCOUTREMENTS OF MODERN CHILDHOOD with an ethos of parenting that seems to warrant their purchase, and Big Baby has tapped into it wisely. A 2006 market report notes the emergence of "a whole stratum of parents who love their young children, but who dislike, even despise, many of the trappings of parenthood." These new parents

> strive to dress themselves distinctively, and are willing to spend more to make their offspring look just as unique. In fact, their babies themselves have shaped up as an identifiable sector of Hipster Babies or Elegant Babies who are decked out in alternative or upscale fashions . . . A child's stroller or car seat or bed is one more opportunity to flaunt style and lifestyle.[17]

Ali Wing, founder of the upscale retailer Giggle, believes the rise of designer baby goods can be traced to a demographic and what she calls a *psychographic shift*. Earlier generations had children at the same time they were setting up their first home, cultivating their first relationship, and navigating the debut of their professional lives. Today, older, successful parents have a better sense of who they are. They have the "space and maturity" to allocate to the next step of raising children. They want greater personalization and products that enhance their lifestyle. In other words, they are fitting children into already established lives, rather than cobbling new lives around them. Call it *lifestyle parenting*.

Wing compares the marketing to these nouveau parents to the tactics of upscale grocery chain Whole Foods. Whole Foods doesn't merely set out bins of turnips and radishes; it sells people on the idea that fresh root vegetables deliver an authentic culinary experience, one that harkens back to the days when every family had its own carefully tended garden and every good cook knew how to dice the latest harvest into a hearty stew. With folksy signs detailing the agricultural philosophies of local farmers, Whole Foods guides customers through its bright, healthy, sun-kissed aisles of fruit, persuading them they are savvy and environmentally conscious, earthy and cutting-edge. Likewise, the new shopping aesthetic for today's parent sells a particular notion of parenthood: The enlightened modern parent is concerned about her child's emotional development and academic achievement, marketers tell us. She cares equally about functionality and high-concept design; she wants to provide an age-appropriate yet grownup-friendly experience. "What we're doing is selling a lifestyle," Wing said. "Just as with Whole Foods, you map your strategy against a broader set of criteria than just, 'I need food.'" Giggle, which began in San Francisco in 2003 and operates five stores and a website, creates this shopping experience by providing a "curated" assortment of products as well as parenting and baby classes. Calling itself a "one stop shop for today's new parents," Giggle aspires to help parents create a smarter nursery. "Our job is to do the homework for parents. We don't sell everything we could possibly sell you—we offer the best options out there and allow *you* to pick which ones best fit *your* personality and lifestyle."

Wing is very good at this, as she should be: She got her training from marketing powerhouse Nike. "I got lucky to cut my teeth with one of the best brand companies," she explained. "They taught me how to build women's brands and lifestyle brands." She spent seven years there, circulating through various divisions, incubating approaches to new and growing markets, including women. "I loved it, but I also knew that for me, I needed to do more than just tennis shoes." So Wing left Nike and enrolled at Northwestern to pursue law and business degrees simultaneously. Upon graduation, she moved to the Bay Area "because that's where growth was happening." Her first job was with Gazoontite, an allergy and asthma retailer with ten stores, a website, and a catalog. There she noticed an interesting discrepancy: The average customer rang up $100 at the cash register, but if the customer was buying something for children, she spent $350. "I thought, 'Wow, *what* is going on here?'" Wing recalled. "It wasn't just the interest and willingness to spend. What was driving it was this new kind of parent, a parent that was educated and self-directed. These parents had an *agenda*."

To Wing, this new mother was like the "Nike woman," though a bit older and in her next life-stage, and she saw in her an untapped opportunity. Wing's first step was to become a consultant to *Child* and *Parents* magazines, helping them to recognize this "Nike Mom"; after a year, she went out on her own. Giggle began small, in a 1,100-square-foot space. Wing used her first store to test products, concept, and delivery, and then in 2005, set up headquarters in New York City's Soho. Later that year, she opened another New York store, then a fourth store in San Francisco's East Bay, then another in Greenwich, Connecticut, with more in development. "I always get asked, 'Is this just New York and California?' and the answer is, *absolutely not!* This is happening throughout the country; these parents are in St. Louis. And Giggle is going to respond to that."

Unlike many independent boutiques, Giggle isn't overly pre-

cious and clutter-stuffed with *objets d'enfance.* Nor is it a cavernous superstore with floor-to-ceiling shelves of baby gear. Instead, Giggle feels like an interactive exhibit at a children's
museum, expertly laid out to encourage shoppers to touch, desire,
and buy. A stroller parking lot with old-fashioned meters greets
visitors, giving the store a nostalgic Our Town feel. A big old sink
topples over with colorful "luxury ducks," which, unlike the bright
yellow duckies of yore, sport mod-colored polka dots and stripes
and sell for $9 a piece. Furniture is outfitted with upscale Dwell
bedding. Downstairs, there's a "giggleroom" for baby classes and a
parent lounge for local parenting groups. Wing runs focus groups
and market surveys to keep up on parents' latest quirks and priorities; she is determined to crack the specialty parent and nontraditional parent markets as well as those of the dominant modern,
traditional, and bohemian parent subcultures. "I know this will
sound really crazy, but I don't consider Giggle a retailer. I see it as
a *brand solution* for parents."

Giggle is also attuned to one of the most significant and priciest
parent market trends: the move toward environmental and organic
products. Shoppers are offered a tip sheet for creating a healthy
nursery. The company advises parents to choose furniture finished
in non-VOC paints (those containing low or no amounts of toxic
volatile organic compounds), select toys made of naturally finished
wood, and use household cleaners free of ammonia and other
harsh chemicals. Teething toys are fabricated from pesticide- and
chemical-free organic cotton, and many of the store's clothing options are organic. Giggle has even created its own line of organic
bed linens.

Eco-luxury is one of the fastest-growing subsets of the deluxe
market. In stores across the country and especially online, parents
can buy premium bedding made from organic cotton and nursery
furniture built using sustainable methods. For example, after
seven years of success in Great Britain, Natural Mat launched in
the United States in 2007. As its president, Mark Tremlett, told
me, "Everyone is going a bit more green, more eco, but no one in

the U.S. has been doing any innovation in the mattress bedding department for children." Traditionally, mattresses for babies have been covered in plastic and other synthetics, with chemical flame retardants added (including ones linked to cancer and endocrine disruption). Natural Mat's crib mattresses, by contrast, are created with lamb's wool, organic coir made from coconut husks and natural latex, horsetail, and mohair and wrapped in recycled packaging.

According to Tremlett, "The green movement is building quite quickly in the states, and a lot of people are trying to get into it. It's one of the biggest consumer trends going on at the moment." A 2007 survey by Babycenter found that more than half of moms say they've become more eco-friendly since having children. Sales of organic baby food were $235 million in 2006, up 14 percent and organic baby formula sales rose 25 percent between 2005 and 2006. The Organic Trade Association tallied 2005 retail sales in the baby personal-care category at $26 million, up 34 percent from 2004. A 2005 market research report on the baby-care industry cites the "natural sphere" as the most exciting arena for higher-priced supplies. "Not to seem cynical," notes the report, "but there is plenty of dollar potential in catering to consumers' fears of unhealthy or outright dangerous traditional products. Shrewd marketers should ask themselves how to make disposables more environmentally friendly; how to replace breathable, cancer-causing talc-based powers; and how to replace the petroleum or harsh chemical components." The report goes on to say that even the old-fangled giants of the diaper-wipe business have "at least made some compromises" to appeal to the eco-market.[18] Cynical or not, the move toward healthier and more environmentally responsible baby gear and clothing is a positive if pricey development. "Green is the new luxury," confirmed Julia Beck, founder of the consultancy Forty Weeks.

ONCE UPON A TIME, THE NURSERY SERVED AS THE FAMILY dumpster, a repository for unsightly hand-me-down furniture and drool-encrusted plastic playthings. It was where things got thrown around and trampled upon, kicked, pushed, tossed aside, spat up on, pooped on, Crayola'd all over, torn into little shreds, and then gathered into a smelly clump upon which a milk bottle could slowly leak out its contents. No longer. The new nursery is a set design for baby, streamlined into the rest of the house's decor in accordance with parents' design sensibilities.

Today, people spend more on nurseries than they do on any other room in the house. Though the number of children five and under has remained relatively stable over the past seven years, the amount spent on decorating nurseries is climbing. Retail sales of infant, toddler, and preschool (ITP) furnishings and accessories surpassed $8 billion in 2005, up 5.2 percent from 2004, and are expected to increase to nearly $9 billion by 2010.[19] Market research firm Packaged Facts attributes the growth to parents' new emphasis on protectiveness and closeness, which, it explain, makes "American parents beautifully susceptible to ITP home furnishings accessories marketers' 'up-to-date designs'—style, high-tech materials, innovation, etc." At least seven hundred companies sell infant, toddler, and preschool home furnishings and accessories in the United States;[20] collectively, they spend nearly $30 million on advertising a year.[21]

Traditional purveyors of nursery furniture are being replaced by boutique start-ups and expensive importers. The takeover began in 2000, when Stokke, the high-end Norwegian design firm, began exporting its ultrahip baby gear. First the compact KinderZeat, a $200 baby chair that its customers cherish ("Please don't say anything bad about the KinderZeat!" one mother implored me), made plastic high chairs feel clunky and shopworn. Next the company brought over the Stokke Sleepi, a $1,000 oval bassinet that converts to crib, toddler bed, junior bed, and finally into two chairs, a coup de grâce against every form of thrify baby furniture. With double-digit growth in U.S. sales each year, Stokke's northern European design aesthetic has permeated nursery design.

"Stokke has been an inspiration to me," said David Netto, owner and designer of the Netto Collection, a line of luxury modern baby furniture. "They showed that in the right atmosphere, where there's a sympathetic climate to the idea, modern baby furniture could be successful."

Celebrated interior designers like Netto are creating their own lines of children's furnishings. Like other entrepreneurs, he experienced the paucity of modern baby design after the birth of his first child, in 2001. Two years later, when he attended the Juvenile Products Manufacturers Association show in Dallas, he realized why the design landscape looked so bleak. "There was this completely disconnected quilt of disparate players in the industry without any coherent aesthetic," he recalled. "It was clear that it had been a *long* time since any aesthetic standards had been imposed on children's stuff, and I just knew there was an opportunity for someone. And I was right. Because here we are three years later."

The Netto Collection launched with a decidedly upscale client in mind. "The philosophy has been, 'It's so beautiful it hurts,'" Netto said. "I'm charging the *most* money I could look anyone in the eye and ask them to pay for a crib." Manufacturing is done on a near-custom basis in Europe. Finishes are labor intensive. Special areas in the factory are set aside so that the fancy spray lacquer can dry without the smallest speck of dust flitting down to mar the crib surfaces. Even without the benefit of a public relations firm, word about Netto's impeccable new collection spread. Then he struck baby luxe gold: Out of the blue, Gwyneth Paltrow cold-called the atelier and bought a set of furniture in the spring of 2004. Shortly thereafter, European fashion designer Valentino bought Paltrow the same set as a gift. Sure enough, *People* magazine got wind of the story and published a picture of the collection. "That was the luckiest thing that could have happened," Netto confessed. Since then, Heath Ledger, Rachel Weisz, Christy Turlington, and Mariska Hargitay have become customers. Jessica Seinfeld talked up the line to the *Wall Street Journal.* "It was easy to guess what these celebrities were buying because what else would they buy?" Netto said. "We were kind of like a couture house where people would come visit us in the studio and order directly from there."

Exclusivity didn't last long. Just four years after its debut, the Netto Collection faced rival start-ups in the market for luxury nursery design. Netto divides his competition into two categories: skilled furniture designers—entrepreneurs like Oeuf and Web sites like Modern Seed—and what he calls "the venture copycat stuff," aka DucDuc, the embodiment of corporate skill applied to the luxury baby market. DucDuc founder and CEO Philip Erdoes, a venture capitalist who has started companies in such diverse areas as film production and overnight delivery services, assembled a creative team that included an architect who had worked with Ralph Lauren and John Varvatos and an experienced interior designer. DucDuc put forth what it calls a four-part philosophy to parents to "share your sensibilities" and develop a child's "aesthetic personality." "A lot of people in the business used to treat nurseries as throwaway," Erdoes told me. "I don't think manufacturers thought there was much money that could be spent on something that would be gotten rid of in two years. But I saw the growth in the luxury market during the 1990s and so decided to go higher end. The way I see it, there are three major trends going on: babies, contemporary/modern design, and luxury—and we're at the nexus of all three." Of course, the way David Netto sees it, DucDuc is "an engineered brand by some venture capitalists who identified a major opportunity" rather than an organic project created by designers and architects.

Whether inspired by artistes or prodded by MBAs, many parents are going mod for their tots, a reflection of Gen X parents' hipster aesthetic. As Laura Wear, co-owner of the nursery-gear start-up Nest, said, "We invested a lot of time and money in design for our living space, but we couldn't find a lot of furniture designs for kids that mingled with our look. Our first idea was to create a toy box that was good looking, simple, and clean enough to mesh with everything else in our living room." Other manufacturers echo that approach, at least in their branding campaigns. Oeuf promotes its products with the line "Good Design for all Ages," and throughout the modern nursery online universe, sites like Modernmini, Babygeared, and ModernSeed display the smooth lines and crisp colors of 1950s American chic. Sparkability offers "better things for kids" like the Svan bouncer ($119), a brown and orange bouncy seat with an early 1960s aesthetic that eschews the toylike features of Fisher-Price's Crayola blue Ocean Wonders Aquarium bouncer.

But it's not enough for these companies to go after a narrow base of wealthy consumers. Because purchase patterns demonstrate that even less well-off parents spring for pricier goods when it comes to their children, marketers consider "mass luxury" the way to ensure long-term profitability. The business model involves spurring middle-income parents to spend more than they ordinarily would by creating "bridge lines" of furniture and accessories— mini-DKNYs for those who can't afford Donna Karan. DucDuc, for example, is planning a line of "lower priced" cribs to get parents who would ordinarily spend $200 on a crib at Target to spring for a $500 or $600 crib instead. David Netto hopes his CUB collection will succeed with the same market. "We spent two to three years establishing visibility for our brand," he explained. "We created a flagship line, as if Hermès had a baby furniture collection. Having done that and remained exclusive in terms of distribution, we're now going to go into a lower market, which will charge less than $500 a crib. CUB will be more humble." Of course, it will still have its aesthetic and its storyline. Netto sees CUB as the nursery embodiment of Sculptor Donald Judd's minimalist pinewood creations in Marfa, Texas. Playful but austere, and very much in tune with their natural surroundings.

THE NEW YOGA MOMMIES, ALTERNADADS, HIPSTER PARENTS, and Elegant Babies naturally need their own magazine, and that job fell to Condé Nast, publisher of *Vogue, Glamour,* and *GQ.* In a landscape dominated by broad-appeal magazines like *Parents* and *Parenting,* there were no parenting magazines for the subscribers of *Vanity Fair* and *Gourmet.* After talking to mothers within the company, a magazine concept for a more affluent, more educated consumer, *Cookie,* was test-marketed to a million people between the ages of twenty-five and forty-four. The response was one of the highest Condé Nast had ever seen. "When we launched, there was this reaction like, 'I could have had a V8!'" recalled Eva Dillon, then the vice president and publisher of *Cookie.* "It was so obvious. The women's magazine category already has so many choices and options, but in this area, it was wide open." *Cookie* debuted on newsstands in 2005 with a blitz of publicity. In one advertisement promoting the magazine, a model mommy sheathed in a ruffled Balenciaga-esque gown sat with legs sprawled in a magnificently appointed nursery, her baby son glowing, a $750 Stokke crib set artfully in the background. "All the best for your family," promised the headline. A direct-mail piece seeking subscribers described *Cookie* as "the magazine for sophisticated parents." The solicitation I received, along with thousands of other new mothers on the same mailing list, opened with, "You enjoy the best in life for yourself, and you want the same for your children."

Dillon bristles at the accusation that *Cookie* is only for the well-off. "There's a complete double standard. Other magazines depict an aspirational lifestyle, but for whatever reason, when the topic is family, everyone wants to show only the attainable and real. The reality is that you *can* have a nicer lifestyle and still have a warm message about the needs and interests of the family. *Cookie* says very explicitly, 'It's OK to have a life," and describes itself as a lifestyle magazine for parents, not a parenting magazine. "With parenting magazines, the message is very negative," Dillon said. "It's ten ways your child can get a head injury. Our message is, here are ten luxury vacations to take with your child." Why should magazines scold parents for caring about things other than their children?

"There's no other magazine that's as high end as ours, but that's not the thrust, it's the gravy," explained Pilar Guzman, *Cookie*'s charismatic editor in chief. If anything, Guzman added, "I have this stealth green mission. Our reader is a little chic, but also a little crunchy. I mean, I live in Park Slope! So there's the Brooklyn mom shopping at the co-op reflected in our pages as well. The thrust is, don't forget yourself. Our reader is someone who is doing things her own way, but also looking for a bit of a road map. We're not terribly dogmatic."

Cookie reads less as a manual and more as a model of inspiration, with brilliantly designed spreads of nurseries and childhood trimmings. The articles are smart, well-written, and grown-up—even when the focus is on childish matters. "There has historically been this divide between woman and mother," Guzman told me. "We're saying, there doesn't have to be." When you read *Cookie*, you don't fear you'll turn into the parents in its pages; they're not harried, fearful, or trapped in the house with a child who has multiple needs and neuroses. Instead, they are calm, confident, and wearing Armani. You *want* to be like those parents. "Every time I open one of the parenting magazines, I always find something interesting to read, but it also makes me feel bad," Guzman said. "We didn't want women to feel guilty for not doing the fifty things a parenting magazine tells them to do every time they opened *Cookie*."

Parents out there need this kind of magazine, emphasized Dillon. She rolled off a list of promising statistics: Twenty-two million households with annual incomes of $75,000 or more have children under age eleven. The upscale baby market is $45 billion. Sales of children's furniture, gear, strollers, and car seats jumped 60 percent between 1998 and 2007. Yet no magazine had been providing the companies selling these goods with a targeted place to advertise. Now *Cookie* does. Upon launch, the magazine promised and delivered an initial circulation of 300,000. In 2007, it raised circulation to 350,000, and the magazine expected to raise its circula-

tion again and increase its frequency from bimonthly to ten issues
a year in 2008. Companies such as Lexus, Cadillac, Gucci, and
Burberry—brands you won't find in *Fit Pregnancy*—have all ad-
vertised in its pages.

Cookie fortuitously landed at the precise moment when parenting became hip. "Five years ago, celebrities wouldn't advertise
the fact that they had kids," Dillon said. "It was uncool, unsexy. It
wasn't part of their PR. Today, children are the coolest thing any
celebrity could have. For better or for worse, parenthood is the
coolest it's ever been." In *Vogue* and *W,* babies substitute for ciga-
rettes as the model's quintessential photogenic accessory. Advertisements for items as diverse as shoes and bottled water feature
infants. Babies are all the rage. "A baby is not an accessory, exactly,
but when you go outside with a baby, all eyes go to the baby," explained Jessica Hartshorn, senior lifestyle editor at *American
Baby* magazine. "All of the sudden, it's not so important to spend
as much money on yourself—you spend on the baby."[22]

Anyone strolling through an upscale neighborhood in America
can see the elevation of infant to status symbol. Children's boutiques sit alongside men's and women's high fashion stores in
America's shopping meccas. Lucy Sykes Rellie, a socialite and children's clothing designer, calls it the *mini-me syndrome:* "There are
so many yuppie families like us who want to project their own image onto their children. They want babies to be sophisticated."[23] It
also works the other way around: "I know I've got something right
when a mommy says, 'Oh, make one for me!' "[24] Many of these
boutiques make no apologies about being ultraexpensive; if anything, the haughty price is the allure. In 2004, a former Giorgio
Armani executive went so far as to open a store called Trust Fund
Baby in New York and Atlantic City and plans to expand to Scotts-
dale, Arizona.

Such stores have no shortage of merchandise to sell. "Fashionista mommies, take heart," decreed *Footwear News* in 2005. "A
new wave of footwear for babies is under way, thanks to adult

brands that are typically known for their high heels, retro sneakers, and comfort looks. Today, they're sizing down to babies' feet, making moms willing to fork out the big bucks for the trendy looks."[25] The numbers reflect such predictions. Overall U.S. sales of infant, toddler, and preschool clothing reached nearly $17 billion by the end of 2005, up 17 percent from 2001. Sales are expected to keep climbing through 2010, to more than $20 billion.[26] According to the *Wall Street Journal,* parents are spending adult prices on jeans for their babies; Paper Denim & Cloth jeans make up 20 percent of Barney's toddler apparel sales.[27] Trendy designers like Juicy Couture, Calypso, Paul & Joe, Tocca, Guess, Diesel, and Roca Wear have launched lines for children, with jeans retailing for more than $100 a pair. Hollywood cult brand True Religion's baby jeans sell for a cool $195. "People are really into that mommy-daughter kind of thing," explained Juicy Couture's co-founder Gela Nash-Taylor.[28]

Formerly composed of hand-me-downs and bargain basement pickups, clothing for preschool is now a prime shopping opportunity. Paul Kurnit, president of the consulting firm KidShop, speculates that after spending so much time and money getting their kids into a top preschool, parents want to make sure their children look up to snuff when they get there. "Back-to-preschool has become a major shopping event," said Kurt Barnard, president of Barnard's Retail Consulting Group.

When designer Marc Jacobs found himself surrounded by the new offspring of friends like edgy fashion photographer Juergen Teller and artist Rachel Feinstein, "We thought, 'Wouldn't it be nice to do cashmere pieces for kids?' Thermals are so standard, and the idea of taking something banal and elevating it to a luxurious level is always great." While dressing children in head-to-toe designer clothing is "tacky," Jacobs doesn't think "there's anything wrong with giving a young kid a taste of the finer things in life, and instilling value, so long as they're taught how to take care of those things." Whether a two-year-old has any sense of how to care for a quality garment, and what it means to buy something so valuable when it will last only a few months, is open to debate. But Jacobs thinks parents are ready to take the plunge. "I can't imagine any of my friends not wanting to spoil their kids rotten."[29] The first year of his collection was so successful, Jacobs quickly expanded into a line of pint-sized T-shirts and jeans, and he is now creating a full-blown "bridge" collection to include shoes and other accessories.

Among the changes in children's wear is the near total disappearance of gender-neutral clothing. You used to be able to buy a red turtleneck that would suit a boy or a girl. Today, the girl's version has a pink heart on the sleeve; the boy's sports a football logo. Unembellished jeans or corduroys to fit either sex are impossible to find. The boy's version is extrabaggy with rugged-hewn edges; the girl's has a pink lining or a flourish of squiggles on the trim. BabyGap practically has a trench line laid down between the sexes. Parents are forced to purchase one of each for either child, making survival on hand-me-downs much less easy. Children's clothing has also begun to reflect the ceaseless whirl of shifting fashions endemic to adult clothing; people have begun to think of children's fashion in terms of collections and seasons, not sizes. And children's clothes aren't cheap. Even a relatively utilitarian wardrobe from BabyGap can set parents back $15,375 over the course of a child's first five years.[30]

High-end women's wear designers like Dolce & Gabbana, Giorgio Armani, Donna Karan, Versace, Moschino, Roberto Cavalli, Tommy Hilfiger, Burberry, and Escada have all launched baby lines because melding the worlds and prices of adult's and children's fashion makes business sense. "Kids' wear gives us the perfect opportunity to attract younger customers," explained Escada's designer to *WWD* magazine. "We can make kids into Escada fans who love the products from early on and we also can attract young mothers who maybe are not aware of how much Escada has changed."[31] While it's more often parents than children who seek brand-name shopping experiences for the pre-K set, children are nonetheless influenced by their parents' shopping. Studies have shown that children as young as one recognize brand names. "In general, the awareness of fashion is getting younger and younger," noted *Cookie's* Pilar Guzman. "Just as we've seen in the teen market, the interest in clothes is fashion- and celebrity-driven, and that interest has been trickling down."[32] Fashion-forward Manhattan boutique Scoop recently opened a children's offshoot, with the tagline "Starting young."

AT CITIBABES, AN EXCLUSIVE CLUB FOR PARENTS IN NEW YORK City, I am received by the security guard at as I would be by the maître'd of a four-star restaurant had I arrived barefoot and with body odor. It is made very clear that I do not belong. I do not have the necessary membership card, so I am shunted aside as lip-glossed mothers with sleek blond ponytails and Tibetan nannies push past me, their charges squealing and kicking in high-tech strollers. To rightfully enter Citibabes (for "We Parents and Wee Children") and indulge in its privileges, one must pay $2,000 for an annual membership, plus $6,250 for the "unlimited" package—which includes spa services, fitness classes, children's classes, adult classes, and childcare; otherwise, it's à la carte, and the services aren't cheap.

Cost, however, is not an obstacle for most Citibabes parents, who may join only if referred by an existing member. Of course, if you can get past its advisory board, composed of New York City's parental elite—a clatter of top fashion magazine editors, designers, mogul wives, and society names, including Brooke and Gwyneth—the assumption is you can afford it. As with Soho House, a private and pricey social club imported from London to New York, if you're not on the list, you are clearly unworthy.

Which is exactly how I felt until the guard at Citibabes's entrance verified that I was a journalist with an appointment. After being allowed into the club's spacious interior, I was welcomed as "one of us" by cofounders, Tracey Frost Rensky and Tara Gordon Lipton. Garbed in loose-fitting gym clothes, pregnant, and reeling with morning sickness, I felt *nothing* like one of them. Frost Rensky and Gordon Lipton look like the kind of moms many women secretly (or not-so-secretly) aspire to be: Slim and attractive, with long blonde hair (no mom-cuts here) and glowing complexions, they are flawlessly groomed and calmly confident; neither has spit-up on her shoulders. Despite having given birth only weeks before, Gordon Lipton was neatly tucked into a pair of dark skinny jeans and a close-fitting top. They each resemble, in fact, the Citibabes logo, which showcases the leggy silhouette of a super-model mom steering a sleek stroller, presumably into a blissful future of top-tier preschools and family vacations abroad.

Gordon Lipton and Frost Rensky were each working on similar ideas for a deluxe baby club when they were introduced by mutual friends and teamed up. (A third partner subsequently dropped out of the venture for reasons they won't discuss.) Since she was not a mother herself when she began contemplating Citibabes (though she has a daughter now), Frost Rensky, an Australian who used to work in finance, concentrated on the parent component of the club. Gordon Lipton, a born and bred-at-the-best-schools New Yorker with a master's degree in early childhood education from the prestigious Bank Street College and two children of her own, took on the child aspects of the enterprise. "As a mother, I knew what the classes out there were like," she explained. "The spaces were below average, even on the Upper East Side. Some of them weren't really classes; they were just entertainment. That's just not what I wanted to go for, and my friends didn't want that either." The goal of Citibabes is to create a place where parents don't have to choose between doing things for themselves and doing something for their children. "Now parents can do both, in a stylish and sophisticated environment," the sleek, spiral-bound membership packet promises.

Frost Rensky and Gordon Lipton ushered me around the

ten-thousand-square-foot loft space, which occupies the full floor
of one of Soho's trademark cast-iron buildings. It reminded me a
bit of Kidville, but where Kidville is sparkly, Citibabes is more
subdued. It actually *feels* more exclusive. The interior is open and
immaculate, a refuge from the gritty sidewalks outside. Architects
Garrett Gourlay and Michael Etzel, creators of the elegant
Equinox Fitness Clubs, envisioned "a modern space that appeals
to the visual and tactile sense of young children" while retaining
the urban aesthetic of their parents. Design group Falcon Perspectives, developers of the Children's Museum of Manhattan,
created the indoor playground. To further divide city from
Citibabes, there is twenty-four-hour security surveillance and a
photo ID system. The entire staff has submitted to extensive background checks by famed private investigator Bo Dietl, a much-
decorated former police officer whose autobiography was turned
into a movie starring Stephen Baldwin.[33]

"As you can see, it's like a country club," Gordon Lipton said.
"You can do everything here." On one end is a lounge furnished
with fashion magazines, business services, and wireless Internet
access; a chic little spa, which offers pedicures, waxing, and hair-
styling; and an exercise room outfitted with the latest equipment
and multiple flat-screen TVs. Members can hire a personal trainer
or facialist while booking "child minding" services. The spa can be
hired out for Little Girls' Manicure Parties. Experts are called in
on a regular basis to lead parenting classes, family wellness seminars, lunchtime lectures, and trunk shows exhibiting the latest in
children's fashion. Classrooms and playrooms line the halls and
open into a huge 1,500-square-foot indoor playground. (As a point
of comparison, most New York City two-bedroom apartments
measure in at around 1,100 square feet.) Inside the playground,
padding covers the floors, which are divided into "activity cir-
cuits," with slides, trampolines, retro ride-on toys, a pretend
greenmarket, and a tree house. At the other end of the club is a
café; behind the stroller parking lot, a luxury boutique is filled with

children's clothing, toys, and baby-care accessories—"the best of the best," as Gordon Lipton described it.

Vibrant, custom-painted murals line several walls, and the bathrooms are outfitted with children's-sized toilets, changing tables, and diaper essentials. Early in the morning, the place already hums with the patter of toddler footsteps and sing-songy preschool teacher voices. By eleven o'clock, the vast stroller park is bumper-to-bumper Bugaboos and sport utility strollers. On the morning of my visit, between fifteen and twenty babies were tumbling around the indoor play area; almost all were accompanied by nannies. Two mothers were chatting in front of the clothing boutique, while their toddlers squirmed in their strollers.

"Charlotte is so funny," said the first mother. "She's so into clothes! She's like, 'I like this shirt.'" Affecting a toddler's voice, she pretended to hold a blouse up to her chest. "So adorable!"

"I *love* the name Charlotte," the other mother replied.

Beside them, a rack of clothing held a $90 cotton tank dress for toddlers by Shirin. A $300 girl's shirt with toile at the shoulders hung next to a $380 blouse with an embroidered bird on the front. Inside were baby clothes designed by Marie-Chantal (one of the Hong Kong duty-free Miller heiresses, married to Prince Pavlos of Greece) and Lucy Sykes Rellie (sister of Plum and a social force in her own right), and boys' seersucker jackets. (In winter, the store stocks fur vests for children and $225 chenille sweaters.) There was a lovely selection of children's books, upscale wooden toys, dolls, and puzzles. A $110 price tag dangled from a rather fetching toy mouse. Baby toiletries from Arbonne, Doctor Bobby, and Cutler lined the shelves.

At the gourmet café, I spotted still more nannies, with the exception of three highlighted mothers at a corner table, their babies fast asleep in strollers beside them. Ravenous in that first-trimester way, I gobbled down my complimentary gourmet lunch and was not disappointed. In addition to homemade baby food by Evie's Organic Edibles, Mini Meals (banana jammer, pretend sushi), and the Toddler à la Carte menu, which featured $2 prepacked containers of fruit, mozzarella cubes, Organic O's, and the like, a full menu of grown-up salads and sandwiches is available.

Many of the assorted minders—nannies and otherwise— seemed to know each other, which is not surprising, considering it's a private club. "Everyone is two degrees of Kevin Bacon," one board member, who attended the exclusive all-girls' prep school Spence with Gordon Lipton, told W magazine. "There's no one there that's totally random."[34] As another founding mother put it, "Motherhood is not enough to forge a friendship. There's this whole idea of 'we bore fruit so let's be best friends,' but with this club, proximity will bring intimacy. It makes the pool a lot smaller than every mom pushing a Bugaboo on Madison."[35] Gordon Lipton defended the membership policy explaining, "The 'real world' has so many cliques—because everyone here is a few degrees of separation apart, there's an automatic sense of community." She said the club's exclusivity is premised on security. "We did a lot of focus groups, and that's what our market wanted. They wanted it to be safe. In New York City, you can't just walk off the street and walk into Citibabes." This is an assurance voiced by numerous children's facilities in the city, as if the streets of New York, the safest large city in the country, were teeming with kidnappers, sexual predators, and other unsavory characters bent on defiling the local zero-to-three population. One wonders whether the children of the elite ever get to play in public playgrounds or parks, or if those are deemed too risky.

Gordon Lipton and Frost Rensky have rightly identified the allure of closed doors. While there is an application form on the Citibabes website, the club is full at six hundred families and has a waiting list. In order to accommodate additional worthies, the owners are actively searching for venues to extend the club's franchise; the Upper East Side, Upper West Side, and Los Angeles are probable locations.

With its comprehensive services and top-of-the-line facility,

Citibabes has an obvious appeal, to those who can afford it. A pregnant woman can purchase a $2,000 "prenatal membership" that offers "$1,000 worth of products and services," including a prenatal spa class, childbirth preparation classes, a private training fitness assessment, unlimited yoga and exercise classes for one month, free parenting books, and discounts from Liz Lange and the Netto Collection. For the child, Gordon Lipton explained, the club's benefits are enormous, especially in a city where most families are confined to apartments without backyards. Gordon Lipton emphasized the sense of community among the club's children. "They make friends in a warm, nurturing environment. And they get to know the place very well," she noted. Plus there are educational benefits. "Children are exposed to all these classes at Citibabes, classes which set the foundation for learning for life. At Citibabes, children learn life lessons."

IT IS IMPORTANT TO QUESTION WHAT "LIFE LESSONS" CHILDREN learn at an exclusive junior country club, because Citibabes is part of a growing nationwide trend. More parents are paying to keep their children out of playgrounds and informal playgroups and instead enrolling in upscale clubs and corporate play areas.

Certainly, the trend is most sharply visible in New York City. In the past ten years, parenting in New York has been transformed by profound social, cultural, and economic changes. The incomes of upper-class households have grown exponentially while the middle class has been edged out, and rich Manhattanites are having more and more kids. The under-five population in Manhattan rose an astonishing 26 percent between 2000 and 2004, even though, according to the Census Bureau, the borough's population rose only 1.5 percent overall. Real estate brokers report that the properties most in demand are three-, four-, and five-bedroom apartments.

The landscape of kiddie-size New York City has been altered

by this influx of well-to-do children. Music classes, junior soccer leagues, and kindergartens fill months in advance, driving up prices. Strollers jam the boutique-lined sidewalks of Madison Avenue and the crooked walkways of Greenwich Village. Tribeca, home to multimillion-dollar lofts, has been dubbed Triburbia, and even the snootiest women's clothing boutiques in the area devote part of their stores to a selection of chic infant clothing. One storeowner whose shop primarily sells Japanese gift items told me that it's impossible to run a store in the neighborhood without selling baby goods. "Every store people come into, they expect to find something cute they can pick up for their baby," she explained. "I had no intention of stocking this kind of thing, but to not do so, you risk alienating the neighborhood residents. It's insane!"

But New York is hardly alone in being consumed by baby shopping mania. In Los Angeles, there's Nana's Garden, a spa, boutique, and café where parents can play while their children are entertained under the same roof. Located in West Hollywood and founded by actress Joely Fisher, her sister, and their actress mother, Connie Stevens, Nana's Garden boasts celebrity fans like Laura Dern, Jenny McCarthy, and Ricki Lake. For $90 a month, members can use the spa and eat in the café while their children are tended by babysitters onsite or enrolled in activities. Clubs that have succeeded in New York are developing extensions so that parents in San Francisco, Chicago, and other metropolitan areas can enjoy the baby luxe life.

Clearly, people who indulge their babies with cashmere blankets and car-shaped beds don't set out to harm their kids. That parents want to give of themselves to their children is, of course, a wonderful instinct. That motherhood and fatherhood alike are currently celebrated in popular culture is a positive step, and it would be difficult to imagine that we could treasure our children too much. Yet many Americans have started to fetishize children and family in ways that aren't particularly healthy. Parents today not only photograph and videotape children incessantly but also dress them up and surround them with exquisite objects, spending unconscionable amounts of money adorning them for themselves and others to admire. Instead of sending out simple birth announcements, we create elaborate, personalized mailings complete with photo collages; in lieu of passing out cigars, we customize golf balls emblazoned with our baby's name, birth date, and weight or send out little packets of pink "It's a girl!" Jelly Belly jelly beans.[36] We devote entire websites and meticulously recorded blogs to every burp and articulation. Making home movies is a classic, universal family ritual that has been gussied up into an artistic endeavor. One company, Hello Beautiful Films, offers parents the opportunity to create professionally filmed and artfully edited movies of their babies for $1,000. For $3,500 more, parents can hire acclaimed documentarian Albert Mayles to shoot the film. Even if you go for the lower-priced package, co-owner Bianca Nejat told me, "we really try to make it look like a piece of art."

This cult of parenthood is something psychologists and other parenting professionals have observed with growing alarm. "You want to make sure a child isn't under the impression that every movement of his life is worthy of memorializing," said Madeline Levine, a psychologist and author of *The Price of Privilege,* an examination of the negative effects of affluent parenting. "Children may grow up to view normal missteps as glaring and unacceptable."[37]

Lisa Spiegel, cofounder of the Soho Parenting Center in New York City, has been working with parents for more than twenty years. After getting her master's in developmental psychology from Columbia, she worked at Bellevue Hospital in New York City, giving parenting classes to teenage moms and teaching them the fundamentals of a child's early development. In 1988, she and her colleague Jean Kunhardt (granddaughter of *Pat the Bunny* author Dorothy) founded their own parenting center, a place where they could offer classes and private consultations for couples, children, and families. She's been doing this for quite a while—and has witnessed some disturbing trends. "At this point, the culture has become so child-centered that it can be stultifying to the family," she said. "If every moment we as parents spend with our child, if every single little interaction is precious, then that creates an enormous amount of pressure, both for parents and for kids."

"There's never going to be a headline that says, 'Your baby lying down and staring at a plant is great,'" Spiegel noted. "There's nothing to sell in that. So what parents *aren't* hearing enough of is the commonsense information about how human beings grow and what they need. They need so much *less* than parents are led to believe they need now." When moms come to Spiegel consumed with guilt and fear about what they're potentially not providing, they're enormously relieved to hear her say, "If your baby is lying on the floor looking at the ceiling fan, happy, *walk away!* That's important for them. You're not being neglectful." According to anthropologist David Lancy, the kind of parent-child interaction where parents are down on the floor manipulating finger puppets and stacking cups with their three-year-old is a purely modern Western invention. Three-fourths of the world's population does nothing of the kind. "American-style parent-child play is a distinct feature of wealthy developed countries, a recent byproduct of the pressure to get kids ready of the information-age economy," Lancy explained in a recent issue of *American Anthropologist*.[38]

The pressure too often pushes people in worrying directions. "There's been a shift in focus away from the internal to the external," Spiegel said. "I think that parents twenty years ago were really thinking about how to build a relationship with their child, how to communicate, be close with them, understand them. It was all about the internal world of the child." She sighed. "Now I feel like there's a great emphasis on what's on the outside. What are the kids doing, what are they wearing, which stroller are you pushing, what classes have you signed them up for? Parents are more worried that if they don't have certain things, then their child is not getting all the opportunities they should get." Spiegel blames the larger consumer culture and its relentless emphasis on materialism for the shift in priorities, but she also understands where parents are coming from. "Underneath this consumerism, I believe, is a pervasive sense of anxiety and helplessness in a world rife with problems," she said. "Obsessing over these things for our children can seem like the antidote. 'If I can just get this stuff, if I can just have my child do this thing, then everything's going to be OK.'"

We try to create an environment of comfort and downy luxury for our children, protecting them from the harshness outside, but fail to take into account the fact that children need to learn to operate in the real world, not a make-believe paradise. People can feel *good*, not guilty, about the fact that they can't afford a deluxe nursery for their baby; indeed some evidence suggests that children fare better when forced to share rooms with their siblings. A child doesn't need to have the matching bedding set on the designer crib or the phalanx of developmental toys that bog down so many households. It isn't necessary that playrooms be decorated to the hilt or outfits be coordinated in the season's latest colors. It puts enormous demands on parents to spend money that does not—and often should not—be spent.

Many parents indulge in products that are not just unnecessary for young children; they're products that inadvertently instill qualities those same parents say they want to avoid: materialism and superficiality. A remarkable 66 percent of American parents believe their kids equate self-worth with what they own.[39] In a crass bit of website copy, the founders of Sparkability, which sells Bauhaus dollhouses for $690, explains, "This business has helped us and others surround our children with products that demonstrate our values and our love. We hope that more and more parents will come to the realization that *we teach our kids our values through the products that we do (and don't) purchase for them.*"

Materialism saps children of the resourcefulness and independence most parents want to impart. A nationwide survey of nearly

1,500 parents conducted in 2006 by the PNC Financial Services Group found that four in ten wealthy parents think their children consider family money a right rather than a responsibility. Nearly one-fourth worries that their money will discourage their kids from working hard in school or in their careers. Studies have shown that for children for whom things have come easily, hardship is more difficult to handle. "There's a clear sense that things have come easier for this generation of kids," said Kevin Haggerty, director of the Raising Healthy Children Project at the University of Washington. "They feel down and depressed when they get older and confront failure."[40] In a study of 1,195 adults who identified themselves as having been overindulged as children, respondents said things like, "I need praise and material rewards to feel worthy," "I feel like I need lots of things to feel good about myself," and "I don't have to grow up because other people will take care of me." Seven in ten reported having difficulty knowing what enough was or what is considered a normal amount of things.[41]

Instead of focusing on their own abilities and what they achieve by applying themselves, or overindulged children focus on external objects and what they can do to acquire them. "Kids from the very beginning are learning that your self-worth depends on what you have and how the market evaluates you," said Juliet Schor, the author of *Born to Buy*.[42]

Allen Kanner, a child psychologist at the Wright Institute in Berkeley, California, has been asking children over the past twenty years about what they'd like to do when they grow up. Their answers used to include occupations such as nurse and astronaut. Today, Kanner said, he is far more likely to hear them say "make money."[43] Children not only value money for themselves but are using monetary markers to judge their peers. He noted, "When they talk about their friends, they talk about the clothes they wear, the designer labels they wear, not the person's human qualities."[44] Novelist Jacquelyn Mitchard recently lamented, "Even out here in the Midwest, little fashionistas are imprinted with what's 'right to wear' startlingly early . . . Already, [my daughter] Mia's pals wear little heels—to church."[45]

This may seem to be a problem to tackle when children start grade school or even preschool. But how can a baby or toddler be influenced by getting a $9 rubber duck? Can an eight-month-old really tell that he's getting barrels full of top-of-the-line toys? Does a two-year-old girl recognize quality linens? Actually, yes. Studies have found that children as young as one year recognize brand labels and characters. Any parent who has seen a toddler obsess over the tags and labels attached to his clothing can believe it, even if you avoid shirts without overt logos. One of the first things my daughter would observe at age one and a half when getting dressed in the morning were the labels that have become ubiquitous on the arms and waistbands of toddler clothing. She would point, forcing me to identify them as *labels* (a word that somehow seems less noxious than *brands*), and would request a particular pair of jeans because of the elephant tag dangling from the waist. She didn't understand which were costly, but she was not untouched by the branding culture.

"Even if they're not aware of it, that doesn't mean it's not affecting them," explained Tim Kasser, an associate professor of psychology at Knox College. "This isn't just Freud from a hundred years ago—many studies show this," Kasser emphasized. "A baby is learning a ton about its world in the first year of life, before it has awareness. Even if a baby doesn't 'know' what's going on, it doesn't mean that its experiences aren't being coded into its neurons. And if you can get a brand insignia, for example, coded down in the neuron level that first year, it's pretty much in there forever." Brand awareness, is, after all, the first big step companies hope to accomplish with advertising campaigns. It's almost as if today's babies are being prepped to receive more overt messages later. Moreover, studies in older individuals have shown that persuasive messages are often more effective when we're *not* aware of what's going on. If we're aware, we try to argue with the messages. "The nonawareness, in a way, is even scarier," Kasser said. It seems the much-documented trend of kids Getting Older Younger (GOY), or *age compression,* as the parenting industry dubs it, begins earlier than even the most pessimistic observers imagined.

According to Kasser, who specializes in the effects of money and materialism on well-being, one message sent by materialistic parental behavior is that love and happiness are connected to material goods and acquisition. In order to be happy, a child is told, you need a lot of stuff. Another lesson noted by Kasser is that the means by which the parent expresses his love is through buying things. Still another is that it's important for the parent to be spending a lot of time outside the house making money in order to buy these things: "Kids learn that all this stuff doesn't come out of nowhere, and that in order for a parent to show his love, in order to make you happy, I need to make money. In this home, money is given a place of primary importance." Several studies have in fact shown that parents who espouse more materialistic values end up with more materialistic children.

We're all materialistic to some degree, but materialism to this extent has negative implications that not all of us are familiar with. Kasser classifies the downside of materialism into three categories. First, personal well-being: People who are more materialistic are less satisfied with their lives, less happy, experience fewer positive emotions, report more depression, anxiety, and alcohol use, and are considerably more narcissistic, according to numerous studies. Second, "social well-being": People who are more materialistic are less cooperative, less likely to engage in positive social behaviors like sharing and helping, and more likely to engage in petty theft. They're also more manipulative, more Machiavellian—children as much so as adults. In a 2005 study of 206 ten-to eighteen-year-olds, children were told they had been given $100 and were offered four ways to spend it: buying something for themselves, giving it to a church or charity, buying someone a gift, or saving it for the future. The more materialistic children chose to give more to themselves and less to charity.

Finally, Kasser identifies the ecological impact of materialism. Materialism demands stuff, stuff uses resources, and resources are limited. Materialistic people are less likely to recycle, turn off lights when they leave a room, ride a bicycle, and reuse plastic bags. Such disinclinations have been noted in children by the time they reach middle school. While part of the movement toward luxury baby good includes environmentally friendly features, the vast majority of luxury gear does not, and people are consuming larger quantities of stuff than ever before.

Psychologists have also found that indulged children can't handle delayed gratification yet feel chronically dissatisfied. "Materialistic rewards are constantly ratcheted up," said Betsy Taylor, cofounder of the Center for a New American Dream. "When children define themselves through things—extraordinarily expensive birthday parties, shoes, bedroom sets—they can never really get to the place where they've achieved an identity because there's always something out there you haven't got or someone who has more. When you train your children to identify themselves through material goods, you're training them for a life of discontent."

Meanwhile, children who receive fewer material goods learn to become more patient and grateful for what they do have, qualities that benefit them as they age. Learning to cope with delayed gratification is considered one of the most important socialization lessons of early childhood. Consider the famous 1970 experiment by the psychologist Walter Mischel in which a group of four-year-olds were told, "You can either have one marshmallow now or two marshmallows in twenty minutes." Some of the kids could wait; others, needless to say, could not—or chose not to. The researchers followed both groups of children and years later found that those who waited for two marshmallows performed much better in schools than those who chose to gobble down one marshmallow right away. They had higher SAT scores, went to better colleges, and had better general outcomes in life as adults.

Children who are indulged with products and services also tend to demand *more* products and services. Already, our culture

bombards children with commercial messages. The average eight-
to thirteen-year-old watches three and a half hours of TV a day,
views forty thousand commercials a year, and makes approximately three thousand requests for products and services annually.[46] In the United States, $300 billion worth of family purchases
are made for children each year.[47] According to a study by economist Juliet Schor, high consumer involvement among children is a
significant cause of depression, anxiety, low-self-esteem, and psy-
chosomatic complaints. "Psychologically healthy children will be
made worse off," she writes, "if they become more enmeshed in
the culture of getting and spending."[48]

Certainly our children don't need us to add to what is already
ubiquitous in our culture. If anything, children need parents to
counteract the dominant ethos of acquisition and expenditure. Ac-
climatizing children to getting by with less not only prepares them
for a future in which they may not be able to get everything they
want, but also enriches them in the present. Rather than things,
children can get attention; rather than accessories, they can benefit
from interpersonal interaction. Parents can take solace in the fact
that rather than require thousands of dollars' worth of baby paraphernalia, their child needs only the most fundamental of parental
activities: holding, singing, dancing, conversation, and playing out-
doors. With a priceless return on investment.

7

Outsourcing Parenthood

"This is going to sound ridiculous," Danielle,[1] a thirtysomething mom, tells the group, laughter flitting nervously into her voice. "It's really my husband's thing— not mine. I'm totally fine with it." The issue is her son, Teddy, who is more into stuffed animals and dolls than he is into trucks and balls. Her husband can't help but wonder if Teddy might be gay. Are there early signs? What *are* those signs? "I personally think it's kind of cute and just a phase, but he's seriously worried, so Donna, can you tell me what I can tell him so that he'll chill out?"

Donna is Donna Halloran, a social worker, infant massage therapist, and infant mental health specialist, who has become a guru to Los Angeles's perplexed moms, and we are gathered in Babygroup, Halloran's weekly mom-and-baby meetings, which take place in a near-empty church in Santa Monica. Instead of getting together informally in a neighbor's living room to chat and gripe and beg for advice, the members of Babygroup have signed up, back when they were pregnant, to meet on a weekly basis with mothers whose babies are the same age, give or take a month, and, more fundamentally, with Halloran, or one of the two surrogates

Halloran has hired to match rising demand. Because the groups are known to have long waiting lists, most moms sign up during their first trimester. Halloran and the two other group leaders steer twenty-eight Babygroups each week, with twelve women in each. After ten of these formal sessions, moms have the option to renew for another ten-week program The moms can continue re-upping until their babies reach eighteen to twenty-four months, at which point, they "graduate."

Over the course of two years together, the moms and toddlers get to know each other well. Babygroups celebrate birthdays to-gether, gather for picnics and barbecues, host special Saturday events with dads, and socialize after class. After graduation, moms continue to get together, organizing playgroups for their toddlers. They also continue to meet occasionally with Halloran, to check in with what's going on in their lives.

In a few weeks, Danielle's group is scheduled to graduate with an accompanying celebration. But for the moment, everyone is fo-cused on the question of gay babies.

A mom seated on the coach opposite Danielle chimes in about how *her* son is also super into stuffed animals. Now there are two nervous sets of eyes. Someone starts talking about someone else's possibly gay baby nephew, then another mom, who happens to be a preschool teacher, says she swears she can tell when kids in her class are gay. A wave of worry, along with more nervous laughter, ruffles the group. Then Halloran walks everyone through an expla-nation of how teddy best love is perfectly normal behavior for any two-year-old boy, giving Danielle an arsenal of facts to take home to her husband.

This is very Donna—empathetic, rational, no-nonsense. Tall and curly-haired, with a soothing manner, Donna Halloran is like your beloved kindergarten teacher, massage therapist, baby nurse, and favorite aunt rolled into one. Born and raised in Indiana, Halloran started as a nanny in Indianapolis; she eventually worked her way up to head nanny for a Forbes 400 family, in which each child was coddled and cared for by two to three nannies. This helped prepare her for Los Angeles, where she moved twenty-two years ago, enrolling at UCLA to earn a master's in social work, working in local clinics as a child therapist, and getting involved with the nonprofit Zero to Three, meeting once a week with a team out of Cedars-Sinai. For eleven years now, she's been running Babygroup.

We're all gathered in a large room, nine hundred square feet, in which toddlers gambol about a large carpeted area on one side of the room, where art tables, puppets, and toys are arranged in nursery-school-style sections, and mothers are on the other. Several caretakers coordinate the toddlers' doings while the mothers, seven women mostly in their thirties, casually dressed, settle into a circle of oversized sofas. Occasionally a wayward child careens toward his mother, showing off a felt collage or sticker, but for the most part, the moms are freed to relax and focus on Halloran, who is seated in a comfortable armchair next to the sofas.

With the mini-exploration of baby sexuality all wrapped up, it's time for Halloran's prepared subject for the week. In the previous meeting, she had handed out an article about overpraising kids for the group to read. "OK, so we were going to talk about the story I gave you, about whether you can praise your children in the wrong way or too much . . . Did everyone get a chance to read it?" The mothers look at each other and at Halloran; a few nod. There is a palpable energy in the air; each mother, I realize, is trying hard not to blurt out her concerns until prompted. Halloran smiles in acknowledgment. "Well, before we go into that, does anyone else have any questions they would like to bring up? Any issues?"

The woman seated to Halloran's left, Caroline, who looks to be about five months pregnant, speaks up immediately. Her daughter constantly wants to be picked up. Isn't she old enough to walk and climb stairs by herself at this point? Why is she suddenly asking to be held all the time? And what should Caroline do, given her expanding girth and aching back? Halloran explains why Caroline's daughter might be going through this phase now, how she may fear her coming sibling and revert to more babyish behaviors. She gives Caroline examples of how to speak to her daughter so that she won't feel rebuffed and will instead feel empowered by her own independence. The other moms, all first-time mothers, are clearly taking mental notes for future use.

Elizabeth, an attractive blonde in sweatpants, whose hurly-burly son sports an exact replica of her surfer-girl features, goes next. She reels off a series of concerns and then abruptly, interrupting herself, reveals that although she told the group she was expecting her second child, she had just miscarried. "No, but it's OK!" Elizabeth protests when the other moms collectively gasp and murmur, pouring forth condolences and support. "Seriously, we're OK with it. I'm just like, 'This wasn't meant to be.' And honestly, all I want is to get my next period so that we can start trying again. I'm just going to move forward." The group is momentarily silenced; several mothers reflexively wrap their arms around their bellies.

Then, a dark, intense woman who also has a son nudges herself into the conversation. "So now he goes into this thing every time I go to work where it's like, 'I miss you, Mommy!' and it just tugs at my heart so much." The other mothers exchange glances; this has clearly been an ongoing issue.

"Yes, but we know where that's coming from," Halloran says, in a firm, though not mean, way. "Have you stopped using the word *miss* with him?"

"Yes, yes, I've tried," the mother, Vanessa, protests. "I *really* think I'm not saying it as much anymore." Once again, other moms chime in with advice, comfort, and support. Halloran occasionally interjects with pointed questions and suggestions. When two children make their way over to show their moms the art projects they've been assembling, Halloran decides to revive the praising issue. "You don't always want to gush about how beautiful and great everything is," she says. "Instead, you can offer more specific responses, just observing what they've done and appreciating it." She turns to one of the boys. "I see you've glued a blue button here. And what's that over there? A string? Wow, is it a red string? I like this green square over here. It's big." The artist hovers, rapt, for a few minutes, then scoots away to rejoin the other toddlers.

His departure leads to a discussion of color blindness. One mother—no, two—are concerned that their sons might be color-blind. At what point should children recognize different colors? Is there reason to worry? Halloran assures them that at this stage, it's normal for children not to know all their colors. Many don't learn them until preschool.

Babygroup continues for the next hour, fielding questions mundane and profound, from nitpicky worries to entrenched problems. Each woman who speaks is greeted with commiseration and counsel from the group and concrete explanations and tips from Halloran. At about every other meeting, Halloran has what she calls a *teaching moment:* ten minutes of telling the group about the importance of tummy time, for example, or a primer on postpartum depression. It's like group therapy, the PTA (without the committees and the responsibilities), a Mommy and Me group, and girls-night-out combined.

Imagine: Right after giving birth knowing a group of local women who are in *exactly* the same stage of frantic sleep-deprivation, sore nipples, and inexplicable crying jags. And their babies are exactly the same age too—teething at the same time, learning to crawl together, blinking at each other and suddenly re-alizing there are other babies in the room. Halloran has created a personalized, interactive *Dr. Spock,* annotated with motherly, neighborly, girlfriendly advice. Whenever I described Babygroup to mothers outside Los Angeles, they practically ached with yearn-ing for such a service. Not only do moms get a group of new friends at precisely the moment when they feel the most isolated, they get a built-in play group as well.

Though she has no kids of her own, Halloran told me, "This has always been my thing." Growing up, she always knew she would work with children someday. In part, that's why her groups all include members' children as well. "It's important for me to get a sense of who their children are," she explained. "I can do an eye-ball assessment if a mom brings up a concern and see if there's something going on that may require additional support, whether it's occupational therapy or speech therapy. I can figure out if a child is developing typically or decide whether I need to speak to another professional."

Much of Babygroup's allure comes down to Halloran, who is damn good at what she does. Wanting to give Halloran a test drive, I presented her with a couple of challenges I was facing with my second-born, Tobey, four months old at the time. Exclusively breast-fed, Tobey balked at the bottle, especially when it came from Daddy. Unlike his sister, he refused to be mollified by the binky, spitting it out when he couldn't nap, flailing his arms and emitting a high-decibel shriek. I went over Tobey's troubles with Halloran, cata-loging the many attempted fixes and failures we had experienced. In turn, she gave me a list of suggestions, and on my husband's next attempt, suggestion number three—running a faucet while feeding him—worked like a charm. Tobey knocked back the milk in one schlorp, and we took a series of celebratory photos of him beaming in my husband's arms, empty bottle by his side. "Have you tried a blankey?" Halloran asked, when I told her about the rejected paci-fier. I was doubtful. The binky had been Beatrice's best friend and our savior. When we tried to introduce her to one of the many little silky blankets we had received as baby gifts, Beatrice turned away her fat cheek, indifferent. But after the bottle triumph, I figured it was worth a try. The next day as Tobey struggled to fall asleep in his bassinet, I passed him a small gray blankey. His response was instan-taneous. He clutched at the blanket, which had a small stuffed dog attached to one corner, as if reunited with my placenta, and rolled over to his side, assuaged. With the blankey soft against his face, he fell promptly asleep. I was officially a Halloran convert.

To any new parent, it's understandable why Babygroup is so popular, even with a cost of $450 to $500 per ten-week course, plus a $50 registration fee. After running the group for eleven years, Halloran has been besieged with requests to expand her services to other areas of Los Angeles and across the country. In 2006, she launched a DVD package so that mothers who can't join Babygroup can learn some of its lessons. "Moms move away and say there's nothing like this where they are. I'm so surprised. I guess I've just hit upon something." She laughed. "I've really just flown by the seat of my pants. I never even thought of myself as an entrepreneur until recently, when people starting referring to me that way." She was recently asked to be a case study in a class on entrepreneurialism at the University of Southern California. "They said to me, You are the *definition* of a true entrepreneur. You love something, and you make money at it."

DONNA HALLORAN ISN'T NOT THE ONLY ONE. TO GUIDE THEM through the daily travails of child rearing, parents are turning to a growing number of professionals: social workers, nurses, and other child development specialists, as well as self-anointed parenting experts. The concept of asking people outside the nuclear unit for assistance isn't new. Parents have *always* outsourced a myriad of child-rearing tasks and responsibilities, but they used to do so within their circle of extended family members and older siblings, not to hired strangers. When families were larger, an older brother might read stories to his toddler sister while Mom gave the baby a bath. A two-year-old's big sister could take him by the hand into the bathroom and help him use the toilet. When families lived closer together and older generations retired at younger ages, uncles could be enlisted to teach toddlers to swim, and Grandpa could assist with learning to ride a bike.

With families smaller and more distant, paid professionals have taken up the slack—and outsourcing has become the kicking dog of the parenting industry, an easy "extravagance" for the media to mock. *"Need to potty-train your kid? Bake class cupcakes? End thumb-sucking? These days there's a pro for every parenting task,"* tsked *People* magazine in a 2005 story, "When Parents Outsource."[2] *"Bicycle Tutor Expands to Play Dates and Repairs,"* announced the *New York Times.*[3] *"Pre-K Prep: How Young Is Too Young for Tutoring?"*[4] and *"Your Infant's First Consultant,"*[5] shouted headlines from the *Wall Street Journal.* In 2006, *New York* magazine offered a tongue-partly-in-cheek guide for *"The Outsourced Parent":* "The hands-free, do-nothing, price-is-no-object guide to rearing a child from conception to college,"[6] while *BusinessWeek* warned, "Entrepreneurs are eager to respond to [parents'] time crunch, creating businesses unimaginable just a few years ago. These companies comprise a rapidly growing Mommy industry, filled with workers ready to do almost anything to help harried parents—even as some experts worry that parents might be delegating too much." One woman confessed to *BusinessWeek* that her daughter burst into tears upon finding out that she had hired help to organize her daughter's birthday party. "I realized that I blew the boundary. To her, organizing the party was part of the event."[7]

Some of the outrage directed at outsourcing parents is unwarranted. Those who scoff at parents spending hundreds of dollars on professional services might consider the benefits of that annotated, interactive *Spock* compared to the costs of a copy of the impersonal book. For an hourly rate ranging from as little as $10 and usually no greater than $50, a parent gets personalized attention that can lead to significant improvements in family life, both immediate and long-term. Hiring someone to improve the chances of a healthy delivery, help clear a clogged milk duct, or toilet-train a recalcitrant three-and-a-half-year-old right before he heads off to preschool can deliver meaningful results. Especially when you weigh the amount of money spent on such services against the hundreds of dollars some parents spend on a set of bedding or a fleet of toys, the expenditures seem trivial and the decision to do so more than justified.

Yet outsourcing also highlights how, in certain ways, children have become little businesses in which parents are supposed to invest. When outsourcing extends beyond solving the problems of child rearing, it enters the murky territory of "achieving" a well-bred baby: attempting to capitalize on each little moment efficiently or depending on experts who, like McKinsey consultants, identify a parent's or a child's "weak spots," ranging from the fundamentals to brand management. Like the perfect product, our children are supposed to project the right image, compete well in the marketplace, and attain their (and our) goals.

In the quest to be a proper parent, we have become accustomed to relying on the readily available expert advice that arrives unbidden even before our babies are born. We are relentlessly told that everything we do is wrong, wrong, wrong, and that we need an expert to straighten things out. Today's expecting mother is urged to hire prenatal personal trainers, prenatal masseuses, and nutritionists. As soon as her baby is born, she must hire a lactation consultant, a postpartum doula, a baby nurse, a mother's group leader, and expert nannies with eight years of experience and four solid references, bilingual skills, CPR training, and a driver's license.

And, as issues, challenges, and quirks inevitably arise, she must consider more specialized help. The freebie parenting gazettes in Los Angeles burst with listings for companies such as Mr. Baby Proofer, "Los Angeles County's original child safety expert," the ad for which points out, "It's much *too important* of a job to try on your own," and a psychologist whose "Helping Kids Shine" service offers parent support, behavior modification, developmental assessment, and social skills groups. An ominous advertisement for the sci-fi-sounding Brain Optimization Institute asks, "Is Your Child Hurting?" Among the positive changes you may see in your child as a result of its ministerings are "increased concentration and focus, improved behavior and interpersonal skills and increased emotional intelligence." On a decidedly more down-to-earth level, Mother's Helping Hand asks, "Just had a baby? Too tired to cook?" and offers professionally delivered comfort to mothers in the form of personalized meal planning, food shopping, and family meals cooked and frozen in your own kitchen.

Donna Halloran's home base isn't the only place seeing the surge in such services. In New York, parents can hire experts to teach toddlers how to adjust to their baby siblings by enrolling them in "sibling prep." In a one- to two-hour-long class, children watch video clips of labor and delivery and learn newborn care using baby dolls; they then share their fears in a support group before touring a hospital maternity ward. "I always make sure the kids get to see a real baby in the nursery," explained one sibling-prep instructor, "and often they're surprised because what they've been expecting is an instant playmate, not a screaming newborn."[8] Also on the subject of screaming, Infant Insights offers house calls in which its consultants serve as "tantrum tamers" and "nanny negotiators." Parents with nannies can also turn to Baby-Safe to do background checks on prospective caretakers and provide nanny surveillance once a helper is hired. Aresh Mohit, Westchester County's "bike tutor," has taught more than 1,800 children to graduate from training wheels. "In the beginning, people were ashamed," Mohit said. "They'd do it secretly." But over the years, "it became more acceptable, and now it's a big thing."[9] The next big thing? Perhaps it's the newly launched Momcierge, a service that charges $50 an hour to help mothers with child-rearing challenges such as organizing a child's home library or finding water shoes in wintertime. Or Nursery 101, "The Premier Resource for New Moms and Moms-to-Be," whose consultants are committed to helping women "make their transition to motherhood easier and less overwhelming." Or perhaps it's the growing spectrum of newborn-care services, including specially trained baby nurses for parents of twins.

Far from a coastal phenomenon, outsourcing services pepper cities and small towns across the country. In The Colony, Texas, parents can hire etiquette expert Lynda White to show children how to use a fork and knife properly and give a good handshake. In Houston, the Texas Lice Squad will come to your home and personally

delouse your children. In New Canaan, Connecticut, home organizer Nancy Belon fills out camp forms, wraps birthday presents,
and packs away outgrown clothes. "Concierge" Lisa McClanahan
of Austin will help with school projects, compile family photo albums, and sew on Girl Scout badges.[10] In Falls Church, Virginia,
and San Francisco, Health e-Lunch Kids and Kids Chow make
and deliver nutritious child-friendly meals. In small towns and
suburbs, parents are hiring birthday party planners, household
managers, kiddie taxi services, nanny tax organizers, mannies, and
home organizers, all taking care of parenting tasks that were once
taken care of by, well, parents.

This dependence on outsiders has become so ingrained that
finding the right name for one's offspring has fallen into the do-
main of the parenting pros. For years, baby name books, websites,
and software programs have helped parents whittle down their
choices; of late, professional baby namers are shepherding the
process, sometimes using mathematical formulas to land on the
right moniker. Other criteria, including phonetic elements, family
history, popularity, ethnic and cultural origins, and compatibility
with surnames, are taken into account by the "professionals," who
charge anywhere from $50 to $475 for their services. Madeline
Dziallo, a thirty-six-year-old beautician from LaGrange, Illinois,
hired Maryanna Korwitts, a "nameologist" based in Downers
Grove who charges up to $350 for a naming package that includes
three half-hour phone calls and a personalized manual describing
the name's history, linguistic origins, and personality traits. Korwitts helped Dziallo pick names for her son Ross and daughter Na-
talie. "She was an objective person for me to obsess about it with
rather than driving my husband crazy," Dziallo explained.[11]

Parents have even begun hiring psychiatrists to examine and
treat their babies, during sessions that typically cost $80 to $250
each, usually not covered by insurance. Apparently, our infants are
suffering from all kinds of previously unseen maladies. In 2005,
the mental health and development diagnostic manual for infants

was revised to include two new varieties of depression, five new kinds of anxiety disorders (including separation anxiety and social anxiety), and six new types of feeding behavior disorder (such as sensory food aversions and infantile anorexia).[12] It's not just troubled babies who are being treated. New therapies address perennial baby "issues" suffered by nearly all infants, such as sleep difficulties and excessive crying. According to the *Wall Street Journal*, "While many of these therapies were initially designed to help kids with early signs of emotional problems, more and more they're being utilized by parents of healthy babies seeking assistance with common parent-infant issues, such as toilet training and separation anxiety."[13] In her book about modern parenting, *Perfect Madness*, Judith Warner tells the story of a woman who takes her eighteen-month-old, who had not yet begun to talk, to see a team of speech therapists. Several hundred dollars later, she is given a report that reads, in part, "He feeds himself with a spoon but he scrapes his teeth. He has trouble gauging fluids from an open cup."[14]

SO YES, IT'S EASY TO GO OVERBOARD, TO LOSE SIGHT OF OUR best instincts. It certainly happened to me after my son Tobey's birth. Whereas my first child, Beatrice, did everything she was "supposed" to do—sleep, breastfeed, nap, take a bottle—Tobey struggled with each new step. From the moment I tried to feed him at the hospital, he refused to latch on properly, howling for hours on end. He didn't seem to sleep for more than twenty minutes at a time. He was perpetually exhausted. He looked uncomfortable. *All the time.* He seemed sad. I didn't think he even liked me. It was a very dark period.

Swaddling, holding, rocking, shushing, swaying, swinging, sashaying, bobbing, bouncing, bouncing off the walls—nothing worked. I fed him more; I fed him less. I held him more; I held him less. I picked him up; I put him down; I joked (sort of) that I wanted to throw him out the window. Finally, in desperation, I called a lactation consultant; desperate for something to blame, I blamed the milk. If *only* my feeding woes could be righted, perhaps all would be well and Tobey would be "fixed." I felt a bit ridiculous, considering I had fed Beatrice with no problem being breastfed for twelve months, surely a feat of über-boober proportions. But pleased or not, I doled out $250 for a consultation.

Out went the fee, in swept the lactation consultant. She was fast-talking, opinionated, and brassy. She castigated the hospital for not addressing the problem on the spot. But I was also to blame: Why hadn't I called two weeks earlier? Tobey wasn't latching on properly at all, and now that four weeks had gone by, the situation had worsened. His jaw muscles hadn't developed properly, and I would need to do three exercises, three times a day, with Tobey's mouth and jaw to get them strong and snappy. This alone left me panicked; I didn't even have time to brush my teeth between Tobey's pitiful wails and my attempts to alleviate them. As anyone who has breastfed (or tried and failed) can tell you, hearing "It's natural, it'll happen!" is like a gawky adolescent being told that the Lindy Hop comes naturally. What's *natural*, for most mothers, is to ask others for help, paid or not.

But there's a difference between someone providing help and support and someone dictating directions and imposing an expertise that may or may not exist. For a mother, parsing the two can make all the difference, especially when, as with lactation consultants and many other variants of parental assistance, there is little to no oversight over the trade. Certainly no parenting "expert" should make a parent feel stupid or powerless, but this is where my lactation consultant went next. First, she pointed out the way in which Tobey arched his back, hunched up his knees, spat out milk, and cried, noting, "I know this is the diagnosis du jour, but I think he has reflux. Look at how unhappy he is when he spits up. He should be looking relieved." I had my doubts about this. Who likes to throw up? "It's definitely reflux," she insisted, filling out a sheath of forms and issuing detailed instructions. I had to keep a food diary. Cut out all peanuts ("Too gassy!") and cut down drastically on fruit. No juice! Could I eliminate dairy too? Hold him with a football grip, not a cross-cradle. No, not that way—like this! Rub olive oil on my nipples five times a day. Make sure he's upright *all the time,* could I let him nap in the bouncy seat? E-mail every day with a list of what I ate and how Tobey reacted. Call every morning between 8:00 and 9:30 AM. "Tell your doctor what I said," she told me. "You'll see."

Well, folks, I believed her. Tobey had reflux, I told myself and anyone else who called to check in; this explained all. I did everything my LC boss said. I pushed Tobey's cheeks and mouth and lips and tongue around three times a day, despite his obvious displeasure. I modified my diet this way and that. Nothing changed, and nothing helped. Each morning, I called the lactation consultant, my devotion fading slightly. When she told me on the sixth morning to cut out the walnuts I put on my salads and replace them with almonds, I balked. "This is *ridiculous*," I said to myself. What the hell was wrong with walnuts?! And what had become of me, a once confident mom who had managed a perfectly acceptable job raising one baby thus far? It didn't sound right.

It didn't sound right to my son's pediatrician either, who rolled his eyes when I told him about Tobey's alleged reflux. "She can't make that kind of diagnosis," he scoffed. Tobey seemed perfectly healthy to him, with an appropriate weight gain. "I don't know who that lactation consultant was, but it sounds like a lot of what she said was way off." He gave me the card of another LC, just in case.

When the Trouble with Tobey continued, I picked up the card my doctor had given me and called. Lactation consultant number two was equally brisk and assertive. She weighed Tobey before and after his feed. He was eating enough. His latch looked OK, she pronounced, though she showed me with a swift grab how to make it *much* better. And that was that. When I broached the question of reflux, she dismissed it outright: "I couldn't tell you that. You would have to ask his doctor." *Phew.* When I brought up the question of walnuts versus almonds, she laughed, and told me that with a few exceptions like caffeine and alcohol, no studies had demonstrated that food passes through breast milk in ways that affect nursing babies. And with that and $200, she departed, leaving me to apply my new strong-arm latch maneuver to Tobey's professionally improved life. (Well, not entirely improved, but more on that later.)

When a lactation consultant is good, she can be a life saver—or at least, she can save a mother hundreds of dollars in formula and give crucial assistance to a mother battling thrush, bleeding nipples, mastitis, and any number of nursing travails. Due to the twentieth-century marketing-to-parents coup by the formula business, most of today's parents weren't breast-fed themselves, so their own mothers aren't able to provide the old standard: free advice. With 90 percent of women leaving the hospital attempting to nurse but usually clueless about how to do so, a wave of consultants has filled that gap. Since 2003, the number of members of the International Board of Lactation Consultant Examiners has increased 15 percent; there are now almost nine thousand certified lactation consultants in the United States alone, and most new mothers can get access to a trained lactation consultant through their doctors or local hospitals.

This wasn't the case a generation earlier. Back in 1982, Wendy Haldeman and Corky Harvey, were working as registered nurses, when breastfeeding began its resurgence. Each held a master's degree in maternal and child health; Harvey served mostly in post-partum, labor, and delivery and Haldeman in pediatric emergency rooms. Soon after, they both left nursing and met as Lamaze instructors. At the time, Harvey was breastfeeding her nine-month-old baby and teaching parent preparation for the Red Cross. Haldeman wanted to put together a class on baby care and decided to pick Harvey's brain. Harvey actually thought Haldeman was asking to partner up, and so they did.

The lactation business was burgeoning. Breastfeeding behemoth

Medela, maker of the illustrious Advanced Pump-in-Style electric pump, had just come out with its first breast pump, relieving women of the graceless task of milking themselves like sows or using onerous manual pumps. In order to get the new machines rented, Lamaze International of Los Angeles asked Harvey and Haldeman to run a rental station with an arsenal of fifty pumps. Moms streamed in at the desperate, odd hours of lactating women. The partners, then volunteers, toiled in the kitchen cleaning out pump parts. As they rented out equipment, Haldeman and Harvey discovered there was an acute need for guidance on nursing. Where else could mothers turn? Pediatricians, mostly male, could offer little assistance. Childbirth educators hadn't been trained. Mothers who frequented the rental station were begging them for help with their feeding woes. That's when they decided to get trained as lactation consultants. After several years, they went into business, and, along with a capital investor, they incorporated the Pump Station in 1986.

Today, the Pump Station operates out of two large connected buildings in Santa Monica; a second store opened in Hollywood in 2005. Spacious, friendly, perfectly attuned to expectant and new mothers' needs, the Pump Station feels like a safe haven, supportive of nursing but without the guerrilla Birkenstock pamphleteering of La Leche League. Its shops are filled with breastfeeding equipment and accessories, nursing and maternity bras and apparel, baby gear, developmental toys, and infant clothing. For $100, it offers private lactation consultations, and for $25 each, Hot Topics lectures on subjects ranging from "The Smart Mama's Green Guide" to "Coping with Pre-school Panic," each taught by visiting experts, including a licensed social worker, psychiatrist, metabolic nutritionist, occupational therapists, attorney, and psychotherapist. There are baby-care classes, breastfeeding workshops, Mommy and Me sessions, second-time mom groups, working mothers' breastfeeding support groups, CPR training, and infant massage. There are even sling clinics to help moms get a handle on how to "wear" their babies. Altogether, Haldeman and Harvey employ thirty people—including, blessedly, a pump cleaner.

In twenty years, they say, not much has changed about the typical woman to whom they cater. According to Harvey, "She's over thirty, educated, nonsmoking. She's middle to upper middle class." And she likes to shop, at least the moms from the affluent neighborhood near the Pump Center do. "I think a lot of parents who walk in our doors think the more things they buy, the better off they'll be. There may be a little bit of keeping up with the Joneses."

This all-in-one outsourcing-and-shopping experience is part of a growing trend of comprehensive "centers" created to serve expectant and new mothers—the mommy equivalent of Kidville. In California alone, several companies compete for precious mothers' dollars. There's the Pump Connection, which offers a pared-down version of the Pump Station to mothers in the Valley, and A Mother's Haven in Encino, with classes in hypnobirthing, "Mother's Gatherings," and breastfeeding support, alongside a boutique selling everything from nursing bras and slings to developmental toys. In trendy Silver Lake, the earthy Love the Belly "maternity spa and family wellness center" provides postnatal massage, pediatric chiropractics, and homeopathy for children; its boutique is stocked with nursing teas and hammock-style baby cribs. An aspiring chain, DayOne, operates two centers in the Bay Area "to provide all the essential baby services, support and products that new parents and babies need during this important time of life—all in one convenient location." Cofounded by Andrew Zenoff, inventor of the My Brest-Friend nursing pillow, DayOne plans to roll out forty-two centers nationwide. As it was for Haldeman and Harvey, expanding from breastfeeding to big business seems only natural.

SLEEPING, TOO, IS SUPPOSED TO BE "NATURAL." BUT TURNER wouldn't do it. Or rather, he wouldn't *stay* asleep. When you tell people you just had a baby, "Is he sleeping through the night?" is the second question they ask, right after "Boy or girl?" Everyone kept telling Turner's mom, Helen Quick, a thirty-nine-year-old attorney in Washington, D.C., to "just wait." *You'll see. His sleeping periods will stretch out; soon he'll be sleeping five- and six-hour stretches. Don't worry!*

Only he didn't. Weeks, then months, went by. At six months, Turner was still waking every two to three hours to feed every night. Quick was nearly done in with exhaustion. "You spend half your time commiserating with other parents at the cocktail party," she told me. "It's the parents whose child is sleeping through the night at six weeks who you want to kill. It is *the* topic of conversation. Sleep is *everything*." And it was something Quick couldn't get.

She swaddled, bought a white-noise device called the Sleep Machine and a cosleeper; she coslept. "I always tried to keep a watchful eye and think, 'What did my mom do when I was growing up?' She didn't have any of these things. Well, she had *Dr. Spock*, but that was it." Thumbing through her eighth edition of *Spock*, Quick said, she tried to find her mother's trusted passages of "classic Spock" buried in "all this other analysis," but found herself attracted to all that expertise. "I suppose you could just read the classic *Spock*," she told me, "but if you have all this other information, of course you're going to read it too." So she decided to read Mare Weissbluth's *Healthy Sleep Habits, Happy Child,* but found that it wasn't practical for her because, as a working mother, she wasn't around to observe Turner's sleep cycles 24/7. She read *The No-Cry Sleep Solution*, which, she said, "if it had been a solution, would have been great." She read all about Ferber's crying-it-out methods but couldn't bring herself to do it. There were always "ifs" with the solutions proposed by the various guru guides. A recommendation would sound plausible but would prove too difficult to implement because the physical setup of their house required that Turner's nursery was on a separate floor from his parents' bedroom. Or the baby didn't do what the books said he ought to do if only she tried Solution X.

Finally, Quick's pediatrician issued an ultimatum. When Quick took Turner in for his seven-month checkup, she was told in no uncertain terms, "This child does *not* need to eat between 7:00 PM and 7:00 AM." The doctor's advice: "Pick a book or pick a system or whatever works, but when I see you at the nine-month appointment, I expect to hear that he's sleeping through the night." That was the final straw. Quick and her husband, Jeff More, a forty-year-old lobbyist, called the Sleep Lady.

The Sleep Lady is Kim West, an independent sleep consultant based in Annapolis, Maryland, well-known thanks to appearances on the *Today Show* and CNN. "We went in with an open mind," reported Quick. "We wanted to hear what she had to say." At the same time, she was skeptical. "I thought it would be smoke and mirrors. That it would be yet another person making money off Type A parents who want to make their lives easier."

West listened while Quick and More explained their troubles. In West's assessment, Quick was doing several things wrong. "Kim's methods are based on Skinner. It's Psych 101, not rocket science," Quick told me. "But her ability to apply that psychology to even the subtlest of techniques was very insightful." For example, Quick patted her son to sleep using a consistent rhythm. According to West, Turner needed random intermittent reinforcement. "She was able to listen to us and pick it apart in a way that was obviously both personal and thoughtful and academic—which was all very appealing to the Type A attorney personality!"

Quick and More went to work. West's system required that they place Turner in his crib and sit, watching patiently over him and dutifully logging everything they did and everything Turner did in response. The next morning, they called West to recount the night's events. "I think I said to her, 'Listen, lady, I don't know if I can do this. It was horrific.' He was *apoplectic*. I was convinced he was having a seizure at one point, he was so upset at being put in the crib." West replied, "If you feel like picking him up, you can do it. But if he stops crying immediately, you've been had." Lo and behold, the next night, when Quick caved and picked Turner up in the middle of his bawling seizure, he immediately desisted. "I realized, 'You're *fine*! You're just really smart and knew what would get me.'"

It took a gut-wrenching six days, but at the end of the week, Turner was sleeping through the night, from 8:00 PM to 7:00 AM. "I was in awe, really." After each bad night, West would give Quick moral support as well as practical advice. "The first night was hard; the second night was harder," Quick said. "But Kim was there every morning to support me and keep me in line. The basic premise, as I understood it, is reinforcement. And learning to be thoughtful about your actions." West's full consultation lasted three weeks, during which she tweaked Turner's program. There were a few hiccups: the first tooth, then the first ear infection. But West personally tailored a response every time a new thorn appeared. For almost a month, Quick and West spent hours on the phone together. The Sleep Lady's bill came to $400, a bargain on an hourly basis for a professional's time. "As much as I despise the concept of all these yuppie parents spending all this money and outsourcing everything and using dollars when common sense should prevail," Quick said, "the money we spent on Kim was well spent because it taught us how to be better parents." At the end of the day, More joked, they paid someone a few hundred dollars to train *them*.

And what about Quick's mother, who supposedly made do without? "My mom told me she wished Kim had been around when I was a baby because apparently I was ten times worse than Turner! She walked the floors with me." One night when Quick was eight months old, she slept for five hours straight and her parents drew straws to see who would go into the room to check on her, they were so sure something had happened. Without the Sleep Lady, Quick hadn't slept though the night until she was four years old. So *this* was how the previous generation "made do."

Sleep consultants are by far the most popular expert parents turn to for help. At every parenting center I visited and with every parenting professional I interviewed, the number one topic was sleep. Sleep training is the most popular offering everywhere parenting classes are taught. When you read about the trials of parenthood in magazines, sleep far outpaces discipline, diapers, and even childbirth. Because sleep deprivation—a highly effective method of torture—drives people crazy. Parents who call in sleep assistance are usually poised somewhere between unbridled anguish and total breakdown.

That parents are desperate, Kim West said, is what makes her job rewarding. West never intended to become a sleep consultant. When she graduated with a master's degree in family and child psychology in 1992, she first worked with families through the court system and employee assistance programs. Then she got pregnant with her first child. "Personally, I love to sleep," West told me. "I'm not one of those people who can function without it. I need a *full* nine hours." Her brother and his wife hadn't slept for the first two years of their first child's life. Their second child had equally terrible sleep troubles. Her brother said to her, "We're not having any more kids or we might get divorced." West thought, "I can't let this happen to me."

She began researching sleep, talking to pediatricians and combining what they told her with what she knew about behavioral science. When her first child was born, she applied what she had learned, and the baby slept through the night at eight weeks. Next she helped her long-suffering brother. Then she told one of the nurses at the hospital where she worked part-time, and word spread. Soon she was helping people she didn't even know, and doing it for free. Her sister-in-law suggested she start her own practice. "After all, you have a job and your own family to take care of."

So West became the Sleep Lady. She has since worked with more than two thousand families, from places as far flung as

Alaska and South America, and her schedule is booked months in advance. In 2004, she wrote a book about sleep training, *Good Night, Sleep Tight*. "I don't feel like I'm working just for the rich," she said. "That's not how I build my practice. A lot of my moms are staying at home, wanting to raise their children themselves, and they are at the end of their rope." Sometimes people e-mail her heart-wrenching stories, and West sends them a free copy of her book. "It's hard for me as a social worker with a big heart not to be able to help everybody for nothing. But I'd burn out quickly and I need to take care of myself too."

While West takes care of government employees and lobbyists in Washington, D.C., on the opposite coast, Jill Spivak and Jennifer Waldburger and crazy busy tending to celebrities like Ben Stiller, Amy Brenneman, and Greg Kinnear as well as regular California moms in the LA area. Founded in 2003, their company, Sleepy Planet, has a two-week-long waiting list and a bundle of "Sleepeasy" products for those who can't afford one-on-one consultations. Spivak and Waldburger both have backgrounds in social work, though Waldburger started off as a writer, working at women's magazines in New York. "I felt like what I was doing was ninety-nine percent sweat, one percent joy," she recalled. She quit her job, moved to Madison, Wisconsin, and enrolled in grad school. She volunteered at Head Start, staffed a crisis line, and felt that she had found her calling. For a while, she worked with child protective services. "A lot of what we do is emotional support," Waldburger confessed, of her later turn to sleep consulting. "Most of the parents we meet are well-educated and smart. They just get stuck because no parent wants to hear their baby cry. It's a very sensitive issue, and one that requires a thoughtful approach."

When I mentioned the Trouble with Tobey, Waldburger fell immediately into gear. Because in addition, and undoubtedly related, to his feeding woes, Tobey napped fitfully and awoke early. Though I had finally coaxed him into a three-nap-a-day schedule and gotten him to go down at 7:00 PM, at four months he would be

up, wailing, at 5:00 AM. Walburger spent an hour with me review-
ing my nap and feeding routines. With her assistance, I eliminated
the "dream feed" at 10:30 PM and got Tobey to fall back asleep on
his own when he woke up early in the morning. Every night she
had me introduce a new tweak, then we had a phone appointment
the following morning to go over what happened the night before.
After ten days, Tobey was sleeping until 6:30. It was still no 7:00
AM (and oh, did that extra half hour matter), but it was better. And
it was nice having someone—other than my husband, who was
as worn out as I was—to consult every morning about Tobey's
progress (or lack thereof).

FACED WITH THE TYPICAL ONSLAUGHT OF UNCERTAINTIES AND
challenges, parents may be tempted to turn to one of the growing
number of consultants who provide all-in-one packages. In the
Washington, D.C., area, Suzy Giordano offers comprehensive
"baby coaching," with several levels of service. The top-tier package covers prenatal prep through week twelve, which includes an
hour of preliminary consulting on preparing for the baby's arrival,
a two-hour home visit before the baby is born, and a week's worth
of "adjustment assistance," including up to three phone calls with
Giordano, after delivery. In the next two weeks, clients can call
Giordano three times; at eight and ten weeks, Giordano again visits
the home, for follow-up assessments. Finally, between ten and
twelve weeks, there is a daily phone consultation, for up to half an
hour per call. The total comes to $1,275, which Giordano discounts
in the package to $1,083. Giordano will travel outside of Washing-
ton for $1,000 per day of service, plus hotel and travel expenses.
She has consulted to families as far away as Santa Barbara, New
York City, and Erie, Pennsylvania, and her client list includes a
number of high-profile names in New York and Washington, D.C.

      To get their four-month-old daughter Reese to nap better and
sleep later in the morning, Courtney Martin, a thirty-three-year-old

teacher turned stay-at-home mother, and her husband, Mark, flew Giordano down to their home in Miami for a four-day stay at a cost of $5,000. "Reese was waking up at 5:00 AM for her little snack bottle and then not falling asleep," Martin explained. But at Giordano's price tag, Martin's first response when her husband suggested the service was, "Are you insane? She better teach the kid to talk and walk!"

Then Giordano arrived on the scene. She promptly introduced a new set of rules for teaching Reese how to fall asleep on her own ("she was passing out right after her bottle") and helping her to nap on a schedule. For two nights, Giordano stayed up all night, seated in the glider inside Reese's nursery to observe the baby's sleeping and waking patterns. "By the second night, Reese was more or less sleeping from seven to seven, which is the most amazing thing in the world," Martin told me a few days after Giordano's intervention. "It's not to be believed. All my friends hate me. I'm still in shock. But honestly it was so worth it."

Giordano's specialty is twins. "When you have multiples you can't afford some of the luxuries or mistakes some parents make," she said. She knows from experience. Her last two children were twins, and she had a two-year-old at the time of their birth; figuring out baby sleep was a priority. "I got into this completely by accident," Giordano explained, and indeed she has no formal training. When she moved to the United States from Brazil fifteen years ago, she was a stay-at-home mother of five. As with Kim West, Giordano's brother figured in her entry into parent consulting. "He was impressed by how well I had my babies sleeping through the night because he had friends who had triplets and they needed three shifts of people coming in and out to help care for them," Giordano recalled. "My brother suggested they see me instead." Within a month, she had her first set of triplets sleeping through the night. She claims to have a 100 percent success rate. "Babies never cease to amaze me; no matter how difficult they seem, they will come through if you do right by them."

But then, Giordano's success would not be possible without the current generation of parents. "People criticize them because these parents are taking advantage of [lots of services] helping them cope with the new realities of the world. Do I think it's because they want everything to be easy? No! What I think is that parents today don't take parenting lightly. They really want to do the best job they can, and they're trying to find something that fits the reality of two parents working." Giordano believes that most of her clients, who are generally in their thirties and forties, don't have the time to let babies figure out sleep on their own. They simply cannot hack the torturous weeks and months of sleep deprivation.

Take Karen,[15] a thirty-four-year-old stay-at-home mom from Bethesda, Maryland. A mere six weeks after giving birth to her son, Karen got pregnant again. In December of the same year she gave birth to her little boy, she had a baby girl. "It was a *very* big shocker," she recalled. "I went to my doctor's office in tears." Karen plunged into severe postpartum depression. "I doubted a lot of things I was doing. The minute something would change with my daughter and I adjusted, something would change with my son." When her son started waking between 5:30 and 6:30 every morning, Karen thought she would succumb to exhaustion. "I just needed him to sleep a little longer!" She hired Giordano ("a godsend!") to help her son stay asleep. "There's something about her that's just so reassuring, even if you have no clue what you're doing," she told me. Since her initial crisis, Karen has consulted Giordano about transitioning her son out of the crib, getting him to give up his beloved pacifier, and teaching him manners around his baby sister. "I've had some ideas of my own on what to do, but for some reason, Suzy has become a crutch for me. She's just a miracle worker."

OFTEN, PARENTS FEEL THEY REALLY DO NEED MIRACLES, INspiring a whole class of outsourcing businesses that can be filed under "Oh no." As in: Oh no, time-out isn't working *at all*. Oh no, what if my child can't get into preschool? Oh no, my daughter *did* get into preschool, but she still refuses to sit on the potty.

The elevation of baby proofing to professional stature is probably the most emblematic of "oh, no" outsourcing. *"Nothing changes your life more dramatically than becoming a parent, from the amount of sleep you get each night to your daily routine to the changes needed in your home to keep your children safe and comfortable,"* warns Safe Surroundings of Elmhurst, Illinois. Marketing tactics in the proofing biz veer from incitement to terror to cuddly comfort and reassurance. Whatever the tack, around the country, professional services like Austin Baby Proofing in Austin, Texas, have popped up, which offer, paranoid parents "a home safety consultant" who does "an extensive room-by-room walk through of the entire house, identifying potential hazards that could cause injuries." Customers like Kim Loftus rave, "I never realized how many possible dangers there were in my home. Now that our home is safer, my son is able to explore our home more and I can worry less!"[16] There's even a website specifically dedicated to helping parents find local baby proofers; it located twenty providers servicing my zip code alone.

More potential trouble lurks ahead. Once you have baby proofing ticked off your list, you can worry about the messy chaos that occurs *within* the safety gates. Though every parent looks forward to the day when her child will finally be out of diapers, she also dreads the prospect of getting him there—public accidents, refusals to sit on the potty, feces-encrusted sheets. Many put off potty training for as long as possible, a practice made easier (though not on the wallet or the environment) by the advent of disposable diapers. Diaper technology has also made it easier for children to postpone training; because today's high-tech diapers don't *feel* wet, toddlers have less incentive to shed them in favor of underpants. (Think there's an incentive here for the diaper industry?) A generation ago, many children were potty-trained as early as age one, and in many other countries, they still are. Today, many American children don't potty-train until they are three or four.

At three and a half, Jesse Sack was pushing the envelope. Despite entreaties from his mother, Amy, a thirty-five-year-old stay-at-home mom in Glen Ellyn, Illinois, Jesse showed "zero interest" in the potty. Seeing his classmates use it during preschool didn't generate the necessary pressure. Watching videos about pooping didn't hold his interest. *Once Upon a Potty* didn't convince him. Over the course of six months, Sack tried various inducements, following friends' examples. She gave Jesse M&M's to reward any contributions he made. She bribed him. She put him in pull-up diapers with Pixar "Cars" on them, which he treasured—so much so that he didn't care to stop using them. Sometimes, he would make his way into the bathroom and then poop in his pull-ups, mission accomplished. Sack tried to tempt him with the new "big boy" underpants she purchased; he didn't care. She set his potty in front of the television, but Jesse sat through an entire hour of *Blue's Clues* with nary a drop. Finally, when the show ended, he peed and announced, "I'll use it again when I'm a grown man."

Sack couldn't wait that long. With summer camp looming and school starting that fall, she needed Jesse potty-trained *now*. In addition to the time constraints posed by Jesse's schedule, there were also the demands of her baby daughter, Samantha. It was then she decided to sign him up for Booty Camp.

"I had seen Booty Camp on the local news in Chicago several years before and had filed it in the back of my mind as something I might need at some point," Sack told me. "I finally got so frustrated and I didn't want to deal with it anymore, so I decided to seek out some help."

"After Booty Camp, you're going to use the potty every time," she informed Jesse.

"That gave us a goal."

The following month, the two of them headed off to Booty Camp with fifteen pairs of underwear in tow, per Wendy "Booty

Camp Mom" Sweeney's instructions. When they got there, Jesse was given a gift bag to hold his underwear in. All the children were asked to undress and pick out their first pair of underpants, and then Sweeney, a nurse, incongruously gave them a huge array of junk food to eat. There was even a Kool-Aid chugging contest to wash it down. Fueled up on salt and sugar, the kids were ready to go.

Once the children had to use the potty, they were instructed to do so. If they didn't go in the potty, Sweeney calmly informed them that their behavior was "unacceptable" and told them to clean it up. (At a certain point, the parents had to pitch in to keep the floor from turning into a cesspool.) When Jesse started dancing around because he had to pee, Sack followed Sweeney's lead and told him, "If you go pee pee in your underpants, you're going to have to clean it up."

"He's putting on a show for you," Sweeney coolly explained. "Once you go away, he'll have to deal with it on his own. Give him the consequences, but *don't* have a big reaction. It's not about you." Sack found her advice helpful. "He was dancing around just to irritate me. He wanted attention, but I wasn't going to give it to him. I had been doing a lot of bribing, but that had made it *my* problem. Now it was *his* problem."

Rather than console the children with, "It's OK, don't worry," Sweeney advised parents to tell them, "It's *not* OK. Look what happened. That's really gross; it's dirty and smelly. You need to clean it up." Her approach emphasizes that "accidents" are not really accidents. At a certain point, children are making a decision.

"Kids are very literal," Sweeney told me. "We have lots of tantrums here, and parents will say, '*It's OK! It's OK! It's OK!*'" She instructs them, "Don't say that. They know they're in a safe environment. Just tell them, 'Take a breath. We're going to work through this.' And then show them what to do." One mom kept saying, "Oh, Jesus Christ, Jesus Christ!" every time her daughter had an accident. The girl got on the potty and said to Sweeney, "She keeps calling for Jesus, but I don't know where he is."

After five hours in Booty Camp, Jesse was a master. "I think he must have eaten about ten bags of Cheetos that day, but it worked," Sack said, astounded. Over the next few days, she followed Sweeney's guidelines to cement the training. She and Jesse spent two days in the kitchen to focus him on listening to his body, away from the distractions of toys. According to Sweeney, "Parents are giving children too much and they haven't earned it." She tells them, "Get a garbage bag and collect the toys and say, 'When you listen to your body and go potty, you can have your toys back.' These kids are trying hard to focus; you can't put them in front of *Barney* while they're trying." Though Sack continued to put Jesse in pull-ups at night, she switched him to underwear during the day immediately after the class. "I feel like if I spent every day with her, I'd be a better parent," Sack said. Sweeney's firm, logical approach seemed to work better with her son than Sack's cajoling and previous attempts at discipline. "Wendy taught me that if I don't react to Jesse as much and just remain calm and matter-of-fact, it works so much better than warning, warning, warning and then getting frustrated and angry." These days, when Jesse questions his own behavior, he turns to Sack and asks, "Mommy, is this unacceptable?"

Imparting this kind of lesson is common for Sweeney. "In today's society, we tend to praise kids just for being in front of us," Sweeny said. "Kids know it's false praise. I try to teach kids to be happy for themselves. And I let parents know that kids need to be proud of themselves." Much of her time, Sweeney noted, is spent educating and training the parents. "A lot of parents give material rewards for going potty before they come to my class, but we don't do that here. I mean, I'm only going to give them food so that they can give it back!"

Sack has no regrets about Jesse's time in Booty Camp. "I had people tell me, 'Oh good luck, you'll be throwing out lots of underpants!' But that hasn't been my experience at all. I just said to them, 'Please try it because it was the best $250 I've ever spent.'"

She laughs. "I don't ever have to even ask him if he has to use the potty!"

Beyond the miracle of potty training, children often make a leap in maturity after Booty Camp, Sweeney said. "Their self-esteem goes up; their independence is boosted. Parents call me and say, 'We have a different relationship now. Some of your techniques have carried over into other areas of parenting. I feel like I'm not yelling all the time and I'm enjoying my kids more.'" Sweeney declared that she's just another parent, albeit one with training and experience. Thus far, about 250 kids have made their way though the class, which she started in 2004. As with other parenting gurus, Sweeney fell into her line of work almost by accident. Working at a pediatrician's office, she was swamped with panicky phone calls from moms asking for advice on toilet training. Having trained her own three children (she now has six) using the book *Toilet Training in Less Than a Day*, she figured she was qualified to pass her success on to others. She was already helping the children of friends and neighborhood parents. "It was taking up huge amounts of time, and one of my girlfriends suggested that I market it," Sweeney recalled. "I was delighted when it worked. It helps pay the bills as well as helping other moms." After adding a set of twins and another baby to her family, Sweeney was especially grateful for a way to work out of her home and manage her own hours.

Sweeney perceives a real need for her services. Most parents enroll their kids after trying for months on their own. Sometimes their children will pee in the potty but not poop. Or vice versa. Some are trained to go only when their parents place them on the potty. "These are normal parents, normal families," Sweeney emphasized. While her initial clients tended to be upper class, Sweeney says most are now middle class or blue collar. Her biggest challenge is dealing with special needs. Kids who are diagnosed with cerebral palsy and Down syndrome, for example, are an increasingly large proportion of her client base; children with autism can have issues with touching things or being around other children, or they can have strong food aversions and don't want to eat and drink the smorgasbord that Sweeney lays out in front of them. Sweeney has thought about expanding or franchising, but hasn't been able to devote time to a serious plan, given the demands of her own young children. People have come to her class from as far away as California and New York. "I've even had parents who have offered to fly me out to where they live, but I just can't do that with a newborn and young children at home."

For now, in any case, Chicago seems like the place to be for intractable kids. It's where parents can call on a host of other "oh no" helpers, such as the Thumb Lady, aka Shari Green, a forty-eight-year-old thumbsucking consultant based thirty minutes away in Buffalo Grove who is one of only two hundred or so thumbsucking specialists in the world. Every day, she treats about six or seven children for sucking, nail biting, cuticle biting, and tongue thrust (a habit of pushing the tongue forward against the front teeth). When a child reaches age four and is old enough to think logically and have some capacity for self-control, Green begins treatment; her fee of $475 covers five visits and a daily phone call with the child, which comes to about $100 an hour. "I don't want to exclude anyone because they can't afford it. Most people have to pay out of pocket and view it as a luxury expenditure." Since Green, who was a pediatric dental hygienist for nineteen years, opened her practice in 1998, her slate has been full. Children from Oklahoma and Wisconsin have traveled to visit her. "I do this full-time," she said. "I'm here all day long, though to tell the truth, I don't consider this working. I love what I do." The great reward is seeing the smile on a child's face once he's kicked the habit. "It's this look of such joy and accomplishment when they realize they can do it."

Yet not all thumbsucking is problematic. "It's *normal* for a baby to suck his thumb," Green emphasized. "And their toes, elbows, and fingers. They're exploring their world. It's acceptable up until age three, and then most professionals get concerned. Half the kids who are still sucking at three will be told by the dentist to stop, and they do. About a third of kids go from the binky to the thumb and are able to wean off after that transition. But for other kids, the thumb goes on and on for years, and that's when you run into a concern." Interestingly, however, Green has started getting calls from parents of children at very young ages—two and three years old. Parents who were once thrilled that their baby "self-soothed," rather than sucking on an endless procession of plastic binkies, are then eager to haul their children in for thumbsucking therapy. "Parents want to get their children to stop before it becomes a problem, especially if they sucked their own thumbs when they were little." Green's advice is to keep them busy—don't let them sit in front of the TV, sucking away without some alternative. "I have parents with babies under one calling me, and I say to them, 'There is *nothing* you can do. At that age, it's just a process babies go through.'" Other parents call because they get paranoid about germs; germs at preschool, germs at the playground, germs in the backyard. One parent wanted Green's advice because the family was traveling to India and was worried her three-year-old daughter would pick up a terrible disease. "I wish I could have given them better news."

In certain cases, a child just isn't ready to give up the habit. "If the child isn't there yet, after the first visit I tell the parents to call me when the time is right. Sometimes the child will be crying, refusing to make eye contact. They'll tell me, 'I'm not ready and my mom made me come.'" Green tries to filter these situations by phone, before the child is brought in.

Five-year-olds about to start kindergarten are her core clientele. "The best motivator for children is teasing, even though it's the hardest thing on the child," said Green. The next big wave comes after the first few weeks of the school year when children shuffle in under a cloud of peer pressure. In some cases, it's not the parents who come up with the idea, but *other* experts their children have seen—pediatric dentists, speech therapists, and orthodontists—who suggest it. "I have parents who take it personally. They feel like, 'Why can't I do this myself as a parent? I should be able to take care of my child by myself.' But I tell them, 'We *all* ask for help all the time in our lives. How is this any different?'"

Parents who have hired outside experts to help them say that the major benefit, beyond the information and tips, is the sense of security, comfort, and support they received—something they couldn't get from reading books or perusing the Web or even consulting their friends. "Honestly, if it had just been us doing the things that Suzy did for us, there would have been a lot of second guessing," Courtney Benjamin said of Giordano's work with her family. "She wrote the book and knew her stuff, which was very comforting. She'd worked with a million people. To have this professional who knew what she was doing made us so much more comfortable with what we had to do to get our daughter to sleep. Suzy knows how to keep parents calm, and that's something we couldn't have gotten from just reading her book."

In some cases, outsourcing aspects of parenting seems so sensible, one questions why such services aren't provided free of charge. Hiring a doula—the word comes from ancient Greece, where it meant a woman who helps a woman (though it could also refer to a slave)—reformulates a long-standing tradition in which women, often family members, assisted each other during childbirth. Birth doulas do everything from prepare women for the late stages of pregnancy to create a birth plan for a cost ranging from $800 to $3,000 per birth. Though the United States requires no certification for doulas to practice, the number of certified doulas in America grew from 750 to 5,842 between 1994 and 2005. Their popularity has been boosted by clinical studies that show the presence of a birth doula during childbirth results in shorter labors with fewer complications; reduces mothers' negative feelings about their childbirth experiences; lowers the need for Pitocin (a labor-inducing drug), C-sections, and forceps; and reduces the mother's request for pain medication and epidurals.

The latest iteration is the postpartum doula, who, according to the Doulas of North America (DONA), charges about $40 an hour to "do whatever a mother needs to best enjoy and care for her new baby." While some women feel guilty over such an indulgence or are quick to castigate others who spend hundreds of dollars this way, countries like Britain and France send similar mother's helpers to new parents' homes *for free* for up to six weeks after a child's birth. Especially useful when extended family is unavailable to provide support, postpartum doulas attend to the needs of the entire family, educating parents, facilitating breastfeeding, and teaching siblings and partners to "mother the mother." According to DONA, "Postpartum doulas also make sure the mother is fed, well-hydrated and comfortable," which certainly has its appeal. The relatively new field, though still small, is growing. The number of certified practitioners jumped from 14 in 2004 to 102 in 2005.[17]

OUTSOURCING DOESN'T OCCUR IN A VACUUM. IN AN AGE OF OM-nipresent and conflicting child-rearing advice, in which parenting has become professionalized, we are both disposed to believe there are "answers" out there for our children and inclined to trust in professional expertise to deliver the right ones. "The idea that the well nurtured child is the product of the skills of his caretakers has proved attractive to many caretakers," explains sociologist Frank Furedi in his book, *Paranoid Parenting*. "However, the belief that parents bear so much responsibility for the development of their children also creates anxieties. With so much at stake, parents have considerable moral incentive to implement the most up-to-date child-rearing practices as possible. As a result, the parent has become dependent on the information and advice offered by professional child specialists." A 2005 U.K. Research and Markets report, observing American parents like anthropologists in the field, notes that for generations, American culture regarded parenting as an ability inherent in the human species. This so called "myth of instinctive parenting" has been dismantled by a multitude of experts in science, psychology, and education. Modern parents are constantly bombarded with conflicting advice on the nutritional, developmental, social, and psychological needs of children. As research on parenting becomes more complex, the parents' expectations of themselves also increase . . . As parents continue to be enticed and confused by parenting theory, they will seek any assistance they can find in navigating the troubled waters of parenthood.

It may also be that in what Judith Warner has called an *age of anxiety* for parents, we are driven to worry about so many potential problems in our children that we turn to experts to preemptively ward off the realization of our fears. Historian Peter Stearns argues that the growing number of professionals specializing in resolving children's "crippling deficiencies" arises from parents' newfound belief in children's vulnerability and the need for a wider array of professionals to guide parents out of their child's particular quagmire.[18] In his history of modern parenthood, *Anxious Parents*, he writes, "The level of concern [over children] is highlighted by the decline of certain traditional guideposts and the emergence of a massive market for outside advice, which is sought both for reassurance and for precise guidance on what should be worried about."[19]

Our propensity to outsource also stems from women's own increased professional experience. "We've come out of the workplace and into motherhood," explained Julia Beck of the consulting firm Forty Weeks. "We leave the workplace at a point where we've achieved a certain level of stature and responsibility and have colleagues and subordinates to delegate to, and resources we can take advantage of. If you do it all yourself on the job, you won't end up a senior vice president." Women apply that same model to motherhood, and we have the same level of ambition—only the model of success in the workplace doesn't quite mesh with the complexities of family life. After all, how do you define success with one's children? Are we supposed to feel like we achieve some kind of goal when our child potty-trains, even though it's a stage all healthy children eventually master? Parental achievement cannot be measured by some kind of check-list of childhood milestones, though our competitive parenting culture fosters that misconception. "We're scared to death of not being successful parents," Beck noted. "To me, that's the biggest sham of all." Babygroup founder, Donna Halloran, questions whether perfect parenthood is even desirable. "Everyone wants to be perfect these days," she said. "Everything gets turned into a project." Parents then transfer their expectations to experts like Halloran. "Parents think that *I'm* the expert, that I necessarily have all the answers or that they can't disagree with me. But I want to say, 'I'm not perfect!' It's not such a terrible thing to make a mistake now and then. Children *learn* from imperfections!"

Why don't we know that? "With parents living farther apart from previous generations of family and moms working more, fewer moms gather in parks to exchange ideas and pass along knowledge," explained Joan Almon of the Alliance for Childhood. "It seems that people have lost their instincts for parenting, but it may be that instead of, or in addition to, losing those instincts, they are losing common knowledge." Today's parents are often less in touch with childhood and child rearing than previous generations. We come from smaller families, and few of us were responsible for caring for younger brothers and sisters. When we babysat for other families, we tended to sit for older children, as baby boomers were less inclined to entrust their babies to teenagers and often sought out professional nannies or experienced mothers—a lesson that has stuck: In some circles today, even hiring a college student is considered risky. No wonder people enter their thirties without having touched a baby. When I gave birth for the first time, I had never seen a newborn; I'd never spent more than an hour with a baby and had only held a child under the age of two once, for about ten minutes, when friends briefly came to town for a visit. The few friends I had who had children lived across the country. As women's lives veered off the predictable graduation-marriage-motherhood track, they began to have children at very different times from their peers; a thirty-year-old mother might find herself the only one of her college friends to have given birth. A forty-two-year-old first-time mother may have no other friends with children under six. "I have a lot of moms come in who say, 'I don't know what to do with a baby. I don't know any songs. I can't remember any nursery rhymes.' They don't have a clue," said Halloran.

No wonder "parents don't feel adequate to the task of raising children," as Almon put it. "They feel it's too big. It's like we don't know how to go about it ourselves, so we better get expertise; otherwise we'll mess up the children." Meredith Small, a pediatric anthropologist at Cornell University, had a more devastating assessment. In the United States, she said, "What I see is a complete lack of confidence in how to parent. People don't seem to trust their positive common sense." Instead of another life stage, parenthood is at risk of turning into an expertise and a profession that requires the best training and the proper equipment. Something that can be taught, learned, and mastered, but that isn't an intrinsic part of us. But while we can all use assistance from time to time, raising children shouldn't require a special skill set. Have we, in a generation, completely lost sight of Dr. Spock's reassurance to relax, to realize that we can do it—to trust that we know more than we think?

It seems so. In our culture of aggressive self-improvement, in which we can remodel ourselves and reinvent our lives with any makeover of our choosing, it's no surprise that *Nanny 911* and *Supernanny* are hits. Televised caretakers-for-hire issue their nostrums while parents nod obediently, cowed by their expertise.

Sharon Pieters, a finalist for a spot on Fox's *Nanny 911*, opened up her parenting consulting business, Child Minded, to provide hands-on advice to families in Los Angeles and Orange counties at $95 plus an hour. One mother asked to be counseled on how to tell if her son is waking from night terrors or from a desire for attention; Pieters visited for two nights in a row, showing her how to calm her son. Pieters said she was a strong candidate for the show because of her "objectivity" observing parents struggle with potty training, eating, temper tantrums, sibling rivalry, and other day-to-day trials of family life. "I think it's because I'm not so emotionally attached to the children," explained the childless Pieters. "Not because I don't have a heart; I love them to death. But I can kind of see the woods from the trees."[20]

Yet is objectivity toward our children—individuals whom we, the parents, know best—always desirable? In some cases, it clearly is. Pediatricians benefit from objective reasoning, and teachers can often provide insight into children that we don't recognize ourselves. But there are other aspects of child rearing that are deeply personal and individualistic. As much as I admire certain ways in which my friends raise their children, I would no sooner have them set my child's nap schedule or select their meals than I would ask them to decide when and how I exercise. Turning to outside experts, people with whom we have no personal relationship, relinquishes us of the responsibility but also the rewards of parenthood. It feels great to help your child stop biting her nails or give up the overnight diaper, yet these feelings of accomplishment cut both ways. Children don't want to be taught how to potty-train or stop thumb sucking by a complete stranger; they want Mommy or Daddy to show them, to be by their side when they face a setback, to clap when they make it to the end of the driveway without training wheels, to brush back their tears when they poop in the bathtub by mistake. They don't want the best person; they want their *parents*.

"A child's sense of security depends on the unconditional trust she develops in her parent," explains Frank Furedi in *Paranoid Parenting*. When authority is transferred to a professional, the role of the parent changes. "The parent now has to listen and defer to outside opinion . . . Parents who are expected to defer to the expert are likely to have a weaker sense of authority than those who do not." Weakened parental authority, he says, becomes particularly troublesome when it comes to issues like child discipline, where a sense of authority, responsibility, and confidence are especially important. Because young children turn to their parents for emotional and social support, they need to develop a sense of unconditional trust in them. "The prerequisite of effective parenting is self-confidence and belief in their role," Furedi asserts.[21] If we constantly, overtly turn to outsiders for help, our children may sense our lack of confidence.

Outsourcing can inadvertently perpetuate our lost confidence. One fortysomething mother I interviewed seemed overwhelmed and stripped of assurance to the point of ineptitude, turning to her Mommy and Me leader for private consultations on a regular basis for a flurry of problems: biting, lack of discipline, not listening, and what she deemed "inappropriate" behavior. "We tried to deal with these things on our own, somewhat," she told me. "But we didn't know exactly what to do. It usually didn't work, or it would work but then stop working. There's always something new to deal with! Every time you conquer your immediate challenge, you blink your eye and there's something else going on." Calling on an outside expert became the immediate recourse. "When you get into the whole parenting thing, you don't realize how complicated it is," she told me, between exasperated sighs. "I always thought I had it going on professionally, but then you become a parent. Where's my training for this? I think it's always good to have a parent expert in your corner because parenting is a process that's always challenging." Well, yes, that's child rearing. But does it require a master's degree?

Or consider the powerful executive who told sleep trainer Kim

West she wouldn't dream of doing herself the things West suggested, and insisted West do them for her. "I remember saying to her, 'What happens if one day your child gets an ear infection? Is that not going to be your job either? My job is to fill your toolbox so that you can do these things *yourself*.' I always wonder what a child would think if I came into the nursery at night. Who is this person? Where's Mommy?" For that reason, West draws the line at visiting people in their homes. "It's important for me to teach a parent what to do and then let *them* do it. I don't want to take away their parenting role." Back before she became a professional sleep trainer, when she was trying to get her own children to sleep, she ignored all outside opinions. "I got to a point where I shut out the literature, the advice, the Internet, and I just listened to my intuition. I listened to myself. And that's such a problem now: I think a lot of parents don't listen to their intuition."

Many of the people parents hire are talented and well-meaning, and they can be extraordinarily useful. But we need to balance those benefits with potential risks, particularly that of going overboard. Not every problem warrants a prescription, a therapy, or a training program. Children need not be taught that something is *wrong* with them every time they exhibit a personality quirk, or that anything—any ability or achievement—can be bought. They should not lose faith in us as parents, to see us as people who don't have faith in our own abilities, and consequently lose faith in themselves unless they have the assistance of outsiders. Rather than having higher self-esteem, such kids may end up feeling insecure. Children who are perpetually given a leg up, with tutors, coaches, and consultants, are taught to distrust their innate abilities—and are not taught to thrive on their own merits.

It's hard to instill perseverance in our children if we don't practice it ourselves. It may be that we do not feel we can dedicate endless weeks or months to trying out seven methods of sleep training (while not getting a wink ourselves) or to cleaning up urine spills in the Pack n' Play. But are we are so horrifically pressed for time and addicted to quick fixes that we can't take time to tune in to our intuitions? Every parenting consultant talks about the busyness, the hectic pace, the business travel, the husbands with late hours, the home businesses, and the competing demands that are propelling parents into their offices. But while many parents I spoke with made serious efforts to overcome whatever childhood trouble they were toiling against, others blew the whistle for aid before the "issue" had even become what could be called a problem. The mother who hired her Mommy and Me leader confessed to e-mailing and calling for help incessantly, often for routine discipline and behavioral issues. As Julia Beck put it, "I *do* think there's room for lactation consultants and sleep experts. If you need help, get it. But what about the notion of taking a stab at it yourself first?" It's not only parents who could benefit from taking more time to overcome difficulties. By hiring outside experts, we may not give our children the room to work through problems for themselves. The baby who refuses the binky at three weeks may get ahold of it by three months; the two-year-old who refuses to give it up may throw it into a sandbox with disdain at two and a half. Sometimes, we don't need to *fix* a parenting snafu; it works itself out with time and dedication.

With child rearing, such common sense often trumps the experts' opinions. Instead of buying into advice from someone who can't possibly know us or our child as well as we do, who won't be there when something goes "wrong" with the prescription, we need to relax and stop giving ourselves such a hard time. When I was facing The Trouble with Tobey, my son didn't need me to cut out almonds and walnuts; he probably just needed me to stop fretting about all the dread scenarios (gastrointestinal reflux disease, failure to thrive, waking at 4:00 AM at age two) and focus on where he was, right then and there. What I really needed was guilt-free support, whether it came for free from family members and friends or for a fee from a qualified sleep consultant or pediatric nurse.

There will always be moments when we need to draw upon others' wisdom, but we must not allow ourselves to become helpless in the process. The need to distinguish between good help and bad, between capable professionals and charlatans, between overburdening ourselves and overreliance on outsiders, only grows as our children get older. Outsourcing doesn't end when a child goes to school; it intensifies. In misbehaving or "different" children, psychiatrists increasingly diagnose disabilities and syndromes that can require years of medication and treatments. For sporty children, the private soccer coach kicks in, while for the chubby ones, the personal trainer goes to work on weight and fitness failings.[22] As children get closer to college application time, a broad array of tutoring, test preparation, and private guidance counselor services beckon. And so on.

With each new round of outside help, we risk creating a cycle of helplessness that not only continues through our children's lives and our lives as parents, but deepens with each successive generation. Tim Kasser, an associate professor of psychology at Knox College, worries that by delegating certain aspects of parenting, we lose vital child-rearing skills. When Kasser moved a few years ago to a working farm, he needed to learn how to milk the farm's goats. "Seventy years ago, it would have been simple to find someone who knows how to milk a goat," he said. These days, it's an ordeal. "I'm struck by the skills deficit in our culture, as more and more of the things we used to be able to do for ourselves get commodified and turned into a business that someone can make a buck off of." Similarly, "There are probably parents who haven't the slightest idea of how to discipline their children or potty-train them," he noted. "It will just cycle and cycle and get worse. They won't be able to teach their own children when they grow up and have kids. This is how skills get lost." The problem isn't the fault of individual parents, in Kasser's view; it's societal. "I'm not trying to blame parents; I'm just trying to identify the system that's creating this dynamic."

The Bottom Line

Remember a time when a child's birthday party was signaled by a few balloons hastily scotch-taped to the front door? A group of ten or so kids would troop over with their parents for rudimentary games like pin the tail on the donkey, or relay races if it was nice enough to celebrate in the backyard. Maybe there would be hamburgers and hot dogs, bowls of potato chips and Cheese Doodles. At some point, the birthday boy would tear open his presents: balls, books, some clothes, a Frisbee. Then the wrapping paper would be shoved aside, and everyone would make for the party's raison d'être: the Carvel ice cream cake topped with a superhero and a few spindly candles. Everyone would get those cylindrical birthday party hats made out of cheap cardboard and rubber bands. A couple of hours after it began, kids would traipse home, crashed from their sugar highs but content, holding a small, striped paper gift bag that invariably contained a superball, a couple of gumball-machine type puzzles, Bazooka bubble gum, and maybe some jacks.

It was thrilling.

Somehow, we have forgotten just how exhilarating those parties were. Given the spectacular possibilities available today, those celebrations of yore no longer seem particularly special. For *our* children, we want more. The birthday party has become our way of communicating to the world just how special and beloved our children are. We're celebrating the anniversary of the birth of our child, which is, after all, a celebration of her very existence. Shouldn't the party proclaim our feelings for her? Shouldn't it be a way to demonstrate to our child's friends, our child's friends' parents, our friends, and our parents just how important our child is? Shouldn't it somehow express the significance of family?

In case we have a moment's hesitation about it, hundreds of services and manufacturers stand ready to remind us, alongside our competitive peers. Instead of the cheapie twelve-packs of store-bought cards our parents sent out, custom ordered and personally engraved invitations have set a new standard. Animal balloon blowers, clowns, famous musicians, magicians, unicyclists, comedians, and cartoon characters are called in to provide diversion. Birthday cakes are commissioned from wedding cake designers. Goodie bags contain gifts that cost as much as the birthday present once did; parents spend upwards of $30 for the three-year-olds in their child's preschool class where once a $5.99 board book sufficed. In New York City, parents pressured or coaxed into hosting elaborate parties resort to special venues to escape the confines of their apartments, sometimes at a cost of $800 or more for a few hours. Koala Banana offers customized parties for children as young as three with themes like Hawaiian Luau, Disco Boogie Fever, and Fashion Diva. FAO Schwarz offers an after-hours party that starts at $25,000 for up to fifteen people, with a complete run of the store, tailored games and activities, and full catering. Our children's birthday parties involve, and reveal, a lot of stuff.

IN SOME WAYS, WE'VE BECOME SUCH SMART SHOPPERS. WE ARE more aware of and interested in addressing our children's developmental needs. Many of us are conscious of the ways in which our purchases impact our personal, family, and collective health, and increasingly, our environment. Nearly all parents want to give their children the best that they can. We want them to be healthy and safe. We want to raise them to be smart and successful, to have them grow up to be resourceful, curious, independent, socially adept, compassionate, and respectful. And we worry about a world in which it seems every other kid is granted the means to attain these abilities and more, while our own children get squeezed out.

More deeply than we realize, we are motivated by that toxic mix of self-recrimination and fear, which leaves us questioning our judgments and our choices. In a nationwide Public Agenda survey, 76 percent of parents said raising kids today is a lot harder than it was for parents when they were growing up. Six in ten rated parents "fair" or "poor" at raising their children. Relatively few believed they had themselves been successful in teaching their kids the values they considered "absolutely essential," such as independence and self-control. Many feared that the world they're raising their children in is a far tougher, less sympathetic world than the one they grew up in, with a far less forgiving economy and few opportunities unhampered by pitiless competition. Thus, we are all the more eager to do whatever we can—given the constraints of time, money, and temperament—for our children.

It's just that many of the ways we spend on our children stifle the very qualities we want to foster in them. There's so much stuff available that *not* buying some of it feels like denial. Just getting through the supermarket buying plain old edible groceries without succumbing to the calls of kiddie cuisine can make a parent feel like a Scrooge-ish tightwad. Why insist on buying plain ketchup when we can get the purple version? Why resolve to buy only plain crackers when we can get bunny-shaped ones? Why *not* buy it, whatever it is, if it makes our children happy? Why not, when we have been taught that acquisition and consumption will make our children happier, that an open wallet equals an open heart? Because if we're the ones who are always making our children happy—by ensuring that their birthday parties are the most socially significant, or that their afternoon snack is not only tasty but hot pink and arranged into a smiley face on an alligator-shaped plate—we deny them the opportunity to learn how to make themselves happy.

While working on this book, I have been exposed to more toys, gadgets, accessories, and contraptions than I could have possibly encountered had I moved into a baby mall for a year. At times, I wanted to haul all my worldly possessions to Goodwill and drag my family off to a cabin in the woods. Yet, along with all the pitfalls of the baby business, there are still significant achievements and a few promising trends. There are, in short, aspects of the parenting industry that can make both parents and children happier.

COMPETITION IS LEADING TO LOWER COSTS

Despite the influx of luxury baby gear with mind-boggling prices, easily affordable baby products persist, and in certain areas, are proliferating. With so many companies vying for the same customer, prices for many kinds of gear—particularly if you eschew the luxury heights—have become a lot more competitive. Baby toiletries can be found at Costco and Target for bargain prices. New companies, eager to claim a large base of customers, often lower their prices to distinguish themselves. Diapers, for example, are sold not only at off-price stores and discounters but also by exclusive Web retailers and online drugstores—each scrambling to offer the most incentives and discounts. The prices of many commodified products have remained stable for a decade, and many basics can be cheaper to buy now than they were twenty years ago.

THE INTERNET IS A BUSY PARENT'S SAVIOR

Shopping for children has become enormously, painlessly *convenient*. Baby products are among the three fastest-growing areas of e-commerce, with 21 percent growth projected between 2006 and 2007, up from 5 percent the previous year. As more parents recognize the convenience of shopping for children online, sales of toys and video games are also projected to grow 20 percent. Ten years ago, if you didn't live near a school supply shop, it was difficult to purchase art supplies beyond the five-and-dime repertoire of crayons and finger paints. Now, multiple web-sites sell classroom materials directly to consumers, enabling parents to fill their playrooms cheaply with pipe cleaners, foam cutouts, and glitter glue.

It's also a lot easier for parents to get used items for free or for less online. In many neighborhoods, parents set up e-mail groups with bartering and trade systems. Craigslist and eBay offer great ways to buy used baby gear and clothing. Swap websites such as Swapbabygoods.com and Swapthing.com allow parents to exchange goods inexpensively or for free. The Internet is like one giant stoop sale.

There's also a lot of advice online for free. In addition to the often snarky message boards at UrbanBaby and Park Slope Parents, extensive social-networking sites for parents are cropping up. Maya's Mom and MothersClick both launched in 2006; each provides MySpace-like features for the with-child crowd. Many supportive virtual communities provide just the kind of exchange of information and guidance that once existed in suburban ranches and garden apartments, where scores of stay-at-home mothers would pass afternoons gossiping and sharing insight into their children. Mommy bloggers like Dooce, Finslippy, and Fussy post the minutiae of their lactation travails into the wee hours, and daddy bloggers like Cynical Dad, Laid-off Dad, Modern Day Dad, and Metrodad offer an outlet for fathers (and insight into them for mothers) heretofore nonexistent.

A slew of niche media such as GoCityKids, available in St. Louis, Detroit, Cleveland, Salt Lake City, and elsewhere, provide local parenting resources. Websites like Babble are tweaking the parenting media formula even further by creating content for what its editors refer to as "Parents 2.0"—educated, culturally engaged, urban hipsters with kids. "I felt alienated by all the parenting magazines I was reading," said Ada Calhoun, Babble's editor in chief. "Everything seemed either really adversarial or treacly." Her aim is to build a centralized resource that's a little edgier and a lot smarter than what's already out there, a site that provides literary satire as well as service, but isn't afraid to go low-brow and report on Kelly Ripa's babies or the latest wacky gadget for harried moms. "We've found that there are a lot of taboos around parenting, as much as we felt there were around sex," explained Babble's publisher, Rufus Griscom, also known as the founder of parent company Nerve. "There are a lot of things you can't say: Like, we wanted a girl, but we got a boy. Or, we're pregnant with a third, but we don't know if we want it. It's a subject about which people feel the most righteous and protective."

New parent portal and aggregate sites aim to simplify and synthesize the enormous quantity of information available and foster communities. Disney's new Family.com hosts a search engine of the thousand websites rated most highly by its online community. "The idea is that if you were to do a search on the entire Web for a topic like potty training, there are a lot of sites that are great resources for parents that might end up buried on page twenty of that Web search," said Michelle Haworth, a spokesperson for the site. "But in the Family 1000, hidden gems will be right on top." Babble, too, includes interactive features, like a video-share service in which parents can post home movies of little Liam getting the hiccups, and extensive community-building components, like profile pages and messages boards where readers can debate the merits of bottle warmers and gripe about the challenges of single parenthood.

MORE MONEY MEANS MORE MEDIA

More money spent by parents means more companies want to advertise to parents, which translates into more offline media targeted to parents as well. While parents can certainly suffer from information overload, some of the new publications have brought welcome changes. Much of the writing in new parenting magazines, as well as in some of the old standbys, is getting sharper. Independent magazines like *Brain, Child* and corporate biggies like *Cookie* and *Wondertime* feature intelligent contributions from talented journalists and authors, often on unexpected topics that steer far away from the perennial "Enliven Your Kid's Lunch." Many attribute this shift to the Gen Xers' ascendancy to parenthood. "I would read parenting magazines and realize, 'I don't want to be any of these people and I don't want to be married to any of these people.' It was all either holy or juvenile," said Shalom Auslander, thirty-six, an author and father of one. "You want to say, 'Listen, I'm an adult and I had a kid. But *I* am not a kid.'" Julia Beck of Forty Weeks sees people redefining parenting rather than businesses doing so. "This is a new generation of parents who are interested in taking their existing lifestyle, sense of self, and priorities into parenting, as opposed to checking them at the parenthood door. They're looking for ways to infuse their existing personality and aesthetic into this new phase of life, and the new lifestyle parenting media reflects that."

GLOBALIZATION BRINGS GREAT IMPORTS

Several years before I had children, I took a trip to Germany, land of beautifully crafted wooden toys. Everything I saw in the little streets of Heidelberg and in the Hansel and Gretlesque Black Forest towns was adorable, but I had no excuse to buy. After I had my first child, I kicked myself for not thinking in advance and getting a bunch of toys anyway. Now, especially with the Internet, purchasing toys from abroad is a snap, as is buying into the latest baby gear from Amsterdam, Sweden, and New Zealand.

ECO-PARENTING IS EASIER THAN EVER

Given the monumental waste generated by baby raising, from drop-in-and-toss baggies so that parents never have to wash a bottle to senseless use-and-dispose plastic cups and utensils, the boom in environmentally friendly products and services can only be greeted with sighs of relief. Even parents who are content to lubricate their homes in industrial strength chemical cleaners and gobble fast food tend to be more cautious when it comes to their children's environment. Everything from sustainable wood furniture produced in labor-friendly factories to organic cotton sleepers sewn without toxic flame retardants infused into the fabric has become widely available. Mass retailers like Target now sell environmentally friendly products for children, such as organic layettes and chemical-lite toys.

In recent years, more than fifty new organic baby food companies started serving American families with flavors like Kickin' Chicken, pear pomegranate, and Baby Dhal and Mama Grain. In the United Kingdom, organic baby food now exceeds conventionally grown in sales. While it remains a niche market in America, with less than 10 percent of sales, in 2005 it grew 25 percent. In 2006, Gerber relaunched its organic line with an expanded number of cereals, juices, and snacks to meet the growing demand. "Organic fruits and vegetables tend to have about thirty percent more antioxidants than nonorganics," said Alan Greene, host of DrGreene.com and a professor of pediatrics at Stanford University. "This is when babies' brains are developing and are most in need of those benefits."

Even cloth diapers seem to be making a small comeback, based on anecdotal evidence. This would be a welcome development considering that an estimated 27.4 billion disposable diapers are thrown away each year in the United States, according to the Real Diaper Association, and disposable diapers are the third-largest item in landfills. Each year, disposable diapers haul in $4 billion in sales, with 16 billion bags of diapers sold, and it's estimated to take between 250 and 500 years for a disposable diaper to decompose. We spend a lot of money on a lot of crap.

THE NIGHT AFTER MY DAUGHTER BEATRICE'S FIRST BIRTHDAY party, I sat down with my husband and in-laws in front of a pile of cheerfully wrapped and gift-bagged presents. Beatrice was asleep upstairs, indifferent to the treasures she had received, but I must admit: I was excited. I couldn't wait to see what "we" got. Like a little kid, I tore open each package with relish, setting aside particularly pretty ribbons for the day when Beatrice's hair would be long enough to give them purpose. One by one, I unleashed toys, books, wooden puzzles. There were frilly dresses and sleek modern dresses, and a bathing suit that Beatrice needed. Inexplicably, there were eight different yellow plastic ducks, which we later photographed in parade, making their way across the living room floor.

But I didn't feel as pleased as I thought I would. I felt, actually, like a kid who had overdosed on birthday cake. What was I going to do with all this . . . stuff? Beatrice, whose wardrobe was well stocked by hand-me-downs from cousins in California, didn't even need clothing. She already had enough toys (thanks, in no small part, to my overpurchasing during those first overzealous months), and she had no place to put more. Her closet was overflowing with out-of-season clothing, extra blankets, and stored hand-me-downs for future siblings.

I know I'm not the only one to feel spent after a birthday extravaganza. In a poll of New York parents, 80 percent said they thought birthday parties had spun out of control and that they've become more about the parents than the kids, a sentiment I heard echoed by parents across the country.[1] But despite such laments, the birthday craze parties on, escalating alongside the parenting business. The shopping spree that consumes babyhood, early childhood, and beyond is encapsulated in these annual affairs, with their coordinated invitations and decorations, their cakes and cookies, their festoons and frippery, the fancy dresses, planned menus, gift giving, and teeming party bags. It's all about buying and giving and getting lots of stuff—and most kids don't even notice most of it, especially when they're under three.

As we haul our kids off to yet another pre-k blowout, awash in commercialism, we might find ourselves wondering if perhaps commerce is trespassing into areas of private life where it ought not to go. There is so much to celebrate about our children and our parenthood that does not require expenditure and material goods. We can take pleasure in the experiential aspects of child rearing that pop up if not on a daily basis then certainly every week. How our two-year-olds mimic the way we exclaim "Oh my goodness!" and impulsively create whales out of noodles, how our eight-month-olds learn to hug us so tight we can hardly stand the bliss of their love. We can take pride in the fact that without anyone ever instructing us to do so, we muffle howls of anguish when we bump an elbow in front of our young children, knowing that their discomfort in seeing us in pain must override our own need to moan and curse. We can greet the onset of parenthood with a degree of greater confidence in ourselves and less dependence on the false promises of Big Baby. Armed with a healthy dose of skepticism and solid scientific data, we can be better equipped to puncture the parenting industry's marketing myths, while still benefiting from the services and products that make sense for us.

Still, there was the question of what to do with my daughter's surfeit of party loot. If her next birthday, and the next, followed this precedent, would she begin to equate family celebrations with material goods? Would she start to expect a gift-wrapped offering every time a familiar face materialized in the doorway? Would celebrations become equated with a barrage of products, and did I want her to have ready access to such material abundance? I remembered how my mother kept a hidden closet where she would periodically hide some of our toys, only to pull them out "new" months later. That weekend, I went on a toy-collecting rampage—gathering excess playthings from Beatrice's bedroom and tossing them into bins to be tucked into the basement. Others went into bags to be donated to charity.

I began to feel a bit better, and Beatrice wasn't any worse off. In fact, she didn't notice. We were grateful to everyone who generously and thoughtfully selected gifts for her, but I didn't want my friends and family to think they needed to buy things for my children; their visits were enough. My husband and I vowed to hold as few (and as low-key) birthday parties for her as possible without her feeling deprived or left out. We could substitute trips to the zoo or other excursions, and the next time we did throw a party, we would ask that guests bring no gifts or swap books instead. For entertainment, no magician or clown; we would roll out sheets of butcher's paper and let the children paint together or resurrect old party games. When she's older, we hope she'll be grateful for what we didn't give her—and what we did *for* her instead.

NOTES

Unless otherwise indicated, quotes come from interviews conducted by the author.

PAGE   **INTRODUCTION: THE MOTHER LOAD**

1   Even during the supposed heyday: Blayne Cutler, "Rock-a-Buy Baby," *American Demographics,* January 1990, p. 35.

2   For example, the government expects: Stephanie Armour, "High Costs of Child Care Can Lead to Lifestyle Changes, Adjustments," *USA Today,* April 18, 2006.

3   "We went into shock": Ibid.

4   In a 2005 survey: iVillage and WPS/Martex, "Motherhood: A Labor of Love," iVillage.com, September 2005, http://parenting.ivillage.com/mom/0,,84f8ht8j,00.html.

5   When the *Wall Street Journal* looked: Eileen Daspin and Ellen Gamerman, "The Million-Dollar Kid," *Wall Street Journal,* March 3, 2007.

6   "Having kids is a privilege": Quoted in Jonathan Clements, "Imagine There's No Children," *Wall Street Journal,* June 4, 2003.

7   "Having a kid is very overwhelming": Alexandra Rockey Fleming, "Big Costs with Baby," *Washington Times,* June 30, 2002.

8   There's also been a massive increase: This phenomenon has been

documented in several excellent books, including *Born to Buy: The Commercialized Child and the New Consumer* by Juliet Schor (New York: Scribner, 2004), *Buy Buy, Baby: How Consumer Culture Manipulates Parents and Harms Young Minds* by Susan Gregory Thomas (Boston: Houghton Mifflin, 2007), and *Branded: The Buying and Selling of Teenagers* by Alissa Quart (Cambridge, Mass.: Perseus, 2003).

1. GEARING UP

1 According to one survey: Hara Estroff Marano, "A Nation of Wimps," *Psychology Today,* November 1, 2004, p. 58.

2 According to Joel Hernandez: Quoted in Rene A. Guzman, "Buy, Buy, Baby" *San Antonio Express-News,* February 11, 2005.

3 "For a brand all about infants and toddlers": Michael Barbaro, "Playskool Expanding to Baby Care," *New York Times,* June 19, 2006.

4 Between 2004 and 2006, Evenflo: Katherine Rosman, "Nursing Moms' Product Niche Grows," *Wall Street Journal,* January 10, 2007.

5 "We showcase tons of products": Quoted in Eileen O. Daday, "Booming Baby Gear," *Chicago Daily Herald,* November 3, 2005.

6 "I thought this sounded like a really great idea": "36 Weeks," the Bright Spot blog, http://thebrightspot.blogspot.com/2007/04/week -36.html.

7 The profusion propelled baby soap sales: "A Baby Booming Success," *Private Label Buyer,* September 2006, p. 36.

8 "probable human carcinogen": "Skin Deep: Cosmetic Safety Database," Environmental Working Group, www.cosmeticdatabase.com.

9 Between 2005 and 2006, drugstore spending: ACNielsen. Note: Figures account only for sales in drugstores with over $1 million in annual sales.

10 "An important part of marketing": "A Baby Booming Success."

11 Given that lavender has been found: At the annual Endocrine Society meeting in June 2006, Clifford Bloch of the University of Colorado School of Medicine presented several cases of young men who developed marked breast enlargement from using shampoos containing lavender and tea tree oils.

12 Invented by Tamara Monosoff: Caitlin Flanagan, "Bringing Up Baby," *New Yorker,* November 15, 2004, p. 46.

13   While parents and babies loved the freedom: Eric Nagourney, "Baby Walkers Found to Be Safer But Still Risky," *New York Times*, March 14, 2006.

14   Nearly half of the country's 75 million recreational hikers: Melissa Schorr, "Look Who's Hiking," *Wall Street Journal*, March 10, 2006.

15   It wasn't until the 1920s: Peter N. Stearns, *Anxious Parents: A History of Modern Childrearing in America* (New York: New York University Press, 2003), p. 37.

16   By World War II, accidents: Ibid. This was also due to a decrease in deaths from disease.

17   "With the technology we have now": Quoted in Nicole Caccavo Kear, "Mommy's Watching," *Time Out New York Kids*, June 2007, p. 10.

18   In 2005, the children's-home-furnishings business: Dana French, "Top Kids Home Furnishings Retailers," *Kids Today*, July 1, 2006, p. 6.

19   Though the majority of baby furniture: Ibid.

20   "more catering to the parents' preferences": Quoted in Sara Shaefer Muñoz, "Kiddie Bedding Goes Luxe," *Wall Street Journal*, March 1, 2007.

21   "Ever more efficient, safer products": Packaged Facts, "The U.S. Market for Infant, Toddler and Preschool Home Furnishings and Accessories," MarketResearch.com, pub. no. LA1173381, February 2006.

22   One-third of parents use teething remedies: Mediamark Research, 2002, http://www.mediamark.com.

23   Nearly half use cold or cough remedies: Ibid.

24   "Kids need to feel bad sometimes": Marano, "A Nation of Wimps."

25   "I think this generation": Judith Warner, *Perfect Madness* (New York: Riverhead, 2005), p. 233.

26   "As the process for interacting": Barbara F. Meltz, "There Are Benefits to Boredom," *Boston Globe*, January 22, 2004.

27   "There's no question in my mind": Quoted in ibid.

28   Crib bumpers interded to protect infants: B. Thach, G. Rutherford, and K. Harris, "Deaths and Injuries Attributed to Infant Crib Bumper Pads," *The Journal of Pediatrics* (September 2007): 271–74.

29   But in an era in which dodgeball: Emily Bazar, " 'Not It!' More Schools Ban Games at Recess," *USA Today*, June 27, 2006.

2. TARGET: PARENTS

1   That year in his laboratory: Harvey Levenstein, *Revolution at the Table: The Transformation of the American Diet* (New York: Oxford University Press, 1988), pp. 122–23.

2   "very same ingredients": Michael G. Schwab, "Mechanical Milk: An Essay on the Social History of Infant Formula," *Childhood* 3 (1996): 479–97.

3   The handbooks added the imprimatur: According to Harvey Levenstein, by the 1890s the impression that artificial feeding was both scientific and modern had gained traction.

4   Still, habits were hard to break: In the United States, where formula was often mixed at home with cow's milk or unboiled water, formula-fed babies tended to have more medical problems than breast-fed infants.

5   "commereiogenic malnutrition": Schwab, "Mechanical Milk," pp. 479–97.

6   "infant formula is currently a commodity market": Yeong Joo Kean and Annelies Allain, ed., "Breaking the Rules, Stretching the Rules" (Penang: International Baby Food Action Network, 2004), http://www.ibfan.org/site2005/abm/paginas/articles/arch_art/302-3.pdf.

7   "In many parts of the world, parents": Ibid.

8   The manufacturers chose to ignore: In 1999, the deputy director of UNICEF condemned these marketers in the harshest imaginable terms. "Those who make claims about infant formula that intentionally undermine women's confidence in breastfeeding, are not to be regarded as clever entrepreneurs just doing their job, but as human rights violators of the worst kind."

9   In 1991, RightStart went public: By 1995, RightStart had been purchased by the company that had bought FAO Schwartz and Zany Brainy, both unprofitable at the time. All three companies were folded together and later went bankrupt, which Fridstein attributes to poor strategy and appalling mismanagement. RightStart was subsequently acquired, and it currently operates thirty-three retail stores in addition to its mail-order catalog.

10 "They spend millions to be right": Quoted in James Heckman, "Say 'Buy-Buy,'" *Marketing News TM*, October 11, 1999, p. 1.

11 Indeed, moms are more likely: Simmons Market Research Bureau, *Study of Media and Markets* (New York: Simmons Market Research Bureau, 2005).

12   When the Sampling Corporation: Heckman, "Say 'Buy-Buy.'".

13   According to Daniel Martinage: Raquel Rutledge, "Exasperated Families Finding Help From 'Parent Coaches,'" *Milwaukee Journal Sentinel,* July 2, 2006.

14   For $29.95 a month, a parent can send: John Johnston, "Need Help With Parenting? Email a Coach," *Cincinnati Enquirer,* February 27, 2006.

15   The average age of American mothers: National Center for Health Statistics, 2002.

16   women are giving birth: National Center for Health Statistics, "Preliminary Births for 2004," October 28, 2005, http://www.cdc.gov/nchs/products/pubs/pubd/hestats/prelimbirths04/prelimbirths04health.htm.

17   Finally, the education level of moms: Silver Stork Research and Packaged Facts, MarketResearch.com.

18   "One of the key reasons these [baby product] marketing": Quoted in Heckman, "Say 'Buy-Buy.'"

19   Moreover, higher-income parents: Juliet Schor, *Born to Buy: The Commercialized Child and the New Consumer* (New York: Scribner, 2004), p. 25.

20   "Companies that understand the underlying fears": "Research and Markets: The American Parenting Market Is Lucrative with 73.2 Million Households with Children Under 18," M2 Presswire, November 23, 2005.

21   The guilt definitely comes out": Quoted in Lisa Moskowitz, "What Kind of Mother Are You?," Salon.com, February 28, 2000, http://archive.salon.com/mwt/feature/2000/02/28/marketing/index.html.

22   "I would so much rather talk": "Parent Coaches Are Trying to Gain Professional Respect," *Marketplace,* National Public Radio (NPR), June 17, 2005.

23   Advertising pages across the category: Theresa Howard, "Upscale Parenting Magazines Discover Eager Advertisers," *USA Today,* March 27, 2006.

24   Seventy percent of parents feel guiltier: "Smart Cookie," *Cookie* (October–November 2007): 34.

25   According to a 2006 survey by the manufacturer PBM Products: "Three Trends That Are Making Waves in Women's Marketing: Organics, Reality, and Boomer Chic," *Marketing to Women,* August 2006, p. 1.

26   The extra cost for organic groceries: Eileen Daspin and Ellen
      Gamerman, "The Million-Dollar Kid," *Wall Street Journal*, March 3,
      2007.

27   In a story on the high-spending myopia: Christopher Palmeri, "In
      Hot Pursuit of Yoga Mama," *BusinessWeek*, November 7, 2005, p.
      128.

28   "We feel that we are suppliers": Quoted in Julia Fein Azoulay, "A New
      Breed, A New Creed," *Children's Business*, March 1, 2005, p. 35.

29   "We just all sat bolt upright": Quoted in Bob Tedeshi, "'M' is for
      the Many Ways Marketers Court Her," *New York Times*, May 8,
      2006.

30   "I had to go to five or ten stores": Quoted in Anne Marie Borrego,
      "Motherhood Gives Birth to Companies, Too," *Inc.*, November 1999,
      p. 17.

31   Mompreneursonline.com attracts 7 million: Amanda Bower, "Meet
      the Mompreneurs," *Time*, May 2, 2005, p. W5.

32   While no statistics specifically track mompreneurs: Ibid.

33   Like women, they are older: Current Population Survey, Annual So-
      cial & Economic Supplement, 2003, http://www.bls.census.gov/cps/
      asec/2003/sdata.htm.

34   In a 2005 nationwide survey of fathers: Silver Stork Dad Survey,
      2005.

35   More fathers also say they share parenting responsibilities: Fathers
      of boys tend to be more involved in their children's daily lives than
      fathers of girls.

36   Only 50 percent care about a brand's cost: Silver Stork Dad Survey,
      2005. Dads are also less likely than moms to be influenced by avail-
      ability, referrals by friends, expert endorsements, and popularity.
      Overall, they are less interested in a product's details and much more
      focused on getting their shopping done.

37   Grandparents now spend an average: Pamela Paul, "Make Room for
      Granddaddy," *American Demographics*, April 2002, p. 41.

38   "I would say 30 percent of my business": Quoted in Thomas J. Ryan,
      "High-End Rebound in Kids," *Children's Business*, September 1,
      2004, p. 6.

39   In 2002, 87 percent of grandparents: AARP.

40   Whereas in the past, a grandparent might buy: Paul, "Make Room for
      Granddaddy."

41   "This is the group that put those Baby-On-Board stickers": Monica
     Hatcher, "The Spoils of Love," *Miami Herald*, February 10, 2007.

42   The baby market is as big: "A Baby Booming Success," *Private Label
     Buyer*, September 2006, p. 36.

3. TROUBLE IN TOYLAND

1   "very important to children's intellectual development": Marco R.
     della Cava, "The Race to Raise a Brainier Baby," *USA Today*, June
     25, 2002.

2   Between 2003 and 2004, the learning toy category: NPD Group.

3   In 2005, 14.6 million American households: Simmons Market
     Research Bureau, 2005.

4   one in four parents purchased an electronic teaching toy: Simmons
     Market Research Bureau, 2006.

5   "As American parenting continues": Packaged Facts/Market
     Research.com.

6   "A robust economy, demographics that have schools": *Publishers
     Weekly*, April 10, 2000, p. 63.

7   The infant, toddler, and preschool toy industry: TNS Media Intelli-
     gence/CMR data, 2004. The figure is for mass media and space ad-
     vertising.

8   "More than thirty percent of babies": Quoted in Barbara Wall,
     "Babes in (Educational) Toy Land," *International Herald Tribune*,
     November 25, 2006.

9   While the households that purchase: Packaged Facts, Market
     Research.com.

10   The prize normally goes to a toy: Susan Gregory Thomas, *Buy Buy
     Baby: How Consumer Culture Manipulates Parents and Harms
     Young Minds* (New York: Houghton Mifflin, 2007), p. 112.

11   Ever since, other toys have been angling: Jane Hodges, "Toy Smarts,"
     MC Technology Marketing Intelligence, May 1, 2000, p. 62.

12   The once traditional Fisher-Price: Packaged Facts, MarketResearch
     .com.

13   With $640.3 million in sales: LeapFrog's performance has tumbled in
     recent years, in part because other companies like Fisher-Price and
     VTech honed in on the electronic toy market with competitive models.

14   "These musical toys utilize": Neurosmith, Small World Toys website,
     http://www.smallworldtoys.com.

15   "infant toys that invite exploration": IQ Baby, Small World Toys Web site.

16   "In terms of basic literary and number skills": Quoted in Christine Rosen, "Too Many Batteries Included," *Wall Street Journal*, December 22, 2006.

17   Consider the textbook meaning of *play*: Kathy Hirsch-Pasek and Roberta Michnick Golinkoff, *Einstein Never Used Flashcards* (New York: Rodale, 2003), pp. 210–11.

18   After holding out for years: Dan Ackman, "Fun Was in Short Supply at This Year's Toy Fair," *Wall Street Journal*, February 15, 2007.

19   The study noted that schoolkids: Jeffrey Kluger and Alice Park, "The Quest for a Super Kid," *Time*, April 22, 2001, p. 50.

20   Sarah: Pseudonym at the interviewee's request.

21   "the baby who needs to be taught": Quoted in Frank Furedi, *Paranoid Parenting* (Chicago: Chicago River Press, 2001), p. 66.

22   The world in which sales of educational toys: In-Stat market research firm data.

23   Current laws make it tricky: A rash of recalls in 2007 led to a call for stricter, mandatory testing across the toy industry, but no legislation had been passed as this book went to press.

24   In 2007, the toys generated: Gretchen Morgenson, "Toy Magnets Attract Sales, and Suits," *New York Times*, July 15, 2007. Earnings before taxes, depreciation, and amortization.

25   Meanwhile, hundreds of chewable, mouthable baby toys: J. R. Barrett, "Phthalates and Baby Boys: Potential Disruption of Human Genital Development," *Environmental Health Perspectives*, August 2005, p. 1056.

26   The average child in America: Juliet Schor, *Born to Buy: The Commercialized Child and the New Consumer Culture* (New York: Scribner, 2004), p. 19.

27   the United States, with 4 percent of the world's children: Dan Ackman, "Fun Was in Short Supply at This Year's Toy Fair," *Wall Street Journal*.

28   "We tend to think of creativity": "Fostering Creativity," *Child*, September 2006, p. 68.

29   "There seems to be a common assumption": Quoted in Margaret Talbot, "The Baby Lab," *New Yorker*, September 4, 2006, p. 93.

30   A nationwide study by the nonprofit: DYG, Inc., *What Grown-Ups*

Understand About Child Development: A National Benchmark Study
(Washington, D.C.: Zero to Three, 2000).

4. LET US EDUTAIN YOU

1 The videos, which hit the market: Sharon Lerner, "They Might be
(Intellectual) Giants," *Village Voice,* August 10, 1999, p. 27.

2 By 2006, more than 1 billion copies: Barbara F. Meltz, "Baby Videos,
Deceptive, Advocacy Group Argues," *Boston Globe,* May 2, 2006.

3 "will stimulate your child": Lerner, "They Might be (Intellectual)
Giants," p. 27.

4 By 2005, the company was generating: The Baby Einstein Company.

5 In 2005, Baby Einstein entered: Though the company initially
claimed to avoid "characters" in favor of real-world experiences, under Disney's ownership its shows for preschools revolved around exactly that.

6 By 2004, the children's video and DVD market: Gerry Khermouch,
"Brainier Babies? Maybe. Big Sales? Definitely," *BusinessWeek,* January 12, 2004, p. 34.

7 Today, a Baby Einstein DVD: Barbara F. Meltz, "DVD Series for Babies," *Boston Globe,* March 22, 2006.

8 "Listening to music at a very early age": Quoted in James Salzer, "State
Set to Give Newborns Music," *Florida Times-Union,* June 20, 1998.

9 "The Mozart Effect is just so much nonsense": Quoted in Janet Si-
mons, "Mozart on the Brain," *Denver Rocky Mountain News,* October 25, 1999.

10 "Although the experimental studies are still few": Daniel R. Anderson and Tiffany A. Pempek, "Television and Very Young Children,"
American Behavioral Scientist 48, no. 5 (January 2005): 505–52.

11 In a 2004 survey . . . 82 percent of parents: D. S. Weber and D. G.
Singer, "The Media Habits of Infants and Toddlers," findings from
a parent survey, Zero to Three, 2004.

12 When asked in a nationwide study: Frederick Zimmerman, Dimitri
A. Christakis, Andrew N. Meltzoff, "Television and DVD/Video
Viewing in Children Younger Than 2 Years," *Archives of Pediatric
and Adolescent Medicine* 161 (May 2007): 473. The top three reasons
parents cited were education, entertainment, and babysitting.

13 "There is no research to show": Quoted in Meltz, "Baby Videos, Deceptive, Advocacy Group Argues."

14   "expose little ones to the world": The Baby Einstein Company.

15   "They can't help themselves": Quoted in Frederick J. Zimmerman, Dimitri A. Christakis, and Andrew N. Meltzoff, "Media Viewing by Children Under 2 Years Old," Child Health Institute, May 17, 2006.

16   A 2006 study in *Pediatrics:* Elizabeth A. Vandewater, David S. Bickham, June H. Lee, "Time Well Spent? Relating Television Use to Children's Free-Time Activities," *Pediatrics* 117, no. 2 (February 2006): e 181.

17   Research has also suggested that while children: Anderson and Pempek, "Television and Very Young Children."

18   http://archpedi.ama-assn.org/cgi/content/short/159/7/619.

19   "Our philosophy is that early alphabet instruction": Preschool Prep, press release, author's emphasis.

20   Kamila B. Mistry, Cynthia S. Minkovitz, Donna M. Strobino, and Dina L. G. Borzekowski, "Children's Television Exposure and Behavioral and Social Outcomes at 5.5 Years: Does Timing of Exposure Matter?" *Pediatrics* (October 2007).

21   Not surprisingly, the American Academy of Pediatrics: Kaiser Family Foundation, 2003.

22   "It's a shame to see": Quoted in David Crary, "Sesame Videos Ruffle Feathers," Associated Press, April 4, 2006.

23   "What we're trying to do is meet" parents: Ibid.

24   But they couldn't have: Quoted in Susan Gregory Thomas, *Buy Buy Baby: How Consumer Culture Manipulates Parents and Harms Young Minds* (New York: Houghton Mifflin, 2007), p. 106.

25   Its JumpStart series: Ibid., p. 89.

26   "There's a shift in need": Quoted in Matt Bradley, "High-Tech Child's Play," *Christian Science Monitor,* November 16, 2005.

27   In a 2006 study of 1,009 parents: Zimmerman, Christakis, and Meltzoff, "Media Viewing by Children," p. 473.

28   the average baby started watching videos: Marilyn Elias, "Study Takes a New Look at Tots and TV," *USA Today,* August 4, 2004.

29   Viacom's Nickelodeon unit generated: Aaron O. Patrick, "In Tots' TV Shows, A Booming Market, Toys Get Top Billing," *Wall Street Journal,* January 27, 2006.

30   Knowing that television viewing: Christakis and Zimmerman, [TK]

31   Surveys show that children six and under: Liz Stevens, "Should Babies Watch TV?" *Fort Worth Star-Telegram,* April 4, 2006.

32 Provoked by this radical transformation: Wendy Melillo, "Senate Calls for Media Study," *AdWeek,* September 14, 2006, http://www.adweek .com/aw/search/article_display.jsp?vnu_content_id=1003122280.

33 "Children invariably love to imitate": "Tech Tonic," the Alliance for Childhood, 2004.

5. CLASS TIME

1   Parents have been [hit]: Sara Mead, "Million Dollar Babies: Why Infants Can't Be Hardwired for Success," Education Sector.

2   Music classes alone cost: Tatiana Boncompagni, "Baby Shall Enroll: Mommy Knows," *New York Times,* May 11, 2006.

3   Since 2000, the international behemoth Music Together: Helaine Olen, "Play Schools for Preschool Kids," *Wall Street Journal,* May 10, 2005.

4   My Gym Children's Fitness Centers: Helaine Olen, "Meet You at the Sandbox—After Class," *Washington Post,* April 30, 2006.

5   "In our market research groups": Ibid.

6   After more than thirty years in the busines: Gymboree, presentation at SG Cowen & Co. Fourth Annual Consumer Conference, January 2006.

7   "Our campaign for Gymboree Play & Music": Quoted in Celeste Ward, "Gymboree Enrolls 'Playful, Strategic' Hive," Adweek.com, November 30, 2004.

8   "build confidence, encourage curiosity": LeapFrog Enterprisesl, press release, October 2, 2006.

9   Sarah: Pseudonym at the interviewee's request.

10 According to the *New York Times:* Winnie Hu, "Parents Take Language Class into Their Own Hands," *New York Times,* September 30, 2006.

11 In 2005, researchers at the Universities of Ottawa and Waterloof J. Cyne Johnston, Andrée Durieux-Smith, and Kathleen Bloom, "Teaching Gestural Signs to Infants to Advance Child Development: A Review of the Evidence," *First Language,* 25, no. 2 (2005) 235–51.

12 "a gleaming, charming, $3 million": Leslie Eaton, "Where Half Caf Meets Double Wide," *New York Times,* February 6, 2005.

13 "the genius of Kidville": Brian Sack, "Spoilt Brats (And That's Just the Parents)," *Independent,* June 27, 2005.

14   "the modern child, with his days": Ruth Frankel, "Child Leisure—A Modern Problem," *Hygeia* 9 (July 1931): 614.

15   "Preschool is never going to be enough": Quoted in Gabrielle Birkner, "Simple Preschool Doesn't Seem to Be Enough These Days," *New York Sun*, August 30, 2006.

16   "How do children learn": Benjamin Spock, *Baby and Child Care* (New York: Pocket Books, 1976), p. 322.

17   "Because fewer men do housework": "When Dad Pitches in at Home, Kids Benefit Socially," *Today's School Psychologist*, July 2, 2003.

6. PAMPERED

1   "Strollers are an image": Packaged Facts, "The U.S. Market for Infant, Toddler and Preschool Home Furnishings and Accessories," MarketResearch.com, February 2006.

2   "Everyone's claiming that they're responsible": Quoted in "Baby Shiloh's Fame Rubs Off on Shirt," Associated Press, June 14, 2006.

3   "There have to be ten companies": Quoted in Michele Ingrassia, "Baby Boom!" *Daily News*, October 5, 2005.

4   "Celebrity babymania is impacting": Quoted in "20 Big Developments," *Children's Business*, October 1, 2005, p. 20.

5   "Any rational marketer": Packaged Facts, "The U.S. Market for ITP Home Furnishings."

6   "Modern design may only represent": Quoted in Kate Betts, "High Style for Small People," *Time*, June 12, 2006, p. 107.

7   "no matter their income": Quoted in Christopher Palmeri, "In Hot Pursuit of Yoga Mama," *BusinessWeek*, November 7, 2005, p. 128.

8   Spending has increased: ESRI Business Information Solutions, 2003.

9   "As a growing pocket": "20 Big Developments," *Children's Business* (October 2005), p. 20.

10   That trend has been captured: Circulation data supplied by *Cookie*.

11   "What's happening in Wisteria Lane": Quoted in Christina Capecci, "Midwest Moms Don't Fit Old Stereotypes, Marketers Say," *Chicago Daily Herald*, November 1, 2006.

12   "The idea behind Genius Jones": Quoted in Betts, "High Style for Small People."

13   "Parents who are looking for high-design": Quoted in Julia Fein

Azoulay, "Market Trend Watch," *Children's Business,* February 1, 2005, p. 66.

14   "We decided to take products": Quoted in Dalia Fahmy, "Making Necessities Stylish and Getting a Higher Price," *New York Times,* March 9, 2006.

15   "It is time to bank on the Hipster Baby": Packaged Facts, "The U.S. Market for Babycare Supplies," MarketResearch.com, August 2005.

16   "What makes parents spend so much": Kristin Carr, "Growing Up," *Footwear News,* January 31, 2005, p. 146.

17   "strive to dress themselves distinctively": Packaged Facts, "The U.S. Market for ITP Home Furnishings."

18   "Not to seem cynical": Packaged Facts, "The U.S. Market for Babycare Supplies."

19   Retail sales of infant, toddler, and preschool: Packaged Facts, "The U.S. Market for ITP Home Furnishings."

20   At least seven hundred companies: Packaged Facts/MarketResearch.com.

21   collectively they spend nearly $30 million: TNS Media Intelligence/CMR, 2004.

22   "A baby is not an accessory, exactly": Quoted in Heather Landy, "Big Niche for Infants," *Fort Worth Star-Telegram,* April 14, 2007.

23   "There are so many yuppie families": Quoted in Alexandra Wolfe, "Children, and Moms, at Play," *New York Times,* June 5, 2005.

24   "I know I've got something right": Quoted in Jennifer Tung, "Lucy Sykes, Everyday Expert," *Cookie,* December 2005, p. 46.

25   "Fashionista mommies, take heart": Carr, "Growing Up."

26   Overall U.S. sales of infant, toddler, and preschool clothing: Packaged Facts/MarketResearch.com.

27   According to the *Wall Street Journal,* parents are spending: Tatiana Boncompangni, "For Real Babes, Denim Gets Pricey," *Wall Street Journal,* April 14, 2006.

28   "People are really into that": Quoted in Lauren DeCarlo, "You've Got to be Kidding," *WWD,* November 11, 2004, p. 10.

29   "We thought, 'Wouldn't it be nice'": Quoted in Jennifer Tung, "On Your Marc," *Cookie,* December 2005, p. 84.

30   Even a relatively utilitarian wardrobe: Eileen Daspin and Ellen Gamerman, "The Million-Dollar Kid," *Wall Street Journal,* March 3, 2007.

31 "Kids' wear gives us the perfect opportunity": DeCarlo, "You've Got to be Kidding."

32 "In general, the awareness of fashion is getting younger": Quoted in Ruth La Ferla, "Fashion Aims Young," *New York Times,* August 24, 2006.

33 The entire staff has submitted to: Quoted in Elisa Lipsky-Karasz, "Peewee's Playhouse," *W* (magazine), January 2006, p. TK.

34 "Everyone is two degrees": Quoted in ibid.

35 "Motherhood is not enough": Quoted in Alexandra Wolfe, "Children, and Moms, at Play," *New York Times,* June 5, 2005.

36 Instead of sending out simple birth announcements: "Goody Bag," *Parents,* August 2007, p. 31.

37 "You want to make sure": Quoted in Kitty O'Callaghan, "Baby Needs New Shoes and a $4,000 DVD Scrapbook," *New York Times,* September 30, 2006.

38 "American-style parent-child play": Quoted in Christopher Shea, "Leave Those Kids Alone," *Boston Globe,* July 15, 2007.

39 A remarkable 66 percent: Valerie Frankel, "Five Parenting Myths You Can Kiss Goodbye," *Parenting,* February 1, 2006, p. 128.

40 "There's a clear sense": Quoted in Bob Condor, "Moi Spoiled? Years of Boosting Kids' Self-Esteem May Have Backfired with a Generation that Feels Overly Entitled," *Seattle Post-Intelligencer,* December 12, 2005.

41 In a study of 1,195 adults: David J. Bredehoft, Jean Illsley Clark, and Connie Dawson, "Indulge the Less, Enjoy them More," Technical Appendix, 2002.

42 "Kids from the very beginning": Quoted in La Ferla, "Fashion Aims Young."

43 "make money": Rebecca A. Clay, "Advertising to Children: Is it Ethical?" *Monitor on Psychology* 31, no. 8 (2000).

44 "When they talk about their friends": Quoted in Miriam H. Zoll, "Psychologists Challenge Ethics of Marketing to Children," *American News Service,* April 5, 2000.

45 "Even out here in the Midwest": Jacquelyn Mitchard, *Wondertime* Summer 2006, p. 64.

46 The average eight- to thirteen-year-old watches: Juliet Schor, *Born to Buy: The Commercialized Child and the New Consumer Culture* (New York: Scribner, 2004), p. 20.

47   In the United States, $300 billion worth: Frankel, "Five Parenting Myths."

48   "Psychologically healthy children": Schor, *Born to Buy*, p. 167.

7. OUTSOURCING PARENTHOOD

1   Danielle: Pseudonym at the interviewee's request.

2   *"Need to potty-train your kid?"*: Quoted in Nancy Jeffrey, "When Parents Outsource," *People*, August 1, 2005, p. 72.

3   *"Bicycle Tutor Expands"*: Merri Rosenberg, "Bicycle Tutor Expands to Play Dates and Repairs," *New York Times*, April 15, 2001.

4   *"Pre-K Prep"*: Suein Hwang, "Pre-K Prep: How Young Is Too Young for Tutoring?" *Wall Street Journal*, October 13, 2004.

5   *"Your Infant's First Consultant"*: Suein Hwang, "Your Infant's First Consultant," *Wall Street Journal*, December 15, 2004.

6   "The Outsourced Parent," *New York* magazine, September 25, 2006.

7   "Entrepreneurs are eager": Rochelle Sharpe, "Nannies on Speed Dial," *BusinessWeek*, September 18, 2000, p. 108.

8   "I always make sure the kids": Quoted in Nicole Caccavo Kear, "Make Way for Baby (Brother or Sister)," *Time Out New York*, March 2007, p. 10.

9   "In the beginning, people were ashamed": Quoted in Jeffrey, "When Parents Outsource," p. 72.

10   "Concierge" Lisa McClanahan of Austin: Ibid.

11   "She was an objective person": Quoted in Alexandra Alter, "The Baby-Name Business," *Wall Street Journal*, June 22, 2007.

12   In 2005, the mental health: Elizabeth Bernstein, "Sending the Baby to a Shrink," *Wall Street Journal*, October 24, 2006.

13   "While many of these therapies": Ibid.

14   "He feeds himself with a spoon": Judith Warner, *Perfect Madness: Motherhood in the Age of Anxiety* (New York: Riverhead, 2005), p. 28.

15   Take Karen: Pseudonym at interviewee's request.

16   "I never realized how many possible dangers": Austin Baby Proofing, www.austinbabyproofing.com.

17   The number of certified practitioners: Data provided by Doulas of North America.

18   "crippling deficiencies": Peter N. Stearns, *Anxious Parents: A History of Modern Childrearing in America* (New York: New York University Press, 2003), p. 40.

19   "The level of concern": Ibid., p. 12.

20   "I think it's because I'm not so emotionally": Quoted in Theresa Walker, "Parenting 1-on-1," *Orange County Register,* January 8, 2006.

21   "A child's sense of security depends": Frank Furedi, *Paranoid Parenting* (Chicago: Chicago River Press, 2002), pp. 185–86.

22   for the chubby ones, the personal trainer: Mireya Navarro, "Playtime at the Health Club," *New York Times,* January 22, 2006.

CONCLUSION: THE BOTTOM LINE

1   In a poll of New York parents, 80 percent: "Parent Poll," *Time Out New York Kids,* June 2007, p. 10.

ABOUT THE AUTHOR

PAMELA PAUL is a contributor to *Time* magazine and the author of *Pornified: How Pornography Is Damaging Our Lives, Our Relationships, and Our Families* and *The Starter Marriage and the Future of Matrimony*. She has written for such publications as *The New York Times*, *The New York Times Book Review*, *Psychology Today*, *Redbook*, *Ladies' Home Journal*, and *The Economist*. She and her family live in New York.